PORTIA

PORTIA

The World of Abigail Adams

EDITH B. GELLES

Indiana University Press
BLOOMINGTON & INDIANAPOLIS

The paper used in this publication meets the minimum requirements of American
National Standard for Information Sciences—Permanence of Paper for Printed
Library Materials, ANSI Z39.48-1984.

Manufactured in the United States of America

Library of Congress Cataloging-in-Publication Data

Gelles, Edith Belle.
  Portia : the world of Abigail Adams / Edith B. Gelles.
    p.   cm.
  Includes bibliographical references and index.
  ISBN 0-253-32553-6
  1. Adams, Abigail, 1744–1818.   2. Presidents—United States—
Wives—Biography.   I. Title.
E322.1.A38G45   1992
973.4'4'092—dc20
[B]
                                                           92-7860
                  1 2 3 4 5   96 95 94 93 92

For
Michael
collaborator in all things
and
Adam and Noah
for the pleasure of their company

Contents

Illustrations follow chapter 3

Acknowledgments

Reflecting on the revolutions, both private and political, that occurred in her lifetime, Abigail Adams wrote to a friend in 1807 that so "rapid have been the changes, that the mind, though fleet in its progress, has been outstripped by them; and we are left like statues, gazing at what we can neither fathom nor comprehend." Looking back over the years that I have spent researching, thinking, and writing about Abigail, I feel a similar sense of awe, especially considering the people to whom I am indebted for their contributions and encouragement. In this sense, the sum is less than the parts, and I can only begin to acknowledge the individuals and institutions that have supported my efforts not only to come to grips with the life of Abigail Adams, but to discover a method for understanding and presenting my portrait of her.

My greatest debt is to my family. After myself, the person who has lived most closely with the Adamses has been my husband, Michael Weiss, who, though he may by now have forgotten, first suggested that I consider writing about Abigail. In this, as in many other respects, Michael's great scholarship, wisdom, and loving encouragement have enriched the book and the process of writing it. My sons, Adam Finkelstein and Noah Finkelstein, have grown from boys to men in the time of this work. They taught me to use a word processor when they were twelve and nine years old and have since rescued me from technological disaster on numerous occasions. They have listened and commented with sophisticated insight and have taught me that a feminist historian can live compatibly with students of physics and math.

I learned to do history at the University of California, Irvine. Since I did not know how to do women's history, the only way I could think of was to write a biography of a woman. I am deeply grateful to the men who supported this effort—Michael P. Johnson, Karl Hufbauer, John P. Diggins, and Keith Nelson—not just for their guidance, but also for their friendship over the years. In 1973 Penny Hansen and I began a discussion about history and women and psychology and life that continues still. Ruthie Ferrell came into my life after Abigail and has been an important spiritual muse.

When I walked into the Institute for Research on Women and Gender at Stanford for the first time and met with its gracious Deputy Director Marilyn Yalom, lights turned on inside of me. I did not know that such an environment existed on this planet; here was a place to do women's history.

The Institute has been my intellectual home, and its scholars, past and present, my teachers, my colleagues, my best critics, and my friends. I am especially grateful to Karen Offen for sharing her erudition and wisdom, and for our continuing dialogue on the nature and theory of women's history. I thank all scholars past and present who have listened to my presentations, and especially those who have over the years read and commented on portions of this biography: Susan Groag Bell, Stephanie Brown, Pamela Eakins, Susan Faludi, Mary Felstiner, Joanna Gillespie, Kathy Henderson, Sonny Herman, Gina Holloman, Phyllis Koestenbaum, Annette Lawson, Iris Litt, Sherri Matteo, Elizabeth Roden, Mollie Rosenhan, Ginetta Sagan, and Karen Wyche.

The Institute may be the center, but orbiting about this little planet is a wider world. I owe a special debt to Mary Beth Norton and Patricia U. Bonomi, who have encouraged me by writing exemplary history, but also because at critical times in this work, each has helped to make this a better book. In conversation and by example, Jay Fliegelman has inspired me to listen keenly to the voices in the letters. Pamela Herr and Barton Bernstein are valued friends and challenging critics. I have enjoyed my long and stimulating correspondence with John Ferling, as he completed his biography of John Adams. I thank Elaine Crane, Eve Kornfeld, and Jean Soderlund; also Bunny Callahan, Jean Kirsch, and Ruth Stimpson. The late, rare gentleman and scholar Gerald White read my entire manuscript and commented gently but in terms that still reverberate as I fall short of his standards. I grieve the loss of a wonderful scholar, friend, and mentor, Rena Vassar. Sheila Cole, Sally Hufbauer, Jean Lave, and Gerre McKenna have been loyal and critical readers as well as lifelong friends.

I have worked primarily from the Adams Papers. All quotations from the microfilm edition of the Adams Papers are by permission of the Massachusetts Historical Society. I am appreciative of many cordial conversations with Dr. Richard Ryerson, Editor-in-Chief of the Adams Papers. I also wish to thank the following: the Massachusetts Historical Society for permission to cite from the Cranch Family Papers and the DeWindt Collection; the American Antiquarian Society for permission to cite the Abigail Adams Papers; the Library of Congress for the Shaw Family Papers; the Boston Public Library for the John Adams Collection; The Historical Society of Pennsylvania for the Benjamin Rush Papers; and Harvard University Press for permission to quote from the letterpress editions of the Adams Papers.

My gratitude to Joan Catapano of Indiana University Press who, on the basis of two early chapters, supported my vision that this could become a book. I thank Terry Cagle for empathic editing.

Several years ago Diane Middlebrook and Barbara Babcock invited me into the Biographers' Seminar that they started at Stanford; I thank the members of that group who have shared their work and their ideas about writing lives as well as their acute and always helpful critiques of my presentations. I have benefited as well from participating in the Stanford Women's History Reading Group, the Bay Area Colonialists, and the Berkeley Seminar on Women's Studies. Finally, two groups of people have helped to maintain health and sanity, so to my friends in the Rinconada Master Swimmers and the Rinconada Runners, I promise to keep working to improve my times. Abigail, while she believed that women must learn history, was also a strong advocate of exercise.

Chronology

1798   *Alien and Sedition Acts*

1800   *Washington, D.C., becomes nation's capital*
        Thomas Jefferson elected president
        Death of Charles Adams (Nov. 30)

1801   Adamses return to Quincy

1811   Abigail Adams Smith has mastectomy
        Deaths of Richard Cranch (Oct. 16) and Mary Cranch (Oct. 17)

1812   *War with Britain*

1813   Death of Abigail Adams Smith (Aug. 14)

1815   Death of Elizabeth Peabody (Apr. 10)

1818   Death of Abigail Adams (Oct. 28)

1826   Deaths of John Adams and Thomas Jefferson (July 4)

Introduction

Abigail Adams has been a popular figure in biography for over a century and a half. Mrs. Adams, whose life spanned the second half of the eighteenth century and the first two decades of the nineteenth, has been chronicled and cited as an exemplary figure among women, primarily because she left a rich legacy of letters from which historians can draw. Still, she has been written about within the traditional framework that views her life in the shadow of the towering figures of her husband and son, who became the second and sixth presidents of the United States. Her independent legacy of letters notwithstanding, biographers have not given her an autonomous stature as a person separated from the men whose lives were integral to the founding of this nation and its political ideology.

I have thought about Abigail and about biography for many years, and it has become clear to me that John is at the center of her biographies because of chronology. As long as Abigail's life is told against the background or context that emphasizes events in which John took a major role during the Revolutionary War and early republican era, the story tends to slip into his world, making his life work the fulcrum of her biography. It follows that a different organizing principle than chronology is needed. This biography of Abigail Adams takes a new shape. It is written topically, focusing on episodes in her life and exploring them for the impact upon her of events in women's world. I call this approach a "collage," because the pieces, or chapters, are constructed from different materials. Each chapter presents an extended analysis of a single facet or topic in Abigail's life, that, in addition to portraying her, has implications for understanding generally the lives of eighteenth-century women. Each chapter is free-standing, in fact, not dependent upon its predecessors for definition or significance.

Taken together as in a collage, however, a whole picture emerges from the separate chapters. Unity comes because the central figure in each chapter is Abigail Adams, but also because the content overlaps from one chapter to another, giving a different vantage to an incident or a quotation. I have also provided a brief biographical chronology and historical context in most chapters to assist the reader. As in a collage, the chapters do not dangle in space, in part because this approach involves the readers, incorporating them into the creative process of imposing unity upon the elements of the subject's portrait. Also as in a collage, there may be many ways to see the picture, but in the end, the portrait is that of a woman, not of her men. Chapter 1, "The Abigail Industry," illustrates the contrast between

topical and chronological approaches by surveying the biographical literature that has been written about Abigail Adams since the first publication
of her letters in 1840.

In one sense, this biography is as much a social and cultural history of
Abigail's time as it is her life story, for it borrows theory from other
disciplines to explain the events of her life. I have chosen episodes or issues
that interest me, and in most cases I have used theories that seemed to me
to clarify and generalize the story. "A Virtuous Affair" borrows from literary studies to establish eighteenth-century letter-writing norms in order to
analyze a flirtatious correspondence between Abigail and James Lovell, a
member of the Continental Congress. Anthropology provides the theoretical context for understanding the function of "Gossip" as it operated in
the courtship of Abigail's daughter and Royall Tyler, her suitor who had a
rakish reputation. The correspondence of Abigail Adams and Thomas
Jefferson is surveyed through the lens of the psychological literature of
gender difference.

My approach acknowledges that women's lives were different from men's
lives, that women lived within an eighteenth-century patriarchy that was
hierarchical and viewed women as subordinate to men. That was also
Abigail's view of her world. The chapter "Domestic Patriotism" describes
how the Revolutionary War upset Abigail's consideration of her place in the
world, when John's responsibilities were shifted to her. Whereas Abigail
did not question the normality of the patriarchy, which she considered
divinely ordained and natural, I, as a citizen of a later age, have a different
perspective that is informed by my late twentieth-century world. I nevertheless believe it is incumbent to recreate the mentality of Abigail's world; I
attempt to write social explanation rather than social criticism.

I view the past through the lens of the recent literature about women, a
literature that has criticized traditional historical narrative as deficient in its
attention to women's lives and is causing a shift in the vantage of historical
discourse to give women a legitimate place in the broad picture of the past.
"The Threefold Cord" describes Abigail Adams's relationship with her
sisters, Mary Cranch and Elizabeth Shaw Peabody, over the course of their
lives, but it also probes the feminist use of the term "sisterhood" as a
euphemism for friendship. This chapter suggests that "sisterhood" borrows from the memory of maternal nurturance, while rejecting parental
authority, at the same time that it both reflects and differs from kin sisterhood.

Abigail Adams's independent reputation derives from the thousands of
letters which she wrote for over a half century and which have survived. I
view Abigail Adams as a writer, an author who composed in the genre
available to her in her time, for she lived before it was socially acceptable for
a woman to write in any other medium. She wrote about the issues that
were of concern to her as an eighteenth-century woman, and her letters are

extraordinary in range of topic, eloquence, and style; they are her best biography. The question is often raised, whether she did not write self-consciously for some public; the response is, of course, positive. She expected the person to whom the letter was addressed to read it and, as was usual in the eighteenth century, to share its contents with trusted friends. As to whether she expected her letters to be broadly read as historical relics, I believe not; the reason is that Abigail wrote primarily for herself. She wrote because it was her way of maintaining contact with family and friends, but she also wrote because the writing process was therapeutic. In the chapter ". . . a tye more binding . . ." I explore Abigail's early marriage to John Adams, but I also argue that she turned to letter writing for therapy in John's absence. Abigail wrote because she possessed a writer's sensitivity. "My wife must write!" John commented.[1]

Abigail's letters rank with those of the great correspondents of her age, which explains why they have been in print since her grandson first published a selection of them in 1840. Often personal, these letters provide unusual access to her private life, but they also capture her age—its social conventions, politics, and people—not just in description but in commentary, giving her the status of a domestic—i.e., American—Tocqueville, a writer whose observations and insights shed light on America and Americans of her time.

While I view Abigail's world as different from men's world, I do not deal extensively with domesticity—caring for her household and her family—which I consider her work. Rather, I examine Abigail's relationships with many people who were important in her life. "Mother and Citizen" focuses on Abigail and her eldest son, John Quincy, noting the Puritan legacy of child rearing with its persistent theme of public service that was later interpreted as "republicanism." "My Closest Companion," which explores the relationship of Abigail and her daughter, especially during the crisis of Abigail Junior's breast cancer and death, argues that mother and daughter were close allies over the span of their lives. The ubiquitous tension that twentieth-century women experience with their mothers may not have been a social phenomenon of that earlier period.

Abigail was modest about her letter writing, often requesting that her letters be destroyed. "You will burn all these letters," she wrote to John Adams in 1774, "least they should fall from your pocket and thus expose your affectionate Friend."[2] As an elderly woman she urged her sister Elizabeth to do the same: "I write very carless—pray destroy these rough unpolishd Letters."[3] She was usually spontaneous and unselfconscious in her rush of writing. To her sister Mary she admitted: "My letters to you are first thoughts without corrections."[4] She rarely copied; she was too impatient; she was too busy. Abigail's letters survived because others did not agree with her assessment of them. Because of them, she survives as an independent noble figure in late eighteenth-century history.

Portia was the pen name that Abigail Adams used during her adult years. She first identified with Portia—the erudite and wise but long-suffering Roman wife of the great statesman Brutus—during the dark years of the Revolutionary War, but she retained the name after she had outlived her worst struggles. The imagery of wisdom, erudition, and humanity implicit in *Portia* satisfied her self-image. It seems appropriate for her biography as well.

PORTIA

1

The Abigail Industry

When a family friend suggested publication of her letters in 1818, Abigail Adams recoiled: "No. No. . . . Heedless and inaccurate as I am, I have too much vanity to risk my reputation before the public."[1] Abigail's response contrasts mightily with the more characteristic Adams eagerness to appear in print; and it contrasts as well with the lack of reticence on the part of subsequent chroniclers who have found her a biographer's delight. Her grandson Charles Francis Adams first introduced her letters in 1840 by publishing a highly edited edition, which proved so popular that it was followed by three more editions by 1848.[2] In the near century and a half since then, enthusiasm for Abigail Adams's letters and interest in her life story have generated a veritable industry in Abigail literature.[3]

Her popularity derives primarily from the letters. The character that shines through the printed words remains to this day as endearing as it is intriguing, and her eloquence and spontaneity of expression give them unique color. In addition, Abigail's relationship with famous men has accorded her visibility. As wife and mother of presidents, she recorded her observations of revolutionary and early national America from a special perspective. She commented upon the salient issues of her time—the war, the economy, the people great and ordinary—as well as upon universal issues of religion, education, child rearing; she noted details of everyday life, such as styles of dress and manners, in a way that is irresistible to social historians; she wrote of philosophy and poetry. She can appear so modern, as in her appeal to her husband to "Remember the Ladies," that this much quoted injunction has been used to support a (false) picture of her as a radical feminist.[4] So many and various have been the claims on Abigail that the Abigail industry warrants analysis as a genre. From such an analysis a pattern emerges that broadly reflects the general depiction of women in historical writing.

We begin with a caveat: biographies of women, even those written during recent years, when rising consciousness of the gender gap in historiography has begun to balance the record of the past between the sexes, have characteristically used the same analytic models that have long been standard for biographies of men. Time is schematized to reflect a male life cycle, success is ascribed to male achievements, value is attached to men's work and interests. The vantage point has shifted over time, but the slant has been male and still remains so. Biographies of Abigail Adams are no exception. The consequence for her, as an exemplary figure in women's history, is that she has been reduced to a derivative place as a woman in a man's world.

This chapter identifies seven more or less overlapping categories in the literature about Abigail Adams. The first, dating from the mid-nineteenth century, sketches an idealized portrait of the domestic Abigail, the New England madonna. Here the subject is less an individualized woman than the qualities that were considered admirable in women. By the twentieth century, this imagery faded into a romantic silhouette of a woman consecrated in dutiful service to her great husband, whose life and activities became the real subject of the story. After the mid-twentieth century, Abigail became more picturesque as sexual motifs were introduced to enliven the portrayal. This characterization, in turn, gave way to feminist revisionism, which took several approaches, and to Freudian analysis. Then the themes of romantic wife and feminist were merged into the "Political Abigail," as admirable as she is anachronistic. Finally, there is an image of Abigail as shrew—an image that shows the destructive nature of historical debunking.

What is largely missing from these several portraits is the character that Abigail's letters reveal. The Abigail who emerges from her own words is a woman of wit, spirit, and emotion. Her thoughts and behavior reflect the culture in which she lived—late eighteenth-century New England; she is therefore domestic in her activity and aspirations. Confronted with circumstances that disrupted her young married life, she altered her ways to accommodate circumstances but remained true to her domestic values, always considering that her changed roles were a form of patriotic service to her country. She commented on politics, she even became political, but not just because she was interested and intelligent. It was the best hold she had on her marriage to a man who was committed more to public service than to family life. The Abigail Adams who emerges from the letters is a woman whose primary concerns derived from her functions as wife and mother, after which she was sister, friend, and patriot. The trend in her biographies, however, following male models of success, exaggerates her public image and suppresses her private domestic concerns because John's career is more valid and dramatic in the historical canon. She is made to mirror his public image whether as a subordinate wife or as a dominant companion. Either approach obscures her real character.

Abigail Smith was born into what was legally, economically, and politically a man's world, on November 22 (new style), 1744, at home in her father's parsonage at Weymouth, Massachusetts. Her parents represented two respectable New England lineages, her mother, Elizabeth Smith, being descended from Quincys, Nortons, Shepards, and Winthrops—"the bedrock of the Bay Colony's Puritan theocracy"[5]—and her father, the Reverend William Smith, from merchants and ship captains. Abigail's youth—indeed, most of her adult life—was spent in the countryside around Boston. As was typical for young women, she was educated at home, where she read literature—popular, classical, and spiritual—and some French, as did her two sisters, Mary and Elizabeth. Unlike her brother William, who was destined for Harvard, she did not learn Latin, which was considered appropriate only for men. Above all, her education prepared her for the one option available to women, the domestic role for which her mother was her noble model.[6]

The great milestone in her young life was marriage to John Adams in 1764, after a lengthy courtship during which the couple exchanged delightfully frank and amorous letters. These letters reveal a compatibility of intelligence, wit, and interests that would endure for over half a century of well-recorded partnership. Upon her marriage, Abigail moved to the modest cottage that John had inherited on the grounds of his parents' farm at Braintree. This cottage would be her primary residence until after the Revolution, although several times in the first decade of marriage John moved his family to Boston for short periods to accommodate his law practice.

Abigail married at nineteen, and within a year gave birth to her first child, a daughter also named Abigail. Within seven years, four more children were born, one of whom, Susanna, died in infancy. Abigail's letters for those years are scant, presumably because she was preoccupied with her duties as wife and mother; those that we have speak of her attentiveness to her babies, of her social life, and of her devotion to John.

By 1774 John was lured into the politics of the Revolution; his service to the American cause soon escalated into a lifelong commitment to public service. This turn of events marked the end of normal domesticity for Abigail; for a decade John was mostly absent from home, and Abigail performed his responsibilities as manager of family resources, in addition to her own domestic responsibilities. She learned to run the farm and deal with tenants; as her confidence grew, she undertook various business enterprises. She speculated in currency, purchased land (in John's name, since by law she could not own property), and sold luxury items that John sent from Europe. She became adept as an administrator and manager, but she always regarded these roles as aberrant and temporary, performed as her patriotic service.[7]

After John's departure, Abigail became an avid letter writer, primarily to her husband at first, but also to other family members and to friends. Those letters have survived, badly spelled and punctuated but noteworthy for their eloquence of style and range of topic. She wrote with equal zest about mundane matters of her social life and great issues of national affairs. Her letters are remarkable for the honesty with which she recorded her observations, feelings, and opinions. She gossiped, she judged, she hurt and hated, but above all, she displayed strength, consistency, and tolerance. The letters grew in number, length, and diversity of topic after she went to Europe in 1784 to join John, who had remained abroad after the conclusion of hostilities to become the first American minister to the Court of St. James's, and during the years when she lived in New York, Philadelphia, and Washington, D.C., where she followed her husband as he rose in public office.

The last twenty years of Abigail's life, like her first decade of marriage, were more private and domestic. After John's defeat for a second term as president, they retired to their home in Quincy, where Abigail resumed her interest in family and community affairs, as well as in household supervision and gardening, which was a passion with her. Her many grandchildren visited and sometimes lived with her, and her letters during this time speak often of her contentment. She also lived through two great tragedies—the death of her son Charles, from alcoholism, and the death of her daughter Abigail Junior from breast cancer. To the time of her own death in 1818 at age seventy-three, she was acutely attentive to her family and friends, as well as to public affairs, and she retained a zest for the business of living that makes her an attractive person to know. For that reason alone, biographers have found her irresistible.

The Saintly Abigail

Elizabeth Ellet's *The Women of the American Revolution*, which appeared in 1848, provided the archetypal portrait of Abigail.[8] This portrait is not truly personal but projects an idealized image of woman. Ellet's reverent tone, formal and elaborate language, unabashed admiration for her subject, and didactic message contour the hagiographic portrait of a New England madonna. "Her character is a worthy subject of contemplation for her countrywomen," Ellet wrote, establishing Abigail as a model of womanly virtues. "With intellectual gifts of the highest order she combined sensibility, tact and much practical knowledge of life." The merit of these virtues—pragmatic virtues, of course—is measured by woman's destiny: "thus she was qualified for eminent usefulness in her distinguished position as the companion of one great statesman, and the guide of another." Other women could aspire to such nobility of character. "Few may rise to such pre-eminence; but many can emulate the firmness that sustained her in all vicissitudes, and can imitate her Christian virtues."[9]

Although biased by convention, Ellet was one of the first historians to acknowledge that the achievements of women deserved a place in the historical record. She made her statement with pride for her sex, and others followed her lead well into the twentieth century. Abigail was typically described as "magnificent . . . the living spirit of the embattled Colonies" by authors who swelled with admiration for her. She was portrayed as "essentially New England—its bigotry inspired to tenacity, its harshness quickened into determination, its austerity illuminated by a fine resolve, its long tradition of sturdy faith and devotion . . . to home, to the land and to God—strengthened and sweetened in the keeping of this gentle, loyal, courageous lady."[10] As recently as 1969, a biography of John (while calling his wife "this bustling little Abigail") extolled Abigail as "soul-mate and helpmate to her husband, place and permanence to her children, mentor to both, loyal patriot to her country" and asserted that "to the man she married, to the children she nurtured she was a rare blessing."[11]

Abigail appears in this class of literature as a heroine—sexless and sainted, toiling and long-suffering, dedicated to husband, children, nation, religion, and charity without restraint or complaint. This theme is repeated as a didactic message. The domestic model becomes abstract; the subject is the ideal position advocated for women in society.

The Romantic Abigail: The Little Woman behind the Great Man

Janet Whitney's *Abigail Adams*, published in 1947, warrants special attention because, until 1980, it was the only full-scale modern biography and is still cited.[12] Whitney's Abigail is a variation on the hagiographic portrait, sketched in greater detail to tell the story of her life; however, the focus has shifted. The heroine remains in the background of this story, whose actual protagonist is John. The book opens when Abigail turns sixteen, at the beginning of her courtship by John, and it essentially terminates with the end of his public career. The story is shaped by the vicissitudes of John's work—the development of his law practice, the Boston Massacre trials, the Continental Congress, his diplomatic missions, the vice presidency and presidency. Abigail stands in the shadows as his dutiful, courageous, uncritical, loyal—and dull—wife.

Despite an impressive citation of manuscript sources, Whitney was writing a romance. She invented dialogue: " 'You won't let the Sons of Liberty draw you out into their doings' [Abigail] murmured. 'No,' said the firm decided voice she trusted."[13] She preached: "It is a hard thing to be on the wrong side of a revolution."[14] She presumed intention: "Abigail, listening to young John Adams, forgot that he also was plump and short-necked: she noticed only that he . . . had the eye of an eagle."[15] She intruded home-spun wisdom: "Abigail was fifty-three and John was sixty-two. They had reached an age when, in the average marriage, mutual interest is at a low ebb."[16] Most important, Whitney fictionalized her biography by making Abigail a romantic adjunct to John. She overlooked Abigail's emotional range—that she could be abrasive as well as docile, that she was inspired by her brain as much as by her heart, that she complained as often as she encouraged. Negative qualities, being unattractive, must be overlooked in such a heroine. Abigail remains a stereotype and a foil for John, whose accomplishments and reputation preempt the story.

Phyllis Lee Levin's *Abigail Adams* (1987), published forty years after Whitney's, has greater scope and depth but also significant similarities.[17] Levin's far-reaching research and extensive use of the Adams Papers make hers the most comprehensive biography to date. Furthermore, although Abigail's youth is typically abbreviated, this biography, unlike others, ac-counts for the last twenty years of her life, after John's retirement from public office.

Yet Levin, like Whitney, has cast Abigail in a supportive role. "To write her life is to write of a partnership," notes Levin in her preface. "Her biography turns out to be as much John's as Abigail's."[18] With that admis-sion, the author surrenders her story to John. She devotes whole sections of chapters to events that occupied John but that affected Abigail only slightly—John's writing of *Thoughts on Government*, the Silas Deane affair, the XYZ affair.[19] In contrast, Levin dismisses in four paragraphs a circum-stance that preoccupied Abigail for almost a year and for which there is unusual documentation—the difficult pregnancy and stillbirth of her sixth child.[20] John's world and work propel this biography, whereas Abigail's world is adjunct and subordinate. At the close of John's public career, Levin shifts her focus to John Quincy's emerging political career to buttress her story about Abigail.

Understandably mesmerized by the elegance of Abigail's letters, Levin was trapped by them. Her heavy use of quotation becomes tedious, es-pecially in the first half of the book. Further, since the author fails to analyze or interpret lengthy excerpts, the projection of Abigail is super-ficial. A paragraph ends with Abigail's call to "Remember the Ladies," and a new topic begins; no further significance is accorded to this famous statement.[21] The letters also control the structure of the biography; by following the content of letters, Levin includes irrelevancies that often obscure the direction of the narrative. Moreover, Levin selects passages in which Abigail whines a lot, lending a doleful aspect to a heroine whom the author asserts in her preface invented "the principle that women should have 'political, economic, and social rights equal to those of men.'"[22] Levin's lack of control over her sources leads to an inconsistent and shallow portrait of Abigail.

What finally qualifies Levin as a descendant of Whitney (whom she also cites as the source for several dubious facts) is the book's tone.[23] Since she quotes so extensively, Levin does not invent dialogue as did Whitney, but her accompanying narrative can be cloying. She describes romance: "After just a few years of marriage, both Abigail and John seemed already to cherish their brief past, as though the elements of happiness it afforded them were forever beyond reach."[24] A later Abigail prefigures Mary Poppins: "Cap in place, children in hand, husband in tow, Abigail descended on Paris." The children were Abigail Junior, age nineteen, and John Quincy, age seventeen.[25] Finally, she becomes the maternal martyr: "For all her anguish, she was probably the proudest mother on American turf."[26] The "Little Woman behind the Great Man" is very much alive as a current model of biography.

The Flirtatious Abigail

If early versions overpraised the ideal woman, a contrary interpretation has disparaged her. In his monumental biography of John Adams, Page Smith dramatized his story and created human interest by modeling Abigail on the age-old double standard.[27] Smith, at best, was sympathetic, even romantic like Whitney. Of the Adamses' marriage he wrote that "Abigail insured [John's] sanity. . . . She gave him, with her love, a gyroscope that brought him safely through the stormiest seas." Smith realized that "a wife cannot be utterly the converse of her husband and thus irreconcilable, not the mirror image and thereby no more than an accentuation of his vices. . . . At the happiest, she is able, as Abigail was, to enter with so much sympathy and understanding into her husband's world, that she makes him more holy, more wholesome, more healthy. And this is what Abigail Adams did for the man who was her husband, her lover and her friend."[28] The wifely mission was thus defined. Essentially, however, Smith used Abigail's romantic presence to lighten the narrative of two volumes of political and diplomatic biography.

Smith asserted that Abigail consciously deployed her sexuality. "The fact was," he wrote, "that there was more than a little of the flirt in Abigail."[29] France was therefore a comfortable place for her to live, for "Abigail who loved to flirt found herself in a world where flirtation was simply a part of the character of social life."[30] Smith did not suggest that John Adams was a flirt, but as a woman Abigail is a vulnerable target. Yet Smith missed the mark, for her letters reveal a different reality: all of her New England prudery emerged during her brief stay in France, and she harangued relatives and friends about the licentiousness she witnessed. "There are some practices which neither time nor custom will ever make me a convert to," she wrote from France in 1785. "If I thought they would I would fly the country and its inhabitants as a pestelence walketh in darkness and a plague that waisteth at noon."[31] Abigail experienced loneliness, displacement, and isolation in France, and no small part of her alienation was due to the cultural climate that contrasted greatly with that of rural New England.[32]

To account for the wife who shared her husband's interest in politics, history, and philosophy, Smith wrote that Abigail "had a masculine edge to her mind that made her especially appealing to intelligent men."[33] He softened this image by merging it with the sexual and the flirtatious:

> She found . . . more comfort and entertainment than she was likely to reveal to John in the several attractive and literate young men of the village. . . . Abigail thoroughly enjoyed the company of witty and intelligent males. She was conscious of her ability to meet them on their own terms without any concession for her sex . . . and she delighted in the play of minds over a subject. . . . Moreover, since she was a very attractive and thoroughly feminine woman with no trace about her of the self-conscious female pedant that her husband deplored, these conversations . . . had a subtle undercurrent of sexual stimulus. . . . There was a certain archness in her glance and speech.[34]

Such juxtaposition of intelligence with sexual imagery detracts from Abigail's intelligence. It demeans her to suggest that in conversations with men (who are never depicted by Smith in blatantly sexual terms) she used sexuality. According to the dictates of the double standard in such literature, a woman's intelligence cannot be described without alluding to her physical attributes.

The Feminist Abigail

During the last decades, feminist efforts to correct the male bias in historical writing have generated a body of literature that reflects both the evolution of women's history and controversies among its practitioners. The first revisionists searched for heroines to match the heroes of revolutionary America, and sometimes they anachronistically cast these women's lives in terms of late twentieth-century feminist ideology. The highly visible Abigail Adams has been an important figure in this new scholarship, for her letters address issues of politics and women's domestic role and education. However, many early feminist writers misappropriated the meaning of her thoughts and attributed to her a greater consciousness of women's subjection than the evidence will support.

Elizabeth Evans's *Weathering the Storm: Women of the American Revolution* (1975) typifies this literature.[35] The tone is polemical: "The most famous advocate of women's rights was Abigail Smith Adams, wife of John Adams, member of the Continental Congress and later President of the United States. Refusing to be an obscure mouthpiece for her husband's views, she influenced many of his political decisions." John becomes the antagonist in Evans's story, a man who "was quite bullheaded about women's rights and refused to take the subject seriously"; in response, Abigail becomes a prototypical feminist activist: "This infuriated the 'lioness' whose growl turned into a roar. She unleashed an angry letter to Mercy Warren, historian, dramatist, and sister of James Otis, asking for support.[36]

For a time in the mid-1970s, this image of feminist Abigail met with sympathy. In his sketch of John Adams in *Seven Who Shaped Our Destiny,* Richard Morris wrote, "Abigail, a committed feminist, often baited her husband about the undue subordination of women at the law and in education."[37] The 1975 television series "The Adams Chronicles" popularized this notion of Abigail as a sturdy type of farm woman and feminist, portraying her working on her farm (in reality, farmhands did the fieldwork), berating John Hancock for his wealth, challenging Thomas Jefferson to discuss the rights of women.[38]

Ironically, this kind of revisionism perpetuates the very misinterpretations that feminist historians wish to correct. The prevailing female role of the eighteenth century—the domestic role that Abigail herself valued as the greatest in her life—is overshadowed by a mythical political activism that reflects late twentieth-century ideology. By diminishing the significance of domesticity, this literature further borrows from male standards of value, achievement, and success to explain women's past.

At the same time, a different current of feminist history rendered a more accurate assessment of Abigail as an eighteenth-century woman whose political aspirations were limited by her acceptance of the domestic culture to which she ascribed. In a provocative 1976 essay, "The Illusion of Change: Women and the American Revolution," Joan Hoff-Wilson claimed that "Abigail Adams was not in any sense demanding legal, let alone political or individual, equality with men at the beginning of the Revolution."[39] Linda Grant DePauw reinforced this interpretation: "Abigail Adams herself, I am now convinced, would have been mortified to learn the meaning that has been read into some of her private—and not entirely serious—correspondence with her husband."[40] Nancy F. Cott has read Abigail's plea to "Remember the Ladies" not so much as a political appeal but as an acknowledgment of the sexual oppression of women: "In Abigail Adams's famous request to her husband . . . her central complaint was not women's political disenfranchisement but husbands' legal exercise of 'unlimited power' over their wives."[41] Mary Beth Norton also stressed that Abigail's "Remember the Ladies" statement was meant to address the legal subordination of married women.[42] Carl N. Degler, in *At Odds,* further supported this view of Abigail: "Rather than denying in any way wifehood or motherhood as the role of women, Abigail Adams merely asked for an improvement in the traditional relationships with husbands."[43]

The two feminist interpretations of Abigail—the one anachronistic, the other sensitive to eighteenth-century thought and behavior—persist in the literature, stimulating a lively debate about the usefulness of historical figures to sustain a contemporary ideology. The most sensitive analyses of Abigail view her as a woman of her times and in her own context.

The Freudian Abigail

Only a small segment of the Abigail industry draws on psychoanalysis, but that work which focuses on Abigail as a parent has had far-reaching effects. For example, in his provocative psychoanalytic study "The Youth of John Quincy Adams," David F. Musto analyzed her eldest son's early breakdown and, probing its etiology, turned to Abigail's influence as a mother.[44] At age twenty-one John Quincy experienced "a period of emotional and physical discomfort" so acute that he was forced to withdraw from his law studies to seek refuge first in his aunt's home and then in the family home at Quincy.[45] Musto attributed this "crisis" to John Quincy's questioning of his capacity to sustain the Adams "family myth," a "view of the family shared by the members yet not subject to rational examination." The Adams myth carried "an imperative for achievement of political power through moral and educational superiority."[46] Musto's meaning becomes more clear as his argument develops.

The myth, according to Musto, originated with John, who in his youth "had a great desire for power and a will to control," as well as great "drive and ambition." John was comfortable with his egoism, claimed Musto, but John Quincy "reacted to his own great egoism with denial, fear or guilt." The critical question in the thesis is, then, "How did the ability to be comfortably aware of one's open ambition become lost for the second generation?" Musto answered his query: "Here the crucial person is Abigail Adams."[47]

The issues of John Quincy's guilt or his crisis as a law student are beyond the scope of this chapter. What is of interest is Abigail's role in relation to her son's emotional breakdown. Musto here followed the common pattern of blaming the mother for her children's problems, sometimes with the scientific "proof" of psychoanalytic hypotheses.[48] His argument was that Abigail compensated for her loneliness during John's long absences by constructing an exaggerated image of his greatness for her children, especially her eldest son. Musto's Abigail is a bitter woman who manipulates her children's lives in order to justify her own sacrifice of normal family life: "Her strength within the family was not simply that of endurance but also of control. . . . It is this powerful ability to control and instill guilt that

Abigail exercised upon her young children during her husband's long years of absence."[49]

This argument contains elements of insight supported by Abigail's letters. She did, when left alone, begin to identify John's service to the country with the good of the country, and she defended against loneliness by promoting an inflated image of him. However, Musto's interpretation of Abigail's negative influence on John Quincy is premised on her single-handed parenting, whereas the boy was actually more often separated from his mother than from his father during his first seventeen years. In his formative years, to age seven, the Adamses experienced a fairly normal family life, except during the weeks when John traveled the circuit for his law practice. Yet Musto proposed that between John Quincy's seventh and eleventh years—when John was often away at the Continental Congress—Abigail so severely crippled the boy's psyche that he suffered a crisis as a young man. This account ignores the effects of war, sickness, and death that John Quincy witnessed during those years, as well as the unsettling influences of material deprivation and erratic schooling. Musto's analysis here, as elsewhere, is too deterministic.

Furthermore, John Quincy was seldom with his mother after he went with his father to France at age eleven. With the exception of a few months' stay in Braintree in 1779, he remained in Europe until the age of eighteen, most often traveling or on his own at school in Amsterdam. In total, Abigail lived with her grown son in Europe for less than a year before he returned to America to enter Harvard.

The flaw in Musto's thesis, as in much psychoanalytic theory, is sexual bias. Musto exaggerated the mother's role as destructive agent, while underestimating, even ignoring, the father's influence.[50] Above all Musto foreclosed John's power to transmit guilt to his son; yet a reading of the correspondence between the two reveals, as Musto acknowledged, unremitting fatherly advice and unvarying filial diffidence in response. John's advice might be read as a form of control, whereas the ultimate expression of John Quincy's diffidence might be labeled guilt. John was no less powerful than Abigail as a manipulator of guilt. Finally, his offices and public reputation, his absence from the household, and his role in the Revolution could have been awe-inspiring to a young son—even without the myth making of an overbearing mother.

Musto was correct in ascribing power and importance to the maternal role, but his analysis fails by interpreting the role negatively, by not exploring the value of mother love and protectiveness. The Abigail who wrote to her sons in Europe, "Neither time or Distance have . . . diminished the . . . affection which I bear you—you are ever upon my heart and mind," was the lonely mother whose expressions of care were not reserved, however, for times of separation.[51]

The Political Abigail

The portraits of the political Abigail in two recent biographies were created for different audiences. Charles W. Akers's brief monograph *Abigail Adams: An American Woman* (1980) was written for undergraduates, Lynne Withey's *Dearest Friend: A Life of Abigail Adams* (1981) for a more popular readership.[52] Both books are notable for their rich contextual development and for their attention to the literature of social history, especially new studies of the lives of eighteenth-century women. They focus on the dramatic events of Abigail's lifetime—events in which she was involved either as a participant or as a relation of a participant. Her role as adjunct becomes, in fact, the center of both books. The importance of John's public offices and activities overwhelms the life of Abigail, and she becomes once again the traditional little woman behind the great man, this time dressed up as John's political alter ego, the outspoken defender if not designer of his policies in office, the power behind the throne.

Withey framed her characterization of Abigail in the preface. Abigail, she asserted, was "maddeningly contradictory"—on the one hand, a "feisty revolutionary"; on the other hand, a "reactionary" in politics. Withey noted that Abigail argued for "legal rights and education for women," yet became "obsessed" with "delicacy" and "moral purity." Within her family, Withey claimed, Abigail tried to control the lives of everyone, yet instilled a "spirit of independence." Given these contradictions, "How does one explain a conservative who advocated independence for America and equality for women?"[53]

In reality, the contradictions in Withey's Abigail derive not from tensions in her subject but from her use of twentieth-century standards to measure a late eighteenth-century woman. Like other Abigail biographers—from Ellet to Whitney—Withey could not separate the heroine from her husband; therefore, she exaggerated Abigail's political character because she was married to a political figure. Withey structured the biography according to the chronology of John's career, used sources to emphasize political issues, and, in the process, lost sight of Abigail's private self. Moreover, when she addressed the political issues of the Adamses' lives, including feminism, she wrote not from the context of the eighteenth century but from the perspective of the present debate about revolutionary politics and gender politics.

Displaced ambition became, in Withey's interpretation, the explanation for Abigail's political rhetoric. She wrote that Abigail "was ambitious, almost without knowing it, and she acted out her ambition in the only way that an eighteenth-century woman could: through her husband. In that sense she enjoyed basking in John's reflected glory."[54] Later, Withey noted that Abigail "had her share of ambition and desire to be at the center of activity. . . . [T]here was a side of her that was bored with her simple domestic life and was ready for the adventure."[55] In other words, at some unconscious level, Abigail longed to be at Philadelphia or Paris herself. This late twentieth-century version of the frustrated professional woman, "bored with her simple domestic life," overlooks the real Abigail who had ambition for neither John nor herself. In reality, when hostilities with Britain ended, she pressed him "to come home, take the farm into your own hands and improve it, let me turn dairy woman in getting our living this way."[56] When Abigail conceded to John's active political life after the Revolution, it represented her reluctant submission to John's ambitions.

Withey wrote that Abigail never asked John to choose between his career and his family.[57] In fact, this was a persistent undercurrent in their correspondence as the years of separation increased to a full decade, and later an open plea when hostilities with Britain ended. In the fall of 1783, while John remained in Europe pining after an appointment to the Court of St. James's, Abigail wrote, "If Congress should think proper to make you another appointment, I beg you not to accept it."[58] A few months later she wrote more directly, "I know not whether I shall believe myself how well you love me, unless I can prevail upon you to return in the Spring."[59]

Abigail's friend Mercy Otis Warren presents a far better example of an aspiring woman who was frustrated by constraints on her sex, who sought fame and influence in the publication of poetry, plays, and history, and who relentlessly promoted her own work as well as the careers of her men.[60] At best, Abigail tolerated a public role for herself, while she rationalized as virtue—as duty, patriotism, and the destiny of unique talent—the irrepressible ambition of her husband.

Withey's allusion to women's work as boring and men's work as adventurous reflects the mentality of the twentieth rather than the eighteenth century. Abigail did not think in such terms. She did not recognize an alternative to domestic life for a woman; she did not view her domestic routine as simple in any sense; she worked too hard at her tasks to consider her life boring; she felt assured of the dignity of her work as housewife and mother. To her cousin Isaac Smith Jr., she wrote explicitly: "Women you know sir are Domestic Beings."[61] When she was forced to support her household during John's absences, she regarded the role as unnatural, a patriotic sacrifice. She wrote to a family friend, "It is no small satisfaction to me that my country will have the benefit of my personal sacrifices though they little [know] how great they are."[62] She took pleasure in her success as "farmeress" and entrepreneur, but she looked forward to the time when John would return to function properly as head of the Adams household.[63]

There is little evidence to show that Abigail thought inventively about politics; in fact, she became a student of history and political thought only after her marriage to John, her mentor and model. Abigail was neither the "fiery revolutionary" nor the political "reactionary" that Withey claimed. Abigail considered herself a patriot, and her words echo the conventional rhetoric of revolutionary patriotism. Her "conservative" views about the most base nature of human beings were part of the Puritan tradition that survived in her New England background. Nor did she in her early life read Wollstonecraft or have any notions about sexual equality.[64] Abigail did live in a political environment. She came from a family of political leaders; she was the wife of a premier architect of the American nation and the mother of a great statesman. Politics was not, however, the overarching concern in her life.

Abigail's religious beliefs, for instance—which few biographers, including Withey, mention, and none have explored—fundamentally affected her life. Religion provided her with perspective for understanding the world and her place in it. Religion explained the vagaries of existence and gave her hope. It described a system of values and a scheme for teaching her children. It explained politics and all other human activity to her. Abigail's religion integrated and transcended worldly affairs, including politics. Withey's Abigail Adams, by borrowing imagery primarily from John's world of politics, reflects his mirror-image rather than her individual character.

Charles W. Akers's *Abigail Adams: An American Woman* insightfully describes Abigail as a woman with "a strong sense of personal worth that seldom failed her in the many unexpected turns of her life."[65] Yet Akers's respect flaws his portrait; he excused Abigail's judgmentalism, her narrowness, her bitter and caustic side, her jealousies, her occasional pettiness. His ultimate distortion of her character results from seeing her marriage as an equal partnership. Akers's Abigail, like Withey's, moves out of the domestic and into the political sphere. In order to make a marriage of equals, Akers must define Abigail as political because the social imagery of the domestic role is not equal to a public role.

The book's great accomplishment is its recapitulation of the revolutionary and early federal eras. "The life of this one woman forms a large window on society during the three-quarters of a century that saw the birth and political maturation of the United States," Akers began, and he succeeded in using Abigail's experience to illuminate the times.[66] However, the depth of biography was sacrificed to this purpose; if, in writing on the Revolution, Akers captured a credible and sympathetic Abigail, she became in the later chapters a lifeless caricature, idealized as the "republican woman" or the "republican mother." By the time she travels to Europe for reunion with John, Abigail is no longer a woman of character but a stereotype.

The overarching story becomes that of the worlds in which John Adams and John Quincy Adams functioned. Abigail is introduced in the book's first two sentences as the wife and mother of great men: she "married a man destined to be . . . the second President of the United States. She gave birth to and nurtured a son who became . . . its sixth President."[67] The title of the concluding chapter, "The Mother of Such a Son," acknowledges the priority of John Quincy's career. Throughout the book, the rhythm of Abigail's life, her womanly concerns, is governed by the tempo of her men's lives.

It follows, then, that Akers missed much of the dynamic in her marriage to John, which he defined as a "marriage of equals," albeit in "separate spheres." True, Abigail and John had a good marriage; there was much sympathy, trust, and loyalty between them. But this was not a marriage of equals. Abigail was, in conventional eighteenth-century terms, submissive to his will and his needs, more so than Mercy Otis Warren, who was "unwilling to give up her husband to the state for long periods."[68] In order to preserve her marriage Abigail acquiesced to the most egregious demands of her husband's well-intentioned but single-minded pursuits in public service. That John felt gratitude, respect, and guilt does not mean that he considered her his equal. Abigail did what was expected of her in her time; she submitted her preferences for a private life to those of her husband; his "sphere" determined hers. "I feel a greater regard for those persons who love me for your sake," Abigail wrote to John in 1783, "than I should if they esteemed me on my own account."[69]

Akers concluded that Abigail's sphere, ultimately, was most nobly defined as republican womanhood, a term that probably derives from Linda K. Kerber's work on women in the revolutionary and early federal periods.[70] Yet Akers did not describe his model of a republican woman; instead, he simply used Abigail as its definition, fitting her views of parenting, education of women, charity, and public service into its framework. As a result, the ideal and the real become indistinguishable, and Abigail ceases to have life; the mission of republican womanhood is confused with republican politics and fused with John's office of the presidency. Akers wrote that "Abigail's greatest satisfaction came from her private role as confidant of, counselor to, and defender of the President. Standing at the center of the nation's political life, she felt the obligation of republican womanhood more strongly than ever before. Her intense concern with the single critical issue dominating the administration of John Adams proved debilitating. She could never rest while her husband's fame—and hers—hung in the balance."[71] Abigail becomes such an exaggerated symbol of the republican woman, such an extension of her husband's career, that at times she and John seem to hold office jointly: "John and Abigail saw no harm in appointing qualified relatives to federal offices"; "Abigail and John sensed that taxes were overtaking foreign affairs as the vital political issue."[72] In using Abigail to provide a window on the Washington and Adams administrations, Akers lost sight of her character.

As republican mother, Abigail is ennobled; she teaches her sons to be patriotic, godly, and good. Her motherly advice becomes politicized, removed from the realm of domestic concerns and shifted to the public arena where it can benefit the nation. Following John Quincy's election to the

Senate in 1803, her "son's rising public career called her back to her duty as a republican mother."[73] This notion of Abigail's maternal duty overlooks the fact that she had always cared primarily about the welfare of her children—their spiritual and moral welfare as well as their physical well-being. She did not care less for those children who did not enter the political arena.

The political Abigail, a construct that fits late twentieth-century concepts of eighteenth-century woman as politically active and ambitious, is not more accurate or appropriate than the romantic Abigail. It views Abigail through her attachment to John, subordinating the content of her life to his enterprises and overlooking other formative experiences that gave meaning and significance to her life.

Abigail the Shrew

Paul C. Nagel explained at the outset of *Descent from Glory* (1983) that his aim was to correct the popular image of the "extraordinary brilliance" of four generations of Adamses. He took as his challenge Charles Francis Adams's comment that his family history "is not a pleasant one to remember. It is one of great triumphs in the world but of deep groans within, one of extraordinary brilliancy and deep corroding mortification."[74]

A gloomy mood pervades the work, implied by its title and sustained by titles of its chapters: "Disappointments," "Struggles," "Tragedy"; the word "depressed" becomes an obbligato. Abigail is depressed; John is depressed; John Quincy is depressed; Thomas is depressed; Louisa is depressed; even nephew Thomas Greenleaf is depressed.[75] Nagel further exaggerates the Adams history with numerous unsubstantiated claims, such as the wild suggestion that Abigail Junior considered suicide or that John Quincy turned to heavy drinking as he fretted over his depraved taste in women.[76] Nagel borrows from the pathology of psychoanalysis—the Adams children collectively "struggle with apprehension, compulsive behavior, rebelliousness, withdrawal and depression"—and summons pop psychology as well: Thomas is engaged in a "search for identity."[77] Altogether, *Descent from Glory* sounds a litany of pessimism and pathos.

Nagel portrayed Abigail as the matriarchal shrew of the dynasty, an ambitious and sexually repressed manipulator who controlled her husband and sons; she fought with her daughter and disliked women. At the outset, he stated that Abigail "was as complicated a personality" as John; yet to compare the two in this facile manner is to miss them both.[78] The struggles that Abigail experienced were not those of unresolvable inner tensions, as were John's. She did not suffer conflicts over her place in the world, her role in society, her guilt, or her ambition. Her suffering was caused by the vagaries of living, heightened by the upheavals of the Revolution and the complexities of her husband's personality. Her responses to adversity were often mournful, self-pitying, angry, complaining—healthy human reactions—and they were as often courageous, wise, and noble. This balanced range of emotional response does not indicate a character complicated by a perpetual internal struggle to define and seek a place in the world. Abigail probably was more stable and secure than John.

Although Nagel stated that managing affairs and people was Abigail's "passion during her first ten years of marriage," he provided no evidence for this and, indeed, could not.[79] During those years Abigail bore five children, including the sickly daughter who lived only a year; she moved her household between Braintree and Boston four times and changed houses in Boston twice. She did not have time to manage the family business and people, much less to develop a "passion" for anything but mothering and housewifery. Nagel simply collapsed the time sequence, for Abigail became involved in family enterprises only in the second decade of her marriage, when John was absent from the household, and she did so initially with the lack of experience and timidity of a neophyte. She did eventually develop expertise, but never a passion for the role.[80]

Nagel described Abigail as a social climber who sympathized with her husband's contentment in rural felicity but "thought that this should not hinder the family's social progress."[81] In fact, Abigail's egalitarian instincts were constant from the time of her marriage to a man from a social background more modest than her own. She wrote in 1783, "I have not sought to vie with the Beau Mond. I have not [socialized] with the frequenters of the Ball or Assembly rooms. I have not extended my acquaintance amongst the polite and fashionable circle of the present day."[82] When she lived in London, as wife of the American minister, she still wrote that "tho I sometimes like to mix in the gay world, . . . I have much reason to be grateful to my parents that my early education gave me not an habitual taste for what is termed fashionable life."[83]

Nagel contended that Abigail was "never a serious student," that she "often claimed that preoccupation with books and ideas threw a person into depression."[84] Whereas Page Smith had Abigail flirting rather than reasoning, Nagel employed his ubiquitous theme of depression to dismiss Abigail's intelligence. In truth, if Abigail developed a passion, it was for books. She read and reflected deeply about literature, history, and political philosophy—the more so as she aged; she corresponded with literate, scholarly women such as Mercy Otis Warren; she wrote disparagingly of women who did not seek to improve their minds: "What is life or its enjoyments without . . . mental exertions—a mere vapor indeed."[85] She lobbied for years in her letters for the improvement of women's education. She encouraged her daughter to learn Latin, highly unusual for a woman in the eighteenth century, and repeatedly urged her nieces to improve their minds. Clearly, she did not think that books and ideas depressed people; she believed that they represented the highest human achievements.

Just as Abigail did not share John's scholarly tastes, Nagel continued, "she usually did not join in his good-humored acceptance of sensuality" (a claim for which there is no proof in the couple's writings) and "became increasingly prudish when she thought of the passion in others."[86] Nagel pieced together bits of Abigail's correspondence from different contexts to argue that she grew increasingly suspicious and bitter when John in Europe did not respond to her affectionate letters. "She clamored: 'I want some sentimental Effusions of the Heart.' 'Lovers and Husbands' who were the 'cold phlegmatick' type were not for her, she insisted. 'I thank Heaven I am not so constituted myself and so connected.' "[87] The theme reaches its crescendo: "Receiving Abigail's reproach and accusations, John broke under his load of frustrating work and personal guilt." Soon after, Abigail, too, came close to "breaking down."[88] Thus marital tension yields to a pathological interpretation.

The case against the shrew mounts. "During their more than fifty years of marriage, John and Abigail Adams appeared to trade roles in the family. He became increasingly calm, tolerant, and unassuming, while she seemed more volatile, caustic, and proud. John grew lovable as time passed while Abigail seemed to intimidate even her children."[89] Nagel further extended Abigail's supposed bitterness to all women, claiming that "she distrusted members of her sex" and had "suspicions of women in general."[90] In truth, Abigail Adams cared for many women and relied on support from her mother, aunts, sisters, daughter, and friends throughout her life. She was charmed by Madame Lafayette in Paris, and she felt great affection for Martha Washington. Abigail respected herself well enough to respect—and trust—other women.[91]

Above all, Nagel built his portrayal of Abigail as shrew upon her role as mother. He suggested but provided no evidence that tension existed between Abigail and her daughter.[92] In fact, the two were always close. "I have frequently been called in the course of my life to very painful separations," Abigail wrote after her daughter's marriage. "But this is the first time that I have suffered a separation from her, and it is more painful, as she has always been my companion and my associate."[93] Tension marked her relations with her sons as well. Since evidence about Thomas's early life is scant, Nagel invented a character—"a very shy lad, slow, clumsy, unsure of himself to a pathetic degree"—who is plagued in adulthood by alcoholism.[94] Abigail hounded Thomas about his weaknesses until the "innocent lad erupted with a cry of indignation."[95] About Charles's death from alcoholism, Nagel wrote that Abigail took a "strange pride in the fact that at least Charles had avoided the appearance of an alcoholic," substantiating this claim with her words: "He was bloated, but not red."[96] Nagel's John Quincy is haunted by his mother's relentless moral teachings, her endless nagging, and her unabashed ambition for him, which "caused him to scorn any [other] woman's ability."[97] Reading this account, one wonders that any of the Adams children became functional.

To be sexless and a bad mother—what is left of the dignity of an eighteenth-century woman? Especially if she is jealous, is uninterested in books, distrusts other women, meddles in the affairs of other people, and possesses among her many passions a "passionate ambition for her family."[98] Nagel even interpreted her charitable activity as a means of extending her "maternal empire."[99] The picture, in the end, is not of Abigail but of the archetypal shrew.

In *The Adams Women: Abigail and Louisa Adams, Their Sisters and Daughters* (1987), Nagel continued his treatise on the Adamses' private lives, this time focusing solely on three generations of women.[100] Many of the themes that informed his earlier book emerge in this one, especially his interpretation of Abigail who, despite some complimentary platitudes, is not cast as a likeable woman. She is formidable as well as stern, prudish, ambitious, condescending, and insensitive; she controls an empire, manipulates her children's lives, is jealous of her sisters, and meddles in national politics, church politics, and sexual politics. Nothing has changed; there is just more of the same.[101]

At times, Nagel deliberately contrasts the Abigail of this group biography with her sisters, her daughter, and the other Adams women: "Abigail's sons received [from their Aunt Elizabeth] an overflowing measure of what [she] quietly recognized they did not get from their stern mother, relaxed and sympathetic affection."[102] Other times, he infers comparisons; both sisters Elizabeth and Mary are described as intelligent, generous, sensitive, and spiritual women against Abigail's more harsh character. Daughter Nabby is burdened with an overbearing mother: "Abigail's demands on Nabby and her brothers for excellence in morals, intelligence, and deportment sometimes obscured her affection for them. . . . Much of [Nabby's] authentic personality was suppressed by resentment and anxiety over the expectations placed upon her."[103] By exaggerating the noble sisters and docile daughter, Nagel draws a contrasting portrait of Abigail that is as unperceptive as it is inconsistent. However, deeper problems flaw this work, particularly Nagel's handling of time.

Because he focuses so closely on the women's lives, Nagel fails to establish a sense of historical time. Although dates are cited, events are not depicted to establish context; without an anchor in the revolutionary and post-revolutionary eras, the private lives of Abigail and her sisters float in space. Contributing to this timelessness is the lack of reference to the scholarship of women's studies, which lends the Adams women a false aura of uniqueness.

A different problem with time is the use of concepts from pop psychology to describe eighteenth-century people, who once again emerge with twentieth-century neuroses. Nagel does not follow the concepts from any one school of psychology to probe character deeply or sensitively; rather, he superficially applies labels: the number of people who suffered (and died) from alcoholism reaches epidemic proportions in this volume; there is lots of sexual tension and frustration; there are the ubiquitous mother-daughter tension and rivalry among the sisters. Abigail's domineering mothering resulted in resentment and anxiety in the daughter and re-bellion in the son; more signs of the "dark side" of the Adams family are described.

For example, consider Nagel's astonishing version of sixteen-year-old Nabby Adams's relations with her father. John was off in Europe all alone while Nabby at home longed to escape from her mother, to establish her "independent self." She "talked more ardently of her own wishes for a new life, one with her father. . . . Surely, Nabby said, a daughter could sub-stitute as a wife and thus bring to her father the 'tender attentions' he so needed. For Nabby, John Adams' life without a feminine companion was distressing beyond words," but, of course, Abigail meddled in her daugh-ter's plans. "By now," Nagel adds, "it was 1782, and Nabby had a pre-maturely buxom appearance which Abigail told John would surely 'grace' his table in Europe."[104] The details are curious, since no portrait exists from 1782, nor is there a description of Nabby's "buxom appearance" anywhere that I know of. The rest of the innuendo—that "a daughter could substitute as a wife"—is preposterous.

Nagel's great forte is his storytelling. Furthermore, he is a virtuoso with the Adams sources. The combination should make for superlative history or biography. But is this history? Or biography? As in his earlier volume, Nagel uses no footnotes, and once again, the story is freed from account-ability. Nagel frequently pushes his material farther than the sources will go. The evidence for Elizabeth's romances, developed here in graphic detail, is slight, beyond some possible references in a letter or two to her romance with the man she married, Rev. John Shaw. Nor does Nagel provide evidence to prove that Shaw and his son died of alcoholism.[105]

The account of Abigail's efforts to engineer a courtship between her daughter and Royall Tyler poses questions about storytelling as well. When Nabby did not respond to Tyler, "the suitor turned to the mother. Abigail Adams never denied that she preferred the company of men. . . . Abigail was then age thirty-seven, with her attractiveness as compelling as ever. . . . Already weary of her mother's pushing and prompting, Nabby's misgivings about Royall Tyler were anything but overcome by Abigail's making the association a triangle."[106] A reading of the sources tells a different story. Nabby was attracted to Tyler and struggled, as did her mother, over his appropriateness as a mate. In fact, Abigail was so distraught over the issue that she wrote to John: "I wish most sincerely you was at Home to judge for yourself. I shall never feel safe or happy untill you are. I had rather you should enquire into his conduct and behavior. . . . I believe it is in your power to put a final period to every Idea of the kind, if upon your return you think best."[107] Her words reveal not a domineering, manipulative mother, but rather a caring and fearful one.

Storytelling and free use of sources reinforce Nagel's negative view of

Abigail. The continued exposition of private issues, secrets, and gossip begun in *Descent from Glory* makes *The Adams Women* a sensational story, but perhaps the low point of the Abigail industry.

Writing to Mercy Otis Warren in 1807, Abigail Adams observed, "If we were to count our years by the revolutions we have witnessed, we might number them with the antidiluvians [*sic*]. So rapid have been the changes, that the mind, though fleet in its progress, has been outstripped by them; and we are left like statues, gazing at what we can neither fathom nor comprehend."[108] Abigail's challenge—to give order and meaning to life—is the biographer's challenge as well.

This investigation into the Abigail industry has attempted to comprehend not Abigail's life but one hundred and fifty years of interpretation of her life, the historiographic story. Although the focus has been on Abigail, the literature written about her reflects broad general trends in the way historians have interpreted women's lives, ranging from romanticism at one extreme to misogyny at the other. Sometimes their biases derive from a cultural vision of woman's place in the world, sometimes from a deliberate effort to put woman in her place. The Abigail industry, furthermore, too often reflects presentism by collapsing the past into the present or, perhaps, emphasizing themes popular in today's literary market place.

The story began in the 1840s with the publication of Abigail's letters, edited to suit the conventions of nineteenth-century mores and tastes. The hagiographers next established a vision of her as docile and domestic, as pure and spiritual, as submissive and passive—a behavioral model for virtuous womanhood. As historians further explored our political, economic, or diplomatic past, Abigail's domestic—and passive—image was contrasted with John's public—and active—life. When the time came in the late twentieth century to infuse the story of the past with a feminine element, her active role was shaped to fit a man's world and interpreted as an exercise of "masculine" power. The constant in this literature has been a masculine orientation, although the image of Abigail Adams has shifted from a figure idealized beyond individuality, to a pure decoration, to a matriarch responsible for her children's troubles, to an aggressive political agent.

The problem that has developed among Abigail's biographers is that even when separating and labeling her attitudes as belonging either to the domestic or public domains, a male interpretive model prevails. The concept of separate spheres reflects social hierarchy, not social difference. Therefore, when biographers have emphasized Abigail's domestic character, she is trivialized or demeaned; when they have emphasized her public life, she is seen as active and dynamic. In both cases she is portrayed as an adjunct to John. By not separating Abigail from his career and reputation, biographers thereby describe her character as a reflection of their marriage.

After years of women's studies, we must acknowledge that a female world and mentality existed in the late eighteenth century that was separate from male experience. The issue is how to address that world for a vision of women, and we start by removing the blinders of the male model.

Abigail's record is her letters, and one must look for an approach to the letters that will separate her character from John and his career. We may begin by viewing Abigail as a writer who composed in the genre most available to her as an eighteenth-century woman before it was considered appropriate for women to write for publication. She was moved by the same compulsion that inspires writers: "There are perticular times when I feel such an uneasiness, such a restlessness, as neither Company, Books, family Cares or any other thing will remove, my Pen is my only pleasure," she confessed, and "My pen is always freer than my tongue. I have wrote many things to you that I suppose I never could have talk'd."[109] If biographers analyze her letters as literature with a focus on content and style, Abigail's character and world emerge. The range of her thoughts and emotions may be scrutinized for meaning beyond their literal content. For instance, though she wrote infrequently about her religious beliefs, she often wrote in a style, a metaphor, and a vocabulary that reflected deep religious commitment. Few authors mention, and none develop, a religious life for Abigail. Abigail was a religious woman. Furthermore, the bonds with her sisters Mary and Elizabeth, and with other women relatives and friends, may be explored for an understanding of female culture. Gossip—in the positive sense of exchanging information about each other—provides a strand of that bond and also provides us with insights into their domestic world.[110] Abigail's relationships with her children may be analyzed in their context rather than in terms of a contemporary model of child rearing. And her relationship with John Adams may be explored apart from later idealized versions of marriage. The eighteenth-century model of marriage was patriarchal, and no amount of republican or psychological gloss can disguise that fact. Abigail did not. Because she was so expressive, Abigail's depth of character emerges from her letters, if they are read in her context and not for the manner in which they suit later models for eighteenth-century woman.

A more accurate assessment of Abigail Adams would acknowledge the preeminence of her domestic role and private concerns as formative experiences. Domesticity and intelligence are not polar opposites: to be wife and mother is not mindless activity. As the best new women's biographies show, the politics of family relationships contain power struggles as complex and subtle as those of national office seeking; the rituals of marriage, childbirth and child rearing are as valid as historical turning points as are declarations and constitutions. In the eighteenth century a woman's primary concerns were domestic, and Abigail was no exception.[111] It was her unique character, intelligence, and talent that distinguished her from other women, not her values or attitudes. Furthermore, through her marriage

Abigail Adams experienced the domestic and the public spheres as a continuity; by acknowledging the interaction of these spheres, we begin to understand her complexity.

The same model that merges public and private life enriches the study of men's lives as well. While the traditional biography that examines intellectual, political, or diplomatic life has dominated the writing about public figures, the story may be enhanced by including domestic affairs. For example, the author of a biography of John Adams attributes his emotional collapse in 1771 to career factors: "In addition to attending the General Court, he served as clerk to the Suffolk County Bar Association, maintained his growing practice, and participated until December in the continuing Boston Massacre trials."[112] The fuller picture of the events of that year includes taxing domestic strains: baby daughter Susanna died, Abigail gave birth to a son, Charles, and was confined by illness for many months. The Adamses, furthermore, moved from a house in Cold Lane to Brattle Square in Boston. Taken together, the public and private forces that operate in lives present a more compelling explanation for the human condition.

The issue that historians of women have confronted—with benefits to the entire historical community—is no less than a transformation of vision. One scholar, surveying her own professional development, noted that "in the mid-1960s few historians considered women a socially significant category."[113] By the late twentieth century, a variety of approaches has made women's past lives a valid and important category in history. The transformation is not yet achieved, as recent biographies of Abigail make clear, but as our understanding continues to grow, we may predict, not only for Abigail, but for women generally, the change that will accord women their appropriate place in the historical record. At the end of the Revolutionary War, Abigail complained that her sacrifices had not been appreciated, that women's contribution as patriots on the home front, domestic patriotism, was unacknowledged. Characteristically, she concluded with a note of personal triumph: "I will take praise to myself."[114] Her boldness and defiance may also describe the challenge and the progress of women's studies.

2

. . . *a tye more binding* . . .

According to Adams family lore, when Abigail Smith married John Adams on October 25, 1764, the Reverend William Smith, Abigail's father, preached the sermon "For John came neither eating bread nor drinking wine, and Ye say, *'He hath a devil.'* " Charles Francis Adams, who recorded this story in his grandmother's *Memoir,* explained the choice of text as the Reverend's response to his Weymouth congregation, that the profession of law was "unknown" in colonial Massachusetts and when it did emerge in this period before the Revolution, a deep prejudice existed against it. Charles Francis continued to explain the less than adulatory text in terms of community and social class—that a "portion of the parishioners" thought that "the son of a small farmer of the middle class in Braintree, was . . . scarcely good enough to match with the minister's daughter, descended from so many of the shining lights of the Colony."[1]

The Reverend Smith's cryptic message may have included his more personal reflections, which Charles Francis, in a typical Victorian manner, attributed to the community. For many reasons, the Reverend Smith and his wife, Elizabeth Quincy Smith, may have disapproved of the marriage of their middle daughter. Abigail was not yet twenty years old when she married, younger than average for the mid-eighteenth century, and she appears not to have had previous suitors to John Adams, whom she met when she was sixteen.[2] That Adams was a full ten years her senior might have weighed as an advantage, had he been other than a lawyer.[3] But Abigail's roots went deep into the colonial elite. Her mother's family were Quincys, Nortons, and Shepards, "the solid bedrock of Massachusetts society."[4] The Smiths, while more recently arrived, represented the other respectable strain of New England society, the merchant class. Adams's father was a farmer and shoemaker.

Given either parental or social disapproval of the match, it is clear that Abigail Smith acted upon her own will when it came to marriage. She chose to marry John Adams because she loved him, and because she believed that they were compatible in spirit, intelligence, values, and energy. During their more then three years of courtship, she had measured his character and tested her own intuition, as he had in return, and in the end Abigail believed that she could live her lifetime in this partnership from which there was no escape.

The Adams marriage has become legendary in American history. Just the mention of "Abigail and John" calls forth an image of an ideal marriage, one founded upon love, loyalty, friendship, and courage, which in many respects it was. However, as is the case with ideals, reality was more complex and gives credibility to Reverend Smith's expressed reservations. The Adamses lived together as a couple for only ten years before the events of the rebellion against Great Britain took John away from home. Then, for a full quarter of a century, he served his nation at distant posts. Sometimes Abigail joined him—for four years of the more than ten that he lived in Europe and for a few of the years that he served as vice president and then president at the nation's capitals. For much of their married life until John's defeat for the presidency in 1800, the Adamses lived apart from one another. This separation does account, after all, for their vast correspondence from which generations of historians have constructed the story of their ideal marriage. The ideal, as read into the letters of Abigail and John, overlooks that the letters survive as a testimony to an ideal correspondence if not an ideal marriage.

The Adams marriage is mythologized for other reasons.[5] It appears modern; in fact, it possessed many of the attributes of modern marriage. It was a love match that endured. It produced one famous son and established a dynasty of great citizens. It overcame adversity intact. It was a match of equals; Abigail's intelligence, wit, wisdom, and strength flourished alongside that of her husband, lending legitimacy to the claim of woman's more equal status. Above all, the Adams marriage is idealized because Abigail is visible, probably the most visible First Lady until the mid-twentieth century. That makes the Adams marriage appear more modern than it was.[6]

In fact, recent scholarship in history and anthropology makes it clear that all human institutions are functions of their culture, marriage as much as any other, if not more.[7] Eighteenth-century New England was no exception from the prevailing patriarchy of western culture. The Adams marriage was predicated upon its existence within this patriarchy. If Abigail chose to marry John, it was the most spectacular act of will available to her for the remainder of her life.[8] Never again would she make a decision of that magnitude to control the direction of her life. There existed no easy exit clause from her decision once her vows were taken. She had little control over the kind of work she performed, over her reproductive life, or probably over her sex life, although that is not an area that can be discerned with the historian's skills.[9] Marriage with its obligations became her destiny in that world that also prescribed very clear separation of male and female spheres that, certainly, were not equal but hierarchically organized. The lens through which Abigail viewed her world revealed a divinely prescribed patriarchy in which it was her destiny to live in the domestic sphere under the terms that John Adams's work and choices about place, manner, and style governed. Abigail accepted that world. "I believe nature has assigned to each sex its particular duties and sphere of action," she once wrote, "and to act well your part, 'there all the honor lies.' "[10]

At the same time, Abigail was neither slave nor servant, and she knew that as well. She had leverage within the marriage bond, because of both her character and John's, and because the patriarchy that existed in New England was flexible.[11] The physical magnetism that charged their early companionship remained alive, mellowed into tender familiarity and a deep loving commitment. Moreover, both of them required intellectual parity in a mate, and Abigail's real education—her own recollections to the contrary—began within marriage to John, with access to his mind, his library, and his dependence upon dialogue with her.[12] Rather than contracting under the weight of domestic drudgery, she developed her intellect over her lifetime, so that she became wise and erudite. Both the emotional and the intellectual aspects of the Adamses' companionship overflowed from life into letters once they were parted.

In the best sense, then, the Adamses represented what historians call the "companionate marriage," meaning a love match in which there exists enduring friendship and respect.[13] It is for that reason that the Adams marriage has been, in the long run, idealized. At its best it presents an ideal accommodation of woman to man in western culture. We know this because they wrote all of this to each other, and we can read quite intimate letters that provide insights into their private lives. The reason is that Abigail, whose eighteenth-century companionate marriage in fact was one of deep friendship and commitment, actually did project her marriage into letters when John went away. The letters were her way of continuing the companionship she had with him when he was at home.

Abigail Smith had grown up in the parsonage at Weymouth as the second of three daughters. Mary, three years older, was her closest childhood friend, and one brother, William, born in 1746, separated them from the youngest sister, Elizabeth. Abigail described a pleasant childhood—"wild and giddy days"—she recalled to her own granddaughter. Among her reminiscences, not many of which were recorded in letters, her greatest regret was lack of a formal education, not unusual for young women in prerevolutionary America. Abigail and her sisters were taught at home by their mother, whose own intelligence and taste were reflected in her daughters' upbringing. They learned to read, write, and cipher, and they studied rudimentary French literature, which was considered appropriate for young women of their station. They also were given free access to their father's library, which included popular eighteenth-century literature, such as volumes of *The Spectator.* Primarily, they learned to cook, sew, spin, nurse, and manage a household, for that would be their occupation. They did not consider their immersion in religion, both biblical and ritual, as education in the sense of its being a discipline or a belief system which could be mastered and possibly examined, questioned, or discarded. Religion informed their apprehension of the world they lived in; it was reality, as much as nature and human existence represented reality, and it existed prior to nature and human existence.

Abigail and John became acquainted as a result of Mary's courtship with Richard Cranch, a good friend of John, and characteristic of two exceptionally literate and verbal people, some of their courting took place in letters. At first playful and flirtatious, they used the metaphor of magnetism to describe the immediate dynamic between them. "Miss Adoreable" he addressed her, "By the same token that the bearer hereof sat up with you last night I hereby order you to give him as many Kisses and as many hours of your company after 9 O'clock as he shall please to demand. . . . I have good right to draw upon you for the kisses as I have given two or three million at least when one has been received."[14] Six months later, John wrote to apologize because weather had prevented his visit the previous day: "Cruel for detaining me from so much friendly, social company, and perhaps blessed to you, or me, or both for keeping me at my distance. For every experimental phylosopher knows," he continued, "that the steel and the magnet and the glass and the feather will not fly together with more celerity, than somebody and somebody, when brought within striking distance."[15]

Over time, their exchanges became more tender: "There is a tye more binding than Humanity and stronger than friendship, which makes us anxious for the happiness and welfare of those to whom it binds us. It makes their misfortunes, sorrows and afflictions our own. . . . By this cord I am not ashamed to own myself bound, nor do I believe that you are wholly free from it," wrote Abigail, signing herself "Diana."[16] He admitted, "Last night I dreamed I saw a lady . . . on the Weymouth shores, spreading light and beauty and glory all round her. At first I thought it was Aurora with her fair Complexion. . . . But soon I found it was Diana, a lady infinitely dearer to me."[17] If Abigail's parents objected to this match, they were powerless to prevent it.

After their marriage, the couple moved to the Braintree house that John had inherited from his father, there to begin a lifelong expedition, they believed, along the same route of rural family life that their parents had journeyed. For ten years Abigail's and John's family life did follow a similar pattern, although in retrospect it is possible to see, in their frequent moves and separations, the twin origins of later disruptions—the escalating pattern of the breach between the American colonies and Great Britain and John Adams's restlessness, born of his deep internal dissatisfaction with himself and his ambition for action on a more global scene than local law and politics.[18]

"Your Diana became a Mamma—can you credit it?" wrote Abigail to a friend in July 1765, still using her youthful pen name. "Indeed, it is a sober truth. Bless'd with a charming Girl whose pretty Smiles already delight my Heart, who is the Dear Image of her still Dearer Pappa."[19] Several months later, John Adams, after first berating himself for neglecting to maintain his diary, recorded that "The Year 1765 has been the most remarkable Year of my Life," continuing then to account for his extravagant assertion: "That enormous Engine, fabricated by the British Parliament, for battering down all the Rights and Liberties of America, I mean the Stamp Act, has raised and spread thro the whole Continent, a Spirit that will be recorded to our Honour, with all future Generations. . . . Our Presses have groaned, our Pulpits have thundered, our Legislatures have resolved, our Towns have voted, "The Crown Officers have every where trembled, and all their little Tools and Creatures, been afraid to Speak and ashamed to be seen."[20] So it was that each of the Adamses recorded the salient events that initiated the only uninterrupted decade of marriage that they would live together until their old age.

At home and in the political arena, conditions developed in tandem. Abigail gave birth five times in seven years. John Quincy, named for his maternal grandfather who had just died, was born in July 1767, followed by Susanna in 1768, who died after one year, Charles in 1770, and Thomas in 1772. Abigail did not become pregnant again until 1777. Her family of four children, one daughter and three sons who lived to become adults, was completed.

Meanwhile, Parliament repealed the Stamp Act in 1766. Abigail, who was "very ill of an hooping cough," was unable to attend the celebrations in Boston, where "Bells rung, Cannons were fired, Drums beaten"; the whole province, John exclaimed, "was in a Rapture for the Repeal of the Stamp Act."[21] John Quincy was born the year that Parliament passed the hated Townshend Acts that levied more taxes on the colonies, resulting in immediate acts of resistance. By the time that Susanna was born, the Townshend Acts had been repealed, except for one that was retained on tea.

The year 1770 marked a crescendo in both domestic and public affairs. The infant Susanna died just months before Abigail gave birth to Charles. The Adamses, who had moved to Boston from Braintree two years previous, were forced to move to a new house on Cold Lane because of the sale of their rented house on Brattle Square. And it was the year of the Boston Massacre, when British soldiers fired into a mob, killing several patriots. This event, if it did not raise popular hostility to Great Britain to its highest pitch, marked a turning point in the career of John Adams by catapulting him into a wholly visible public role.

John recalled that his first consideration upon hearing news that evening of the "massacre" was for his wife, at home alone with the servants. She was "in circumstances and I was apprehensive of the effect of the Surprise on her. . . . I went directly home to Cold Lane. My Wife having heard that the Town was still and likely to continue so, had recovered from her first Apprehensions, and We had nothing but our Reflections to interrupt our Repose." He added: "These Reflections were to me, disquieting enough." In that momentous and terrifying evening, the effects of the impending political rupture reverberated along many dimensions of their private lives, forecasting the intrusion of great public affairs upon the privacy of their home life. It signified as well the interwoven texture of John's and Abigail's marriage, his concern for her well-being and her sharing of his reflections.

The next day, John was asked to defend Captain Preston and the British soldiers, a call that he accepted, because, "Council ought to be the very last thing that an accused Person should want in a free Country."[22] After the three long trials in which John successfully defended Preston and the British soldiers—"the most exhausting and fatiguing Causes I ever tried," he recalled—John suffered from a physical and emotional collapse that resulted in the Adamses' return to Braintree.[23] For Abigail, who preferred rural life to the city, and whose health flourished when she lived in the country, her "humble Cottage" represented freedom: "Where Contemplation P[l]umes her rufled Wings / And the free Soul look's down to pitty Kings." While she did not always quote great poetry, she did aptly choose a political metaphor to describe the pleasure that she experienced at home in the country.[24]

The Adamses returned to Boston after eighteen months in Braintree, where Thomas was born. In another few months, the crisis over tea developed. "The tea that bainful weed is arrived," Abigail wrote to her friend Mercy Otis Warren. "The flame is kindled and like Lightening it catches from Soul to Soul. Great will be the devastation if not timely quenched or allayed by some more Lenient Measures." Abigail understood the temper of Boston. To John it meant the disruption of his business, for in the wake of the Tea Party, Boston's courts were closed, and he, who had risen to have "more Business at the Bar, than any Man in the Province," had no business to conduct.[25] Clearly, it would be a matter of time. "Altho the mind is shocked at the Thought of sheding Humane Blood, more Especially the Blood of our countrymen, and a civil War is of all Wars, the most dreadfull," Abigail continued to Mercy, "Such is the present State that prevails, that if once they are made desperate Many, very Many of our Heroes will spend their lives in the cause, With the Speach of Cato in their Mouths, 'What a pitty it is, that we can dye but once to save our Country.' "[26]

In late 1773, Abigail's eldest child, her daughter, was eight, and her youngest just one year. She had moved from Braintree to Boston and back again, changing houses three times on her first sojourn and twice this time until John purchased a house on Brattle Square. She did not write frequently; she did not have the time. But when she did, her letters resonated with the impact of her reading and her conversation with John and their friends. Her world had not yet separated from John's.

In fact, Abigail and John had experienced many short separations during this period, due to the structure of the legal system. Whether John maintained his primary offices at home in Braintree or in Boston, he needed to travel the court circuit to obtain a sufficient living. During the second half of 1767, for instance, he attended the Plymouth Inferior Court in July and the Suffolk Superior Court in August; in September he tried cases in Worcester and Bristol, in October in Plymouth, Bristol, and Cambridge, and in December in Barnstable and Plymouth. He traveled north to Maine and south to Martha's Vineyard. His journeys lasted sometimes as little as a few days, sometimes for weeks.[27]

During those periods Abigail remained at home or visited her parents in Weymouth, but she was always lonely. In late 1766, she had written to Mary, "He is such an itenerant . . . that I have but little of his company. He is now at Plymouth, and next week goes to Taunton."[28] To John she wrote: "Sunday seems a more Lonesome Day to me than any other when you are absent."[29] After eight years of marriage, she still wrote: "Alass! How many snow banks divide thee and me and my warmest wishes to see thee will not melt one of them. My daily thoughts and nightly Slumbers visit thee."[30]

John's law practice thrived as he traveled the circuit; Abigail tended their home and their children grew; and meanwhile the events that would lead to revolution escalated. "Such is the present Situation of affairs that I tremble when I think what may be the direfull consequences—and in this Town must the Scene of action lay," Abigail wrote to Mercy from Boston. "My Heart beats at every Whistle I hear, and I dare not openly express half my fears.—Eternal Reproach and Ignominy be the portion of all those who have been instrumental in bringing these fears upon me."[31]

She expressed fear once more when John was elected by the Massachusetts General Court to be one of three representatives to the Continental Congress that gathered in Philadelphia in 1774, but she did not prevent him from going. "You cannot be, I know, nor do I wish to see you an Inactive Spectator, but if the sword be drawn, I bid adieu to all domestick felicity and look forward to that Country where there is neither wars nor rumors of War in a firm belief that thro the Mercy of its Kind we shall both rejoice there together."[32] John departed on August 10 in the company of fellow delegates Samuel Adams, Thomas Cushing, and Robert Treat Paine. Five days later, Abigail wrote to him, and with that letter initiated the correspondence which would become a torrent in the years to follow. Inspired by loneliness, her writing became a substitute for speaking with him. She, of course, did not realize that war was imminent or that her separation from John would be so lengthy, any more than she understood the roles they would play in the course of the developing revolution. She only recognized that events impelled action and that John had been called to be an actor.

For some time both Abigail and John were sustained by the spirit of the growing rebellion. "There is in the Congress a collection of the greatest Men upon this continent," John wrote with enthusiasm from Philadelphia.[33] "I think I enjoy better Health than I have done these 2 years," Abigail responded from Braintree.[34] Time passed and John wrote: "The business of the Congress is tedious, beyond Expression. This assembly is like no other that ever existed. Every man in it is a great Man—an orator, a Critick, a statesman, and therefore every Man in every Question must show his oratory, his Criticism, and his political Abilities."[35] At home Abigail became impatient: "I dare not express to you at 300 miles distance how ardently I long for your return. I have some very miserly Wishes; and cannot consent to your spending one hour in Town till at least I have had you 12. The idea plays about my Heart, unnerves my hand whilst I write, awakens all the tender sentiments that years have encreased and matured. . . . The whole collected stock of ten weeks absence knows not how to brook any longer restraint, but will break forth and flow thro my pen."[36] Separated for two months, they had begun the practice of transferring their private conversations to paper. John wrote about what affected him most—frustration or boredom; Abigail wrote about her loneliness. Of course, they wrote much more, but their moods were partly expressed by these intimate confessions to each other.

John returned by the end of October, but the forces that led to Lexington were set on course. Abigail wrote to Mercy in February 1775, "Is it not better to die the last of British freemen than live the first of British slaves?"[37] Mercy, who was mother to five grown sons, wrote: "Which of us should have the Courage of an Aria or a Portia in a Day of trial like theirs."[38] She referred to Portia, wife of Brutus, the Roman statesman. Abigail found the image appealing.

By the end of April 1775, John Adams traveled to Philadelphia, no longer to mediate, because Lexington had occurred. John returned to wage war, and so ended the first decade of the Adamses' marriage. "What a scene has opened upon us," Abigail wrote Mercy. "Such a scene as we never before experienced, and could scarcely form an Idea of. If we look back we are amazed at what is past, if we look forward we must shudder at the view. Our only comfort lies in the justice of our cause." She signed herself Portia.[39]

One historian of marriage points out that social groups tend to legitimate their practices by considering them "natural."[40] Abigail Adams entered into marriage with many expectations that she considered structurally "normal," only to discover the corruption of her expectations over time because of both the unanticipated transformations caused by war, and the shift of her husband's career. Ideologically, Abigail described her accommodation to circumstances as a patriotic sacrifice. "Tis almost 14 years since we were united, but not more than half that time have we had the happiness of living together," she complained in the summer of 1777. "The unfealing world may consider it in what light they please, I consider it as a sacrifice to my Country and one of my greatest misfortunes."[41] As a practical consideration, she began to replace John's presence by writing him letters that substituted for their conversations. This is illustrated by two episodes that developed within the early years of the Revolutionary War.

In the fall of 1775, soon after John departed to serve as one of the three Massachusetts delegates to the Continental Congress in Philadelphia, an epidemic of dysentery swept through the Boston area. Abigail's entire household, herself included, was afflicted. Despite the weakening effects of her own illness, Abigail, assisted by her mother, became the primary nurse and physician in the hospital that her household became. In that time of widespread sickness, when no outside help was available and her own servants were sick and dying of the disease, the majority of responsibility fell to Abigail.

"Since you left me I have passed thro great distress both Body and mind," she wrote to John in early September, indicating that her hardships were emotional as well as physical. Isaac, her servant boy, had been taken with a "voilent [sic] Dysentery" and "there was no resting place in the House for his terible Groans." Abigail's descriptions to John would invoke sound and odor as well as image. After a week, Isaac recovered, but "two days after he was sick, I was seaz'd with the same disorder in a voilent manner." Abigail recovered, but next her servant Susy was ill. "Our Little Tommy was the next, and he lies very ill now. . . . I hope he is not dangerous. Yesterday Patty [a servant girl] was seazd. . . . Our House is an hospital in every part and what with my own weakness and distress of mind for my family I have been unhappy enough."[42] Abigail wrote not just to keep John informed of conditions at home but to dispel her feelings.

One week later she described her mounting misery: "I set myself down to write with a Heart depressed with the Melancholy Scenes arround me. . . . We live in daily Expectation that Patty will not continue many hours. A general putrefaction seems to have taken place, and we can not bear the House only as we are constantly clensing it with hot vinegar." Abigail continued to cite the number of deaths among her neighbors and friends.[43] Another week passed and she wrote, "I set down with a heavy Heart to write to you. I have had no other since you left me. Woe follows

Woe and one affliction reads upon the heal of an other."[44] Abigail tended to locate her emotions physically, so that her heart became the bearer of her hurt.

One week later, grief overflowed into her letter to John: "Have pitty upon me, have pitty upon me o! thou my beloved for the hand of God presseth me soar," she pleaded. Her mother had died. "How can I tell you (o my bursting Heart) that my Dear Mother has Left me, this day about 5 'clock she left this world for an infinitely better." Abigail wrote this grief as she would have spoken it: "At times I almost am ready to faint under this sever and heavy Stroke, seperated from *thee* who used to be a comfortar towards me in affliction."[45] Her grief was compounded, Abigail informed John. She grieved for her mother, but also her separation from John, whose role it had been to comfort her. She did not reprimand him, but rather she emphasized the unnatural condition of their separation; he was supposed to be with her during this crisis. Her writing became the substitute for his presence. She comforted herself by this means.

Another week passed, and Patty still lingered, "the most shocking object my Eyes ever beheld, and so loathsome that it was with the utmost difficulty we could bear the House . . . a most pityable object." Then Patty died, and the epidemic had run its course.[46]

Throughout this time, while she wrote about her woes, Abigail worried as well about the effect of her letters on John. "I know I wound your heart," she wrote. "Ought I give relief to my own by paining yours?"[47] Another time she wrote, "Forgive me, then, for thus dwelling upon a subject . . . I fear painful. O how I have long'd for your Bosom to pour forth my sorrows there, and find a healing Balm."[48] With these words she described her continued expectations of the relationship between a wife and husband, to describe what their relationship had been when they were together.

John's responses were consistent as they were immediate. "I feel—I tremble for you," he admitted when her troubles began. "Surely if I were with you, it would be my Study to allay your griefs, to mitigate your Pains and to divert your melancholly thoughts."[49] Later he wrote to relieve her concern about troubling him: "If I could write as well as you, my sorrows would be as eloquent as yours. but upon my Word I cannot."[50] John consoled Abigail, also by letter, as he might have in person—but he did not return. If there was an undercurrent of requesting his presence in her letters, if John felt great tension between his country and his family, his greater loyalty was expressed by his behavior. He wrote comforting letters to her from Philadelphia.

Another episode developed less than two years later. John finally had returned from Philadelphia for a visit in the winter of 1776, and Abigail became pregnant. They knew about the pregnancy before John's return to Congress, and he wrote shortly after his departure: "I am anxious to hear how you do. I have in my Mind a Source of Anxiety, which I never had before." Because of eighteenth-century reticence about pregnancy and also because mail was often intercepted by the British, John continued cryptically: "You know what it is. Cant you convey to me, in Hieroplyphicks, which no other Person can comprehend, Information which will relieve me. Tell me you are as well as can be expected," he wrote, demanding good news as a means of relieving his conscience for leaving her.[51]

"I had it in my heart to disswade him from going and I know I could have prevaild," Abigail admitted to Mercy Otis Warren, "but our publick affairs at that time wore so gloomy an aspect that I thought if ever his assistance was wanted it must be at such a time. I therefore resignd my self to suffer much anxiety and many Melancholy hours for this year to come."[52] Abigail had not abandoned her expectations for marriage, but she certainly had suspended them. To Mercy she cited patriotism, probably even as she rationalized John's departure to herself. Once more she located emotions in her heart, her desire to dissuade John from leaving her, but used her reason to overcome her feelings. That reason may have incorporated her understanding of John's now driven need to participate, which was re-shaped in her own mind to a vision of patriotic service by her uniquely qualified husband. Her reasoning represented as well the historic transformation of spiritual into secular calling, and she resigned herself to carrying on her marriage in letters.

Using "hyroplyphicks," she wrote to John in March, "I think upon the whole I have enjoyed as much Health as I ever did in the like situation—a situation I do not repine at, tis a constant remembrancer of an absent Friend, and excites sensations of tenderness which are better felt than expressd."[53] Her protestations to the contrary, Abigail did express the intimacy that pregnancy represented to her, a different dimension of the "companionate marriage" in which children were the consequence of a loving relationship rather than the purpose of marriage.[54]

One month later, Abigail wrote in a different vein, as a friend of hers had died in childbirth: "Everything of this kind naturally shocks a person in similar circumstances," she admitted. "How great the mind that can overcome the fear of Death!"[55] Eighteenth-century women were acutely aware of the risks of childbirth under normal circumstances. During wartime, the fears multiplied. By May she was reporting, "I cannot say that I am so well as I have been."[56] And within weeks she wrote explicitly about fear. Troops were passing her house day and night, and she believed more fighting might take place. "I should not dare to tarry here in my present situation, nor yet know where to flee for safety," she wrote John with mounting concern over the rumors she was hearing: "The recital of the inhumane and Brutal Treatment of those poor creatures who have fallen into their Hands Freezes me with Horrour. My apprehensions are greatly increasd; should they come this way again I know not what course I should take."[57] Pregnancy had weakened Abigail's resolve and had made her vulnerable, indecisive, and afraid. Soon her fear turned to anger.

She complained: "I loose my rest a nights . . . I look forward to the middle of july with more anxiety than I can describe." Rising to an emotional crescendo, she exclaimed: "I am cut of from the privilidge which some of the Brute creation enjoy, that of having their mate sit by them with anxious care during all the Solitary confinement."[58] In late eighteenth-century terms, hers was a bold wifely indictment, perhaps a transference into letters of a confrontation that could have occurred between them. Or perhaps, the letter allowed her more distance to complain, to express her autonomous feelings of indignation at a world that was violating her expectations—of a world that appeared brutal and uncivilized to her.

Further signs of physical complications developed on the eve of childbirth: "I sit down to write you this post, and from my present feelings tis the last I shall be able to write for some time if I should do well," she wrote mildly, this time understating her anxiety. "I was last night taken with a shaking fit, and am very apprehensive that a life was lost. As I have no reason to day to think otherways; what may be the consequences to me, Heaven only knows."[59]

Abigail did not describe her household during this crisis. It is not clear what children were present, whether her sisters, or even a midwife, were with her. Her entire concentration in her letters of this period was on John, upon telling him what was happening to her, on recording the events and her feelings. She brought him into her chamber during childbirth by writing her ordeal, and she closed out the rest of the world but him and herself.

"I received a Letter from my Friend," she wrote, "begining in his manner 'my dearest Friend.' That one single expression dwelt upon my mind and playd about my Heart." This time she allowed both her mind and her heart to experience her affections. "It was because my heart was softened and my mind enervated by my sufferings, and I wanted the personal and tender soothings of my dearest Friend," she wrote explicitly. Then she shifted to her topic: "Tis now 48 Hours since I can say I really enjoyed any Ease. . . . Slow, lingering and troublesome is the present situation." She was in labor. "The Dr. encourages me to Hope that my apprehensions are groundless . . . tho I cannot say I have had any reason to allter my mind. . . . I pray Heaven that it may be soon or it seems to me I shall be worn out." By "it" she meant the birth of her child. Then she wrote the most astonishing statement: "I must lay my pen down this moment, to bear what I cannot fly from—and now I have endured it I reassume my pen." Abigail wrote to John through her labor.[60]

The child, a girl, was stillborn, and Abigail lived. Within a week she was writing to John: "Join with me my dearest Friend in Gratitude to Heaven, that a life I know you value, has been spaired . . . although the dear Infant is numberd with its ancestors."[61] Abigail revived physically and in spirit, and her life continued. As in the earlier episode of the dysentery epidemic, Abigail had written to John during her pregnancy and childbirth in order to recreate in her fantasy the conditions of marriage that fulfilled her expectations for wife and husband. During the time that she wrote, she was able to retreat from the reality of their interrupted companionship and sense that they were together.

Because of these experiences and others, Abigail learned about letter writing as a means of dispelling her emotions, and in time her writing became abstracted from John, serving its own end. She began to write with the intensity of one who enjoyed the process itself. She discovered that writing allowed her the satisfactions of recreating her world in letters as well as the therapy that came from this method of confession. Abigail also began to redefine her vision of her marriage from that of normal companionship to separate living. She accepted John's participation as their patriotic sacrifice in wartime and further justified his repeated choice to serve as mandated by conditions that required his unique genius.

In 1777 the Revolutionary War was not yet at midpoint, nor had John departed yet for Europe, and while a few of her worst experiences had passed, many were yet to come. In time, circumstances like the dysentery epidemic and pregnancy compounded her self-confidence, and she began to trust her ability to function alone. She even learned how to survive economically as the major source of support for her household during the war. However, her experience and accomplishments to the contrary, she never considered herself an independent unit, but always as the subordinate partner in marriage. To do otherwise would deviate from the socially prescribed form of marriage in the late eighteenth century. Abigail never considered such an option.

3

Domestic Patriotism

The Revolutionary War not only increased Abigail's traditional domestic responsibilities, but it shifted to her as well the primary responsibility for supporting her family. For ten years, Abigail served as the primary source of support for her family, a position to which she never adjusted comfortably; yet it was a function which she performed energetically and competently.

Since their marriage in 1764, the Adams family income had been derived from two sources: John's law practice and his farm at Braintree, large parts of which were rented to tenants. The law practice disappeared with the advent of war, and thereafter the only sources of income were the farm and the portion of his congressional salary that John could spare from his own expenses. The responsibility for managing the farm fell directly to Abigail, and for approximately four years she struggled with crops and nature as well as an acute labor shortage and spiraling inflation, before she abandoned the farming business to concentrate on other enterprises. Throughout those years and in the subsequent six years of John's absence, she focused her efforts on remaining free from debt and on not losing their property. Abigail did avoid debt, and she even added to their property holdings.

The trend of shifting the support function to Abigail began with John's first trip to Philadelphia in 1774. He wrote, "You must take Care my Dear, to get as much Work out of our Tenants as possible. Belcher is in Arrears. He must work, Hayden must work. Harry Field must work, and Jo Curtis too must be made settle. He owes something. Jo Tirrell Too, must do something—and Isaac. I cant loose such Sums as they owe me—and I will not."[1] John mentioned as many as six tenants, some of whom in later years were hired as laborers by Abigail.[2] John, apparently, had not dealt effectively with his tenants, since all were in arrears, and he now alleviated his concern by shifting the responsibility to Abigail. Later he wrote: "Keep the Hands attentive to their Business, and [let] the most prudent Measures of every kind be adopted and pursued with Alacrity and Spirit."[3] As soon as his own attention turned to national politics, John began to delegate responsibility for managing their affairs to Abigail.

For a long time Abigail did not write about the farm, explaining to John: "As to your own private affairs I generally avoid mentioning them to you; I take the best care I am capable of."[4] Furthermore, she was challenged and noted with pride: "I hope in time to have the Reputation of being as good a Farmeress as my partner has of being a good Statesman."[5] Abigail viewed the new responsibility as her contribution to the war effort, but also she did not wish to burden John with family business concerns. As time passed, however, she began to chafe under her burden. "I miss my partner, and find myself unequal to the cares which fall upon me; I find it necessary to be the directress of our Husbandry and farming. . . . Retirement, Rural quiet, Domestick pleasure all must give place to the weighty cares of State."[6] Farm management was becoming an oppressive responsibility.

Throughout this four-year period the onerous chore of hiring men to work was aggravated by inflation which drove the cost of farm labor to unprecedented heights. "Hands are so scarce," she wrote, "that I have not been able to procure one, and add to this that Isaac has been sick with a fever this fortnight, not able to strick a Stroke and a Multiplicity of farming Business pouring in upon Us. In this Dilemma I have taken Belcher into pay, and must secure him for the Season, as I know not what better course to stear."[7]

She described her frustrations to Mercy Otis Warren: "I find it necessary not only to pay attention to my own in door domestic affairs, but to every thing without, about our little farm etc." She further complained to her friend: "The man whom I used to place dependance was taken sick last winter and left us. I have not been able to supply his place—therefore am obliged to direct what I fear I do not properly understand." So, in short order, Abigail, whose background had not prepared her for farm management, much less for the complete responsibility of supporting her household, learned a new kind of work, and she learned under pressure. "Frugality, Industry and economy are the lessons of the day—at least they must be so for me or my small Boat will suffer shipwreck."[8] Frugality and industry were not only ethical principles; they meant survival.

To John she wrote in a lighter tone, "We have had fine Spring rains which make the Husbandry promise fair—but the great difficulty has been to procure Labourers. . . . Isaac [whom she had nursed to health through dysentery] insisted upon my giving him twenty pounds or he would leave me. He is no mower and I found very unfit to take the lead upon the

Farm."[9] After lamenting the difficulties of finding a replacement for the apostate Isaac, she finally settled on the ubiquitous Belcher, her tenant. In another month, she had more to say about Belcher: "If he should purloin a little I must bear that; he is very deligent, and being chief engineer he is ambitious."[10] She had learned that management required pragmatism as well as tolerance, but she also asked John to write an encouraging note to Belcher, as a word from the man of the household might secure Belcher's loyalty.

The saga of Abigail's frustration with farm labor continued in her report of the Hayden affair. "I have met with some abuse and very Ill treatment. I want you for my protector and justifier," she declared to John. Hayden, a tenant of long standing, refused to vacate his cottage when Abigail wanted it for a family of Boston refugees. "He said . . . he could not be stirred up, and if you was at home you would not once ask him to get out, but was more of a Gentlemen." Outraged, she continued, "It would be needless to enumerate all his impudence. Let it suffice to say it moved me so much that I had hard work to suppress my temper. . . . I feel too angry to make this anything further than a Letter of Business. I am most sincerely yours."[11]

John responded with indignation from Philadelphia: "I will not endure the least disrespectful Expression to you. I send you a Warning to him to go out of the House immediately."[12] The warning proved ineffective, however, for months later Abigail still complained: "Hayden does not stir. Says he will not go out of the parish unless he is carried out."[13] For almost three years Abigail quarreled with Hayden but finally announced: "I know you will give me joy when I tell you that I have wrought almost a miracle. I have removed Hayden out of the house, or rather hired him to remove."[14] She purchased her triumph over Hayden by paying him to leave.

If Hayden, the stubborn tenant, would not leave the premises, other farm hands were only too eager to leave for more lucrative opportunities. "The late call of Men from us will distress us in our Husbandry. I am a great sufferer as the High Bounty one hundred dollars, have tempted of my Negro Head [this in MS probably meant Hand] and left me just in the midst of our Hay," she wrote in August 1777. "The english and fresh indeed have finished, but the salt is just coming on, and How to turn myself, or what to do I know not. His going away would not worry me so much if it was not for the rapid depretiation of our money. We can scarcely get a days work done for money and if money is paid tis at such a rate that tis almost impossible to live. I live as I never did before, but I am not going to complain. Heaven has blessed us with fine crops."[15] The double bind of labor shortage and inflation persisted.

Abigail struggled to preserve their small fortune. "Debts are my abhorrance. I never will borrow if any other method can be devised."[16] With wifely if not patriotic pride she occasionally recounted her success to John: "I hardly know how I have got thro these things, but it gives me great pleasure to say that they are done because I know it will be an Ease to your mind."[17] John's praise was extravagant, as well it might have been, since he was relieved of the distracting duty of supporting his family: "I begin to be jealous, that our Neighbors will think Affairs more discreetly conducted in my Absence than at any other time."[18] He further noted that "Gen Warren writes me, that my Farm never looked better, than when he last saw it, and that Mrs. ——— was like to outshine all the Farmers."[19]

For four years Abigail struggled with farming, and despite inflation, the scarcity of labor, and her own lack of experience which contributed to her dislike of the responsibility, the farm was maintained. She had discharged this duty in order to free John for political service, expecting all the while that it would be a short-lived duty. Only after years, when it became apparent that John would not return immediately, did Abigail decide to rid herself of this odious responsibility. She wrote to her sister Elizabeth, "I am endeavoring to put the Farm I am in possession of out of my Hands which will relieve me from a load of care, and be more Beneficial to my Interest I believe than to struggle along as I have done from year to year."[20] Not long after, she announced to John, who was abroad, that she had rented her farm: "I will tell you after much embarrassment in endeavouring to procure faithful hand I concluded to put out the Farm and reduce my Family as much as possible. I sit about removing the Tenants from the House, which with much difficulty I effected, but not till I paid a Quarters Rent in an other house for them. I then procured two young Men Brothers newly married and placed them as Tenants to the halves retaining in my own Hands only one Horse and two Cows with pasturage for my Horse in summer, and Quincy meadow for fodder in Winter." With relief she reported that "My family consists at present of only myself, two children and two Domesticks."[21] Abigail was at last rid of a chore which, despite her success, she abhorred.

Inflation, which as much as any other factor had contributed to Abigail's troubles in maintaining her farm, was a constant and persistent enemy of domestic life. John was well aware of Abigail's struggle. "What will become of you, I know not. How you will be able to live is past my Comprehension."[22] Paper money, legal and counterfeit, came and went, most often as worthless as the paper it was printed upon. Abigail learned this lesson the hard way: "A most Horrid plot has been discovered of a Band of villains counterfeiting the Hampshire currency to a great amount, no person scarcely but what has more or less of these Bills. I am unlucky enough to have about five pounds LM of it," she admitted.[23] John responded, "How could it happen that you should have five of counterfeit New Hampshire money? Cant you recollect of who you had it of."[24] Abigail's reply was equally reproachful: "If I do not explain the matter I fear you will suspect me of being concerned with the Hampshire money makers."[25] She was able to redeem her money for its true value from the people who had innocently given it to her. Nor was John less harsh several years later when Abigail again confessed that she had been caught with paper money. "I am sorry to learn you have a sum of Paper—how could you be so imprudent! You must be frugal, I assure you,"[26] he wrote from Amsterdam.

As costs spiralled year after year, Abigail regularly recounted to John her own economic struggles and her observations on the general monetary situation. In mid-1777 she wrote, "A Dollar now is not equal to what one Quarter was two years ago, and there is no sort of property which is not held in higher estimation than money."[27] Later she reported that "money is looked upon of very little value, and you can scarcely purchase any article now but by Barter."[28] She wrote, "Our money will soon be as useless as blank paper."[29]

More specifically Abigail's accounts reveal her ongoing struggle with ruinous inflation over the years. "Butter is 3 shillings, cheeses 2, Mutton 18 pence, Beef 18 pence, Lamb 1 & 4 pence," she wrote in 1777.[30] The next year when the situation was more bleak, Abigail reported that "a hundred Dollars will not purchase what ten formerly would, common sugar is 200 dollors per hundred, flower 50, cider 12 pounds a Barrel, and other articles in proportion."[31] A whimsical Abigail wrote in the summer of 1781, "Our old currency died suddenly, the carkases remained in the hands of individuals, no burial having been yet provided for it. The New was in Good repute for a time, but all of a Sudden and in one day followed Elder Brother—so that with old and New in my hand, I can not purchase a single Sixpence worth of any thing. . . . Barter and hard money is now the only trade."[32]

With money out of control, Abigail had to devise new schemes to sustain her family. Her standard of living dropped as former necessities became luxuries, and she explained, "I live now as I have never lived before." But some expenses were unavoidable, notably taxes, which had increased to pay for the war. Food and clothing were compelling needs, along with some repairs to her house and farm. In addition, Abigail considered the education of her children a necessary expense. Abigail learned to balance her expenses with the injunction to practice "frugality and economy."[33]

One source of income was John's often erratic and always insufficient remuneration from Congress. When he left for France in mid-1778, she reported, "As to my own affairs you may recollect the sum you left with me was between eleven and twelve hundred dollars, seven of which I placed in the public fund, there was a debt due the clerk of court which amounted to fifty dollars which I discharged and another to the Black Smith accounting fifty-five. My Rate Bill amounted to fourty-nine pounds, and the continental Rate to fifteen, the ministereal rate raised by contribution. These sums with the payment of my winter labourers left me destitute enough but I struggle along hoping to receive some assistance from you . . . but never having received anything."[34]

When he was abroad, John advised Abigail to draw "bills" upon him, which meant that Abigail gave her personal note, one of exchange not of indebtedness, to a person who would arrange a trade for hard money from John's account in Europe. "You inquire how you shall pay Taxes?—I will tell you," John wrote from Paris. "Ask the favor of your Uncle Smith or some other Friend to let you have Silver, and draw your Bills upon me. The Money shall be paid, in the instant of the sight of your Bills, but let it be drawn in your own Hand Writing. Any body who wants to remit Cash to France, Spain, Holland, or England, will let you have the Money. You may draw with Confidence, for the Cash shall be paid here."[35] Abigail used this method on many occasions. "I can receive four pounds of Lawful money here for one pound Sterling paid in France," she wrote. "I have therefore run the venture to draw upon you for fifty pounds Sterling payable to my cousin Smith."[36] John replied, "I approve very much of your draught upon me, in favour of your Cousin. The moment it arrives it shall be paid. Draw for more as you may have Occasion. But make them give you Silver for your Bills."[37]

Fortunate as she felt to receive any financial assistance from John throughout the period of his service to Congress, Abigail was still forced to struggle, and she became a competent money manager under conditions which required financial wizardry to survive. Greed and corruption flourished as many enterprising citizens manipulated the economy to their personal benefit. Abigail survived by means she considered moral and honest, by becoming a shrewd manager of her economic life.

Quite by circumstance, Abigail discovered an opportunity to develop her entrepreneurial skills; she became, in effect, a merchant. In order to ease the family's hardship while he was abroad, John began to send Abigail goods from France to supply family needs. These were items which Abigail had not the hard cash to purchase, or which, perhaps, were not available to her in Braintree. Soon after his arrival in Paris in 1778, he wrote, "I have several Times sent some Things to you and shall continue to do so."[38] Abigail quickly grasped the opportunity: "In your last Letter you mention having sent some articles. . . . There is no remittances you can make me which will turn to a better account than Goods, more especially such articles as I enclose a list of but I believe a ship of war is the safest conveyance for them. Doctor Tufts son has lately set up in Trade, whatever I receive more than is necessary for family use I can put into his hands which will serve both him and myself."[39] Later she wrote, "Remittances made in goods, provided it could be done with any safety, will fetch hard money, or may be parted with as occasion required."[40] Abigail had discerned that she could earn money from the sale of her husband's gifts.

Such were the simple beginnings of a business that was to become more complex and important as a source of income in the six years ahead. As it became apparent that John could provide European goods to his wife without too much trouble to himself, the amount and variety of goods escalated. Requests and lists of goods disbursed traveled back and forth across the ocean: "With regard to remittances calicos answer well especially chocolate ground, as they are called Blew ground or Green ground. They should be coloured stripes or flowers; ribbons are still more profitable qauze tape fine threads handkerchiefs Bandano handkerchiefs couloured tamies or Calimenos, black serge denim Bindings either Shoe or Quality."[41] On occasion John was wont to beg for more information about the meaning of some of these requests. Better were Abigail's lists:

    6 lb. best Hyson Tea
    2 China Coffee Pots
    1 doz: handled Cups & Soucers—China
    2 doz: Soup Plates & a Tureen
    doz. flat do
    doz. small long dishes
    2 pr Pudding do.
       (2 or 3 brushes)
    3 or 4 house Brushes[42]

John wrote, "I have sent you, one yard of fine Cambrick, at 14 Livres an Ell, two of a coarser sort at 6 Livres an Ell. Eight India Handkerchiefs at 6 Livres each and three of another Stamp at 6 Livres a Piece. These seem monstrous dear, but I could not get them cheaper."[43] Tea and handkerchiefs were good sellers, Abigail reported, and she became quite dependent upon this new source of income.[44] She wrote, "Nothing could have been more fortunate for me than the arrival of the few articles you ordered for me from Bilboa, just at the time when the calls for large sums of money took place. (The Quarterly tax for the state and continental amounts to 7 hundred pound Lawfull, my part.)"[45]

Over time Abigail's enterprises became more complex. After arriving in France for the second time, John became acquainted with the family of "The House of Joseph Guardoqui and Sons," merchants. He recommended them to Abigail. "You may write to Mr. Guardoqui, for any Thing you want."[46] Although the full extent of her dealing with Guardoqui is not clear, since orders have been lost, and some letters and goods probably did not survive the ocean voyage, Abigail did maintain direct commerce with a supplier of goods.

The conveyance of merchandise across the ocean presented other obstacles; shipping was not dependable, nor were ship schedules precise. Frequently goods directed to Abigail would be sent in care of friends in Philadelphia from there to be accounted for and forwarded. James Lovell, Massachusetts delegate to the Continental Congress, and a friend to John and Abigail, served as one such agent. A typical report came from Lovell: "Your Effects, expected in the Alliance, came in the Ariel. Yesterday two Cases were brought to my Chamber, the Size of which I give on the other Side to govern your future Directions as to Transportation . . . I was agreeably disappointed in finding that the Damage was not equal to my Fears. It was such however as to oblige me to pass over every Article separately; for those which are not really injured were in a warm fermenting moisture."[47] Transportation was not reliable; goods arrived on the wrong ship to a distant port, damaged or mildewed. Nevertheless, Abigail pursued her business.

Abigail sold some items from her own home, but she also sold goods through merchants such as her cousin Tufts or friends. Mercy Otis Warren, who lived at Plymouth, became her agent, and once warned Abigail: "A word or two on Trade and Commerce. Have not sold a single Article nor Can. The town is full of Hank a chiefs. Your price is too high. They are dull at a Doller."[48] Abigail responded, "The black handkerchiefs sent the other day were a mistake, the flowered papers had always contained the coloured handkerchiefs and I did not think to open them."[49] So it was that Abigail became a modest merchant, selling items which came from Europe through the good offices of her diplomat husband.

In contrast to her farm management days, Abigail did not consider merchandising so burdensome an enterprise. In fact, she appears to have been challenged by business and to have enjoyed being a merchant. Had she been a man, she might have capitalized on these beginnings to become a merchant by profession, as did many wartime opportunists. Abigail's horizons never reached such proportions; she never regarded herself as doing more than supporting her children and sustaining the family fortunes in the absence of her husband. She did not express ambition to go into the public sector, or disappointment at the limitations on her success. Instead, she occasionally acknowledged the difficulty of her aberrant role. "The fluctuating state of our currency and the exorbitant demand for every necessity of life, together with the high taxes renders it more peculiarly difficult to be deprived of a partner at the day," she wrote to James Lovell.[50]

Although it is apparent that Abigail sustained her family and added to their fortunes in small ways, she did not record the exact dimensions of her enterprises. If she took the time to keep a record of her accounts, it does not survive. Items were lost at sea, her orders as well as her instructions. The fragmentary record suggests only that she learned trade well enough to support her family.

Abigail's success may be calculated from one index which is also a measure of her enterprising nature. She negotiated for and acquired property during the time when her husband was abroad. Her ability and foresight in land purchase, perhaps a legacy of her New England background, was profoundly ironic, because she could neither purchase nor sell property in her own name.[51] Married women could not legally own land, so Abigail negotiated and acquired property in John's name, oblivious as an eighteenth-century woman to the situation's irony.

For her initial transaction Abigail purchased property from the widow of her deceased brother-in-law, Elihu Adams, who had died during the dysentery epidemic. In this venture Abigail sought John's advice and followed his instructions. "I am desired by Sister A—— to ask you if you will take 28 acres of woodland."[52] And John gave his assent: "I am willing to take the woodland sister mentions,"[53] he answered. This experience educated her, and later she concluded several purchases on her own, informing John of her intentions without seeking his permission. Although John disapproved of one such transaction, this did not deter Abigail, who by this time was a confident businesswoman and manager of property.

In early 1780 Abigail informed John that she was negotiating for more property: "I have some prospect of making a purchase of the House and land, belonging formerly to Natell. Belcher who died this winter. I have been trying to agree with the Heir, he asked the moderate price of 20 thousand Dollars when the exchange was at 30, it is now 60 and he doubles his demand," she wrote of the unstable bargaining situation. "There are several persons very eager to purchase it, which has determined the owner to put it up to vendue, if he does I shall endeavor to buy it."[54] Abigail referred to this property several times more, but it is not clear that she ever succeeded in making the purchase.[55]

Abigail's Vermont venture represented the work of a speculator. It also represented her fantasy for John's return as she proposed future happiness in a new land. "I have a desire to become a purchaser in the State of Vermont," she informed John in 1781. "I may possibly run you in debt a hundred dollars for that purpose. . . . I know you would like it, so shall venture the first opportunity a hundred and 20 or 30 dollars will Buy a thousand acres."[56] Months later she wrote, "I will purchase you a retreat in the woods of Vermont and retire with you from vexations, toils, hazards and publick Life."[57] John did not like it: "God willing, I wont go to Vermont."[58] Justifying her speculative venture, Abigail repeated the old adage: "Nothing ventured nothing have; and I took all the Lots 5 in number 4 of which I paid for, and the other obligated myself to discharge in a few months."[59] Since she could not own property in her own right, she was obliged to inform John that "You are named in the Charter as original proprietor, so no deed was necessary."[60] Ironic indeed that John now owned over 1,600 acres of Vermont which he did not want, purchased by Abigail, who had the courage to speculate and the cleverness to negotiate for land she could not legally possess. If this situation appeared unjust to Abigail, she did not write about such a reaction in her surviving letters.

Business and domestic concerns aside, Abigail expressed her great loneliness during this long period by referring to herself as a widow. John's absence coincided with the decade between her thirtieth and fortieth years, and during the time that she lived without him she supported an awesome record of industry, but she found the time to read and to write. In both cases much of the stimulus must have been escape or relief from loneliness.

That Abigail read both classical and popular literature is apparent from the references in her letters, but she also quoted freely from Molière, Milton, Rousseau, Shakespeare, Pope, and Addison. Her interest in contemporary literature is clear from the exchange that developed when she requested a copy of "Lord Chesterfields Letters."[61] John responded: "Chesterfields Letters are a chequered sett You would not chose to have them in your Library, they are like Congreeves Plays, stained with libertine Morals and base Principles."[62] Abigail acquiesced to John's censorship: "I give up my Request for Chesterfields Letters submitting intirely to your judgment."[63] Curiosity rankled, however, and four years later Abigail admitted to Mercy that "A collection of his Lordships Letters came in my Hands this winter which I read, and tho they contain only a part of what he has written, I found enough to satisfy me, that his Lordship with all his Elegance and graces, was a Hypocritical, polished Libertine, a mere Lovelace."[64] John's admonition notwithstanding, Abigail had performed her own experiment before she accepted his judgment. Clear as well from her remark, she too was familiar with *Clarissa*.[65]

Abigail also read political treatises, poetry, and travel literature; she received numerous journals related to contemporary politics. She began to read history seriously during this period. This was undoubtedly the effect of John's predilection for history and the availability of his library. "In America . . . so few Ladies have a taste for Historick knowledge, that even their own Country was not much known to them until the present Revolution,"[66] Abigail wrote, reflecting the commitment of the convert. Her letters to one and all drew lessons from ancient Greece and Rome, as Abigail applied history to her contemporary world.

The vastness of her correspondence is apparent. Letter writing became more than communication to Abigail; it was a form of therapy. "There are perticular times when I feel such an uneasiness, such a restlessness, as neither company, Books, family Cares or any other thing will remove, my Pen is my only pleasure and writing to you the composure of my mind," she confided to John.[67]

In addition to her family, Abigail maintained several other regular correspondences, none more suggestive than the exchange with James Lovell. "Must I write to you in the Language of Gazetts. . . . It seems I must be taxed a Flatterer," wrote Lovell.[68] To which Abigail remonstrated: "I know not whether I ought to reply . . . indeed Sir I begin to look upon you as a very dangerous man."[69] This correspondence provided some sensation during an otherwise tedious and lonely period of Abigail's life.

The revolutionary years and those following were times of great industry and readjustment for Abigail Adams. She accepted adversity as a theory of life because she was of New England background; she accepted adversity in practice as a necessity. Over the long run of years she emerged strong of will and powerful of personality. The dominant figure of her home and family, Abigail was matriarch to the microcosmic social group that was her household. Both she and John knew that. They knew as well the limitations of her power.

"Portia" was the pen name used by Abigail Adams into her middle age. A clever device, the imagery which Abigail chose to reflect was the patient and long-suffering wife to the great Brutus. Abigail's model was the obscure wife of a great politician, above all, a domestic figure—a Roman wife.

There are, however, some contradictions in this domestic vision. Aside from assuming a "masculine" role by supporting her family for so many years, which can be explained by her rising to the needs of the occasion, Abigail recurrently made statements that express dissatisfaction with the feminine role in society. Whether Abigail had radical ideas about women for her time; whether she was a feminist who advocated change for the position of women in society; whether she was ahead of her time, an early representative of the women's rights movement; or whether there was a different significance to her expressions of discontent—all these questions have emerged as results of some of her statements and activities.

In fact, Abigail disapproved of women who breached the prevailing code of female behavior. However much she was compelled in the absence of her husband to assume activities which fell outside the traditional domestic sphere, she believed her performance was extraordinary, aberrant, expedient, and unnatural. She continually referred to her new situation as a patriotic sacrifice for her country.[70]

At the same time, domesticity did not signify weakness or silence to Abigail, so she freely expressed her opinion on a number of controversial topics that interested her. In the spring of 1776, for instance, she wrote to John: "I long to hear that you have declared an independancy," adding a bit of advice, as was her custom: "and by the way in the new Code of Laws which I suppose it will be necessary for you to make I desire you would Remember the Ladies, and be more generous and favorable to them than your ancestors." Her remarkable request continued, making a specific recommendation that resonated with the public rhetoric of 1776: "Do not put such unlimited power in the hands of the Husbands. Remember all men would be tyrants if they could."[71]

It was not only the events in revolutionary America that convinced Abigail about the corruptibility of men, but also her deep roots in Puritan New England. A year earlier she had written, "I am more and more convinced that Man is a dangerous creature, and that power whether vested in many or few is ever grasping."[72] During stressful periods throughout her life, Abigail reverted to the Puritan notion of depravity to explain human behavior.[73]

As an eighteenth-century woman, Abigail did not question male authority, but in the spirit of the revolutionary era, she was concerned about justice: "That your Sex are Naturally Tyrannical is a Truth so thoroughly established as to admit no dispute." She continued to press her point: "Why then, not put it out of the power of the vicious and the Lawless to use us with cruelty and indignity and impunity." Abigail argued for the protection of women from abuse. It was not a demand for political or social equality; it was a plea for humane treatment. Her poignant summary best described her feminine faith: "Regard us then as Beings placed by providence under your protection and in imitation of the Supreme Being make use of that power only for our happiness."[74] Her own experience to the contrary, Abigail concluded that women were subordinate to men, just as all human beings were subjects of the Supreme Being; her analogy suggested the extreme case of caste structure in the relationship of women to men.

Yet, Abigail's plea for constitutional protection of women reflects unusual gender awareness for her time. Her proposal that there could be legal guarantees of just gender relations—albeit a patriarchal arrangement—was a daring step. She did not persist when John jokingly dismissed her petition, but she complained to her friend Mercy before dropping the issue entirely.

The topic of women's education, however, preoccupied Abigail throughout her life. Therefore, another of her recommendations to John for the new body of laws that he and other Founding Fathers were drafting in 1776 incorporated her concern "that our new constitution may be distinguished for learning and Virtue." In this case, she allowed, "If we mean to have Heroes, Statesmen and Philosophers, we should have learned women."[75] This time John agreed: "Your Sentiments on the Importance of Education in Women, are exactly agreeable to my own."[76]

Abigail's commitment to the improvement of women's education remained consistent. To John Thaxter, John's young law clerk and secretary, she wrote, "It is really mortifying Sir, when a woman possessed of a common share of understanding considers the differences of Education is attended too. . . . Why should children of the same parents be thus distinguished?"[77] Abigail's justification for female education reflected her traditional vision of domesticity: "Why should the Females who have a part to act upon the great Theatre, and a part not less important to society, (as the Care of a Family and the first instruction of children falls to their share, and if as we are told that first impressions are most durable), is it not of great importance that those who are to instill the first principles should be suitably qualified for the Trust. . . ."[78] Her belief in female education was compatible with domesticity; it was a prescription that she had sustained long before the war disrupted the way that society operated. Her different approach was to propose that the national law should ensure women's education equal to men's. In that respect, Abigail advocated ideas whose time had not yet come.

When the time came that Abigail regretted being a woman, it was because war and separation from her husband for so many years had burdened her greatly. She did not fight back or demand change; she submitted to biblical orthodoxy. "Desire and sorrow were denounced upon our Sex as a punishment for the transgression of Eve," she wrote in a time of despair. "I never wondered at the philosopher who thanked the Gods that he was created a Man rather than a woman."[79] Her dour outlook did not last, because she was not naturally a depressive woman. "I am not Naturally a gloomy temper nor disposed to view objects upon the dark Side only," she correctly observed.[80] During the Revolutionary War, however, when the press of events and loneliness gripped her most, she reverted to the ancient biblical doctrine. Perhaps, as well, she was trying to tell John that it was time to come home.

Abigail Adams by Benjamin Blyth, 1766. Courtesy of the Massachusetts Historical Society.

Portrait said to be that of Abigail Adams, artist unknown. Courtesy of the New York State Historical Association, Cooperstown.

Abigail Adams by Gilbert Stuart, 1800–1815. Courtesy of the National Gallery of Art, Washington.

Elizabeth Smith Shaw Peabody by Gilbert Stuart, 1809. Courtesy of the University Art Collections, Arizona State University.

Abigail Adams Smith, after a portrait by John Singleton Copley, 1786. Courtesy of the Massachusetts Historical Society.

Charles Adams, artist unknown, 1797. Courtesy of the Massachusetts Historical Society.

Thomas Boylston Adams, 1794. Courtesy of the Massachusetts Historical Society.

John Adams by John Singleton Copley, 1783. Courtesy of the Harvard University Portrait Collection. Harvard University, Cambridge, Massachusetts. Bequest of Ward Nicholas Boylston to Harvard College, 1828.

John Quincy Adams by John Singleton Copley, 1795. Courtesy of the
Museum of Fine Arts, Boston.

4

A Virtuous Affair

Scholars of every historical discipline aspire to a share of the American Revolution, and most have achieved partnership, if not monopoly. Political historians tell of the exchange of power between men at the conference table; military historians describe men on the battlefield. The tension between the men who served and those who stayed home and profited, and the discord between classes of men are included in the tale of the social historians. Intellectual history probes the conflicts between ideologies that gave energy and impetus to the men on all sides.[1] But the Revolution was experienced in another forum as well, the domestic forum, and with the recent emergence of women's studies, the issue of women's role during the Revolution has become significant. No longer is it possible to ignore the fact that women, too, participated in the history of the revolutionary era, though their voices resonate differently.[2] We may now restructure the past by acknowledging women's contribution in the more traditional story of man's war for liberation. Further, we may ask if and how women benefited from that quest for liberation.[3]

While the Adams Papers are richly informative about the politics and diplomacy of the Revolution; while Abigail Adams's letters, too, are regarded as rich in the social history of her times, a small portion of her letters is especially revealing on the issue of woman's status in revolutionary America.[4] The correspondence between Abigail Adams and James Lovell has attracted Adams scholars for some time for the reason that it contains a distinctly seductive motif. Mrs. Adams, the respectable, courageous, clever, articulate wife of the eminent Founding Father, and James Lovell, the distinguished, dedicated patriot, Massachusetts delegate to the Continental Congress, attentive husband and parent, exchanged letters which, in addition to describing wartime politics, contain an unmistakable sexual element. A different kind of politics emerges from this exchange.

This correspondence took place over a period of five years, between 1777 and 1782, and consequently by late twentieth-century standards the sexual references appear tame and lustless, shrouded in innuendo. Only in their eighteenth-century context do the exchanges between Mrs. Adams and Lovell assume the force of sensation. Most twentieth-century Adams scholars, struck by the incongruity of this exchange amidst the more decorous content of the Adams correspondence, have interpreted the letters as a mutual flirtation.[5] The exchange does, in fact, appear flirtatious. However, with deeper scrutiny a different design emerges from the correspondence. By inquiring whether a friendship could exist between a man and a woman who were not married to each other, if friendship implies equality, the Adams-Lovell letters may be used as a barometer to measure women's status during the revolutionary era.

Ordinary discourse between men and women was governed by clearly understood formal conventions, gallantry by the male, signaling dominance, modesty and discretion by the female as a sign of submission.[6] This is observed in many extant sources, even among the Adamses. The famous John Adams–Mercy Otis Warren letters, communications between two people who were good friends over a long period of time, adhere to these conventions, despite the great tension which motivated the later exchange.[7] Abigail Adams's letters to any number of male correspondents remain polite and mannered.[8] The conventions of addressing people by their surnames, of restricting content to impersonal topics, of structuring the language in euphemisms to avoid personal issues, all these conventions prevailed, except in the letters between close family members.[9]

By the late eighteenth century, letter-writing conventions drew on a literary tradition which had developed two modes of expression. On the one hand its triumph was measured by the canonization of the epistolary novel: *Pamela, Clarissa,* and a host of lesser classics. In its other mode, letter writing, as communication, had developed as an art form, lending the age distinction as the "golden age of letter writing."[10] Manuals of style became popular, promoting idealized versions of proper letter types, business letters, social correspondence, family letters. These manuals became an important part of the education for gentlemen, and young women were expected to spend several hours each day practicing letter writing. These conventions reached from England to its American colonies.[11]

The causes for the flourishing letter-writing tradition in the eighteenth century were manifold. The inception of the penny post in England at the end of the seventeenth century, when for the first time a convenient and reliable postal service became available, was a primary cause. At the same time English prose style was changing. Reacting against a formulaic Latin style which had prevailed since the Renaissance, authors in the eighteenth century strived to achieve a "natural" style that took spontaneity and candor as important attributes. The eighteenth-century correspondent was encouraged "to compare his letters with polite conversation."[12]

An important component of conversation was courtesy; ladies and gentlemen were courteous in conversation through gesture, manner, and behavior. Therefore, literary conventions developed that translated manners to prose style, for "too much casualness would have suggested some measure of insolence."[13] A function of letter-writing manuals, then, was to teach conventions, so that writing style would incorporate the politeness of body gesture into prose style. These manuals ensured that letters, like polite conversation, were civilized, that the forms of address among ladies and gentlemen were above all courteous.[14] Educated people in the colonies were schooled in this prevailing literary ethos.

Such was not the case in the Lovell correspondence. Lovell referred to Mrs. Adams by her familiar pen-name "Portia," though he was not an intimate; he went further and called her "Lovely Portia." In subtle ways he mentioned the unmentionable, as when he flippantly congratulated her, John having been away in France for eleven months, on not being pregnant![15] Some of the letters have the thrust and parry of a political negotiation—a testing of positions between two clever people, an aggressive challenge from one side, a perseverant probing from the other. This correspondence violated the ordinary eighteenth-century standards of formal discourse between a man and woman who were virtual strangers to each other.[16] A pattern emerges from the Abigail Adams–James Lovell letters which illustrates the imbalance of the relationship between man and woman that characterized gender politics in the eighteenth century.[17]

Throughout the time of her correspondence with James Lovell, Abigail, who was then in her mid-thirties, was living in her family home, a rustic cottage by our standards, in Braintree (later Quincy), Massachusetts.[18] Her husband had left home to serve his nation at the outbreak of the conflict with Great Britain in 1774, and except for a few visits of several months' duration, she did not live with him for a decade.[19] A variety of people, who came and went, lived in her household during the war years: her four children, Abigail Junior, John Quincy, Charles, and Thomas; several servants; the children's tutor, John Thaxter; and her niece Louisa.[20] Still, it was a lonely and anxious time, for she was solely responsible for this household, and in every sense of the word, she supported its members throughout the decade. It was during this period that her letter writing became rife. It was also during this period that her correspondence with Lovell took place.

James Lovell's name does not appear on the Declaration of Independence; he was in a British prison in 1776. Nor is he associated with the drafting of the Constitution, for by 1783 he had returned to Boston, having served the longest uninterrupted tenure of any delegate to the Continental Congress. Lovell was renowned neither as a profound political thinker nor as an ambitious statesman or courageous military man. His service to the nation was performed in the chambers of Congress, and in his own time he earned a reputation as a diligent worker. The other part of his reputation accounts in part for his historical obscurity; he was reputedly a most abrasive person.[21]

Lovell had been a schoolteacher in Boston when the conflict with Britain developed. The son of a schoolmaster, he graduated from Harvard in 1756, the year after John Adams, and he was subsequently acknowledged in Boston as somewhat a scholar and orator. His reputation inflated to heroic proportions with the outbreak of hostilities, for while other citizens were evacuating Boston during the British occupation, Lovell deliberately remained behind. His self-proclaimed motive was to care for the property of those patriots who had departed, a mission which he zealously executed.[22] But in addition, he probably did intelligence work, for he was arrested by the British after they confiscated a letter from him describing British military positions in Boston. Lovell was imprisoned for nearly a year in Boston and then transferred to Halifax when the British evacuated the city. In late 1776 an exchange of prisoners was effected; he was released and returned to Boston where he was soon elected to the Continental Congress.

Lovell served a full five years in Congress while others, less dedicated or less energetic, came and went. He became a good friend of John Adams, whom he had known since they were students at Harvard, a friendship confirmed by their journey together from Boston to Baltimore, where the Congress convened for a short time in early 1777.[23]

In Congress Lovell was known for his diligence, for the long hours he worked, for his service as translator for French visitors, and for his chairmanship of the Committee on Foreign Affairs,[24] but he was also known for his irreverence and sarcasm. Always a controversial figure, he returned to Boston after the war, and for the remainder of his years, he eked out a penurious existence for his family as a civil servant. He never became rich; he never achieved fame; he was ostracized socially because of his incurable irreverence for convention. He never did become "one of those grovelling politicians" whom he publicly disdained.[25]

James Lovell initiated the correspondence with Abigail Adams, writing a brief note from Philadelphia in late August 1777, to accompany a little present for her, a map he had drawn of the battle area in Pennsylvania. "I send you a copied sketch of the part of the country to which the Gazettes will frequently refer," he explained, because he knew she was interested in following the events of the war. Then he added, "This knowledge is only part of the foundation of my affectionate esteem for you. Nor will I mention the whole." To esteem an unfamiliar person is entirely within the scope of acceptable discourse, but "affectionate esteem" for a stranger so violates propriety that Adams must indeed have been unsettled. But then, "not to mention the whole," in its ambiguity, established a style that would become characteristic of Lovell's letters. He teased. Only at the conclusion of the note did he explain that "your having given your heart to such a man (John Adams) is what, most of all makes me yours, in the manner I have above sincerely professed myself to be."[26]

Abigail replied promptly, in a spontaneous style that became typical of her. And in this case, she might just have been putting Lovell in his place. "I cannot describe to you the distress and agitation which the reception of your Letter threw me into. . . . I dared not read it. Ten thousand horrid Ideas rushed upon my Soul. I thought it would announce to me the sickness or death of all my earthly happiness."

Less an ingratiating introduction than an assault, Abigail's reply may have been quite innocent. Or she may have been offended by his familiarity and making clear her respectability by reaffirming her primary loyalty to her husband. "Your professions of esteem are very flattering to me," she continued. She thanked him for the map and praised him as a "Virtuous" public servant.[27] After this little exchange, except for a desultory response from Lovell, the correspondence lapsed. But the seeds of a small power struggle had been sown.

The next letter four months later was an inspired outburst from Abigail. John had come home from Philadelphia for a brief visit, when he received an appointment to serve in Paris as a commissioner to negotiate a treaty of alliance with France.[28] This was quickly followed by a letter from James Lovell, urging him to accept the appointment.[29] Abigail reacted to the appointment in a communication to Lovell: "O Sir you who are possessed of Sensibility, and a tender Heart, how could you contrive to rob me of all my happiness?" Her tirade continues. She could understand how others at Congress could be insensitive, but not he, Lovell, who was a loving family man. "How could you so soon forget your sufferings and risk your Friend." Abigail discharged anger and fear, but at the same time she attempted to reason with herself as she struggled to adjust to what she knew would be, at best, an inevitable lengthy separation from John. She recognized the compliment to him and she appreciated that Lovell himself was torn by this decision, but "can I Sir consent to be separated from him whom my Heart esteems above all earthly beings, and for an unlimited time?" She continued to reason: "I know you think I ought or you [would] not have been accessary to the Call." She acknowledged the inappropriateness of her agonized outburst: "I beg your Excuse Sir for writing thus freely, it has been a relief to my mind to drop some of my sorrows through my pen. . . ."[30]

Time and again during the years of separation from John Adams, Abigail employed her pen to this purpose. She knew intuitively that confession was a form of therapy, and she possessed the ability to put words on paper to describe her great emotional distress. She then took the additional step of sending the letter, of giving away her distress, in effect. Abigail's reputation in her lifetime, and certainly in history, is attributable to her emotional strength, to her ability to function effectively in abnormal circumstances and to triumph over circumstances. No small part of that stability, what her great-grandson Henry Adams called "stern stuff," came from the therapeutic effect of her letter writing.[31] Usually, however, the recipients of these therapy sessions in letters were her intimates, family members or close friends. In this case, however, with her outburst to Lovell, she had misjudged her audience. For as much as Lovell was sympathetic to Mrs. Adams, he played the part of flirtatious male with her, a part that inherently negotiates for power.

Several letters followed in which Adams continued to address Lovell in her honest and direct manner. She sought to enlist him as a friend, trusting that as John's friend, he would extend that courtesy to her. These letters described her anxieties about John and eleven-year-old John Quincy, who had accompanied his father to Europe. Months had passed and she had not received news of their arrival in France. Perhaps Lovell could convey information from Philadelphia.[32] Lovell's language compounded Abigail's problems. "Call me not a Savage," he had written in April, "when I inform you that your 'Alarms and Distress' have afforded me *Delight* . . . if you should expect that your griefs should draw from me only sheer Pity, you must not send them to call upon me in the most elegant Dresses of Sentiment and Language: for if you persist in your present course," he warned, "be it known to you beforehand that I shall be far more prompt to admire than to compassionate them."[33]

Lovell's message was not lost on Adams, and for several months she did not write to him. If she thought she had written to a friend, certainly she was unsettled by his shift of tone in the dialogue; perhaps she did not know how to respond. Finally, she wrote: "I know not whether I ought to reply to your favor of April the first, for indeed Sir I begin to look upon you as a very dangerous man."[34] The obvious question arises: Why, then, did she reply? She "Cannot but acknowledg Mr. L[ovel]l as a most ingenious and agreeable flatterer," she wrote, perhaps coyly. But coquetry, as Lovell would later affirm,[35] was not in her character, not even as a lonely, middle-aged woman, living alone with children and servants in a rustic cottage in rural Braintree.

The reason that she persisted in this correspondence was that Abigail Adams needed James Lovell. She continued this correspondence for years, despite the escalation of Lovell's impudent remarks, because he performed services for her that no other person could or would do. He was, in the first place, the best placed person at Congress to receive information about John. He served as secretary of the Committee on Foreign Affairs, which, in a later age, would be tantamount to secretary of state. Dispatches from

Europe, where John was serving, were directed to him or came to his attention immediately upon their arrival. Furthermore, he genuinely admired John Adams, not only because they were fellow delegates from Massachusetts, but because he was devoted to John by principles and statesmanship.[36] Abigail trusted him because of his admiration and affection for John.

But, furthermore, and most important, Lovell was the only person at Congress who *would* help her by keeping her informed about John and about the developments in Congress. She had attempted to get information from other Massachusetts delegates. Elbridge Gerry, she pointed out, was a bachelor, "a stranger to domestic felicity and knows no tender attachment than that which he feel[s] for his country . . ." a "stoicism" which intimidated her.[37] She tried Sam Adams too: "I wrote to Mr. SA—— . . . but not a syllable of information have I yet collected from him."[38] And again, "I need not add that Mr. SA is too much the politician to attend to the purtubations and too much the philosopher to realize the thousand anxieties that distress the tender heart of our frail sex." She added, "I think I have the right to say this since he has not even wrote to me a line . . . tho he could be no stranger to my perplexity having received a message or two from me. . . ."[39]

Lovell, however, did respond to Adams's pleas for news and assistance. Many times Abigail literally begged for news of John when his infrequent letters to her were either lost at sea or delayed. Upon hearing a rumor, in March 1778, that Benjamin Franklin had been assassinated, Abigail wrote to Lovell of her "terror." "When ever any perticulars arrive with regard to this black affair I must beg of you to acquaint me with them."[40] She was, of course, most alarmed about John's safety in this situation. And Lovell replied that the rumor was unfounded.[41]

She asked Lovell for information. "Am I entitled to the Journals of Congress, if you think so I should be much obliged to you if you would convey them to me."[42] He sent her the Journals regularly. She asked Lovell for confidential information: "I have not the pleasure of intelligence which used to be communicated to my Friend with the perusal of which he always indulged me. I dare venture to say this only to you, since a hint of this kind would restrain many Gentlemans pens possessed of less liberal sentiments."[43] She learned to take the good with the troublesome. "You will see, lovely Woman," impertinently began his response, "that I regard, esteem and respect you and will certainly write you as often as I possibly can."[44] And again "I send you a Continuance of the Journals. . . . How do you do, Lovely Portia, these very cold Days? Mistake me not willfully; I said Days."[45]

Abigail was acting the role of manager of family finances and had ventured into currency speculation by this time. She requested information from Lovell about action in Congress that would affect the currency exchange. "I find that congress are Drawing Bill(s) at 25 for one. . . . Have they any prospect that their draughts will be answered. . . . Why may I ask do they demand only 25 when 30 has been currently given here. . . ."[46] Nor was she misguided about her informant. "It is recommended to redeem the Continental currency at 40-1," he responded.[47]

Congress adjourned from its exile in York after the British abandoned Philadelphia in late 1778. Lovell was the person who took charge of John's belongings that had been left behind. He sorted, itemized, and packed clothes, books, and papers, sending them to Abigail with an inventory and noting that he had resisted reading her letters which were part of the consignment.[48] In the ensuing years, John shipped items of various sorts to Abigail from Europe, which she in turn sold for a profit. Several times, these shipments arrived in Philadelphia, and again Lovell took charge of them. "Your effects, expected in the Alliance, came in the Ariel. Yesterday two Cases were brought to my Chamber. . . . I found them not much injured. I thoroughly examined, wiped and dried them properly for second Package."[49] Again months later, "I feared moths—have opened your Goods—aired and shook the Wollens—added good tobacco leaves and again secured them for Transporation."[50]

For years Lovell rendered services to Adams, easing her struggles in the ways that he could. At the same time, like the irrepressible youth that was part of his character, he persisted in a series of outrageously flirtatious remarks. Sometimes he wrote sensitively: "Yesterday the Letters of Portia . . . came to my hand . . . I will only tell the sudden Effect which it produced, upon the quick glancing of my Eye over it . . . it forced from me, almost audibly, in a Grave Assembly where I broke the Seal, 'Gin ye were mine ain Thing, how dearly I would *love* thee!' "[51] Other times he became quite ribald: ". . . I doubt whether I shall be able to keep myself void of *all* covetousness. I suspect I shall covet to be in the Arms of Portia's [and here the page ends to be continued on the overleaf] Friend and admirer—the Wife of my Bosome [his wife]. . . ."[52] Sometimes he teased, referring to his "Correspondent as one of the ____est and ____est and ____est women."[53]

Abigail Adams continued to put up with James Lovell for over five years because he helped her. The issue is, then, how did she cope with his irreverence? Not comfortably, to be sure. She found herself in a situation that called for a reaction beyond her repertoire of natural responses, and she struggled to find her voice with Lovell, a voice that would not concede to his terms. At first, she modestly ignored the issue. Then she called him "flatterer," perhaps thinking that he would be dissuaded by name calling. This ploy did not work: "Amiable tho unjust Portia! . . . Must I write to you in the language of Gazettes. . . . It seems I must or be taxed a Flatterer. . . ."[54] Then Abigail stopped writing to him altogether, and when he inquired about her silence, she replied: "But can Mr. L____l soon forget that he had prohibited (me) from writing by prescribing conditions . . . *that he knew she could not practice.*"[55] For a while she attempted to tease in return. Lovell sent her a copy of a code that he had invented. She wrote: "If Mr. L[ovel]l will not call me Saucy, I will tell him he has not the least occasion to make use of (the code) himself since he commonly writes so much in the enigmatic way that no body . . . will ever find out his meaning."[56] This was not a tone she could sustain, so she upbraided him in her strongest language, calling him "wicked man."[57] Finally, she tried to proscribe his language by explicitly defining the terms he could and could not use: "amiable and agreeable are bearable," but "lovely" and "charming" are proscribed.[58] All the while she scolded him.

Still, the suspicion remains that Adams might have encouraged the flirtation. Perhaps her tactics appear coy, encouraging his advances in a subtle manner, a manoeuvre used by women to negotiate power with men. If the doubt remains, another kind of evidence supports the credibility of Adams's serious position in opposition to Lovell's advances. Her strict New England upbringing in the household of a clergyman established standards of virtuous behavior for women; but that is not enough. That she remained loyal to John for over half a century, despite his own divided loyalties between family and nation, is not enough. More persuasively, the subconscious issue, which Abigail concealed with all her rational strength, would have deterred her: the possibility that if she violated, in even the most modest terms, the spirit of her marriage contract with John, he was much better placed in France to do her harm through disloyalty.[59] Never could she risk by her own example any violation of the marriage bond.

The primary evidence, albeit indirect, derives from Abigail's acute awareness of the risks of interception of mails by the enemy, resulting in publication of letters in the popular press. This publication not only provided the enemy with easy access to information, it compromised reputations. The threat was real; the problem was pandemic. From the time John Adams left home in 1774, he had cautioned Abigail to be careful about the content of her letters to him because of the danger of interception.[60] On a regular basis she observed the capture and publication of mails, even her own. She learned this lesson well and observed it carefully. To believe, then, that Abigail would risk her reputation, and her husband's reputation, by participating in a *risqué* correspondence goes in the face of her intelligence and common sense. Abigail would not have been so careless.

Indeed, one such episode of capture and publication touched closely on Abigail's exchanges with Lovell. A Lovell letter was intercepted, and for some time Abigail did not know its destination.[61] She was mortified but discovered to her relief that it had been addressed to Elbridge Gerry in Boston. The letter, of typical Lovell extraction, contained some phrases that even today might provoke sensation in the case of a public official, and it provided local gossipmongers with enough entertainment to last for weeks.[62] Adams in her best form confronted Lovell with a blistering denunciation. "If what I heard is true, I cannot open my lips in defense," she wrote, admonishing him as thoughtless and irresponsible. She continued to write to him, she concluded, addressing him in the third person, only because she stood in need of his services, and because she considered him loyal in the discharge of them. That bound her to him as a friend.[63] Calmer by the time she next wrote, she equivocated: "I wrote you by the last post with a freedom which perhaps you may think I had no right to make use of. I was stimulated to it by many severe speaches that I had heard. . . . All former excuses were worn out by *time*. . . ."[64] Abigail was confounded by this issue. On the one hand, she felt loyalty to the only man at Congress who had consistently done her service. On the other, his letters, aside from perplexing her, threatened her reputation.

For his part, Lovell was sobered by this incident—temporarily. He reassured her that none of their letters had been captured.[65] Then for the first time in almost four years of correspondence, he wrote seriously about himself. He explained the questionably obscene phrase in the intercepted letter. "As to *the* letter Madam, there is one Expression or rather one Mode of Expression that I wish was not there. I am very unwilling that it should be submitted to the Eye of one so very much my friend as you profess yourself to be. My Enemies are welcome to read it a thousand Times over. It was an unbecoming Levity, and quite unfit for a 'Senator.' " The "unbecoming Levity" referred to his wife, and Lovell explained to Abigail that "It is not that which will give Pain to my affectionate Wife. She will be pained with what you will smile at. For she is more Apt to fear than dispise the Enmity of Little-Great-Folks." Referring to his wife, he wrote, "You have a very small acquaintance with the Lady, and as little personal Acquaintance with the Gentleman connected with her. Had you greater with both, you could not fail to think more highly of the former, and not so well or so ill of the latter."[66] That Lovell explained the letter, that he described his wife and himself to Abigail is a gesture of consideration, of caring, of wanting to maintain her sympathy and friendship. He knew himself to be in grave jeopardy with Abigail this time. He abandoned his former posture.

Sensing her advantage, Adams became assertive, and, claiming that she had discovered the remedy for Lovell's rapidly waning reputation in Boston, she advised him to come home at once. After all, four years of absence did appear suspect, and his presence would demonstrate that he cared for his wife and family.[67] Again Lovell responded, fully vulnerable at first. Much as he cared for his wife and children, he could not return. He wrote, "I must now be very serious," and he confessed that his solitary income was derived from his "pay for Time and Service as a delegate, which *ceases that day I arrive in Boston,* tho my Wife and Children expect to dine the day after and per adventure they will be extravagant enough to expect it the third Day also." With this his seriousness gave way to bitterness; he railed against the men, many his former students at the South

Grammar School, who stayed at home throughout the war, building their fortunes: Will they call "to pay their compliments to the *Honorable Delegate of Congress*. . . . Do those who condemn my absence mean to take me into their stores as a Clerk?"[68]

Then the bitterness became anger and the darts were turned on Abigail. "And now Madam, do not think that this serious Subject shall prevent my taking occasion to censure your Sophistry. . . ." In a series of paragraphs he assailed her point by point, citing the catalogue of rebukes for what he considered false social values: her scruples about his choice of words, her reputation as a married woman, his loyalty to his wife. Having gained the offensive, he reached his crescendo by assaulting her patriotism: ". . . your fine tuned Instrument cannot be an American one; it must be english with which we are at war."[69]

Nor did Abigail cower before his onslaught: "Uncandid do you say? You will never find Portia so," she shot back. She supported her flank by calling in additional forces, the forces of gossip. Her friend Cornelia, a pseudonym probably used to protect Mercy Otis Warren, had reported the gossip, and the rumors proved to be widespread and nasty. Lovell, she persisted, was the object of derision, and she had only repeated to him as his friend what others were saying to deride him.[70]

The letters have changed tone. They have achieved a level of confrontation in which each attacks and defends with uninhibited and equitable strength. Adams and Lovell do political combat; they argue. But the argument, instead of setting them apart, instead of separating them altogether, brings them closer together. Lovell has become vulnerable: "Why do you strive to make me vile in my own eyes," he had written to her.[71] Now he confessed, "I really do not foresee how I am to begin the world at 42 without any of what are called the 3 learned professions, without farm or Stock in Trade: and yet if you will believe me I do not feel distressed, for tho slanderous Females will speak slightly of my morality I know that I am one of the most religious men in the world."[72]

She never really believed the gossip in the first place, Adams generously allowed. She had only listened and repeated it because she cared about him. Now that Lovell appeared vulnerable, now that she sensed the advantage was hers, she became magnanimous. "You have sometimes given latitude to your pen which I thought exceptionable and I have ever told you so," she reiterated triumphantly, leading to her final sally: "But to be very sincere Sir I do not think female Slander has been the busyest—you might possibly find it [she means gossip] in the city where you reside."[73]

An evolution had occurred in the five years of correspondence between Abigail Adams and James Lovell. An increasingly caring, honest, and understanding relationship had developed; the correspondence had produced friendship. Lovell, for all his irreverence had secured Abigail's trust. She wrote, "In truth Friend thou art a Queer Being—laugh where I must,

be candid where I can.—Your pictures are Hogarths. I shall find you out by
and by—I will not build upon other people's judgments. Thus I do run on,"
she continued, "because I know you take an Interest in my happiness and
because I know I can make you feel. I hate an unfealing mortal. The
passions are common to us all, but the lively, sweet affection(s) are the
portion only of a chosen Few. Laugh and satirize as much as you please,"
she went on, "I laugh with you to see what a figure your inventive Genious
makes in picking up terms—tis necessary to keep a watchful Eye over
you."[74]

No longer equivocal, Abigail Adams has found her voice with Lovell. She
writes with the assurance of a friend. No longer testing his character or her
own approach, she subscribes herself to him thereafter as "your real
Friend." Lovell's affection and respect for Abigail induced him to abandon
his impious facade, to reveal the caring individual he had so carefully
masked in impudence, wit, and sarcasm. And Lovell responds: "Perhaps
after my Profession of Respect it will be incongruous to hint that you also
Madam are a 'queer being.' "[75] Later he writes seriously, "Your good sense
and your Friendship make the second claim to my attentions after the
sovereign one which Mrs. L—— secures by an avowed, uniform, unabid-
ing Love and a prudent confidence which is sure not to be abused. . . ."[76]

A few more letters were exchanged before the Revolution ended and
Lovell returned home to Boston. This little corpus of letters—some ninety
of them exist—is concluded. It represents a friendship, unique in a number
of ways. To begin, the letters represent the essence of the relationship. The
friendship lived in the letters alone. It did not survive into a personal
relationship. After Lovell's return to Boston, there is little contact between
them. In a desultory letter in late 1782, he apologizes for not visiting her
upon his return, and there is no evidence that he ever did.[77]

This correspondence between a married man and a married woman
ventured outside the bounds of eighteenth-century social conventions,
and within it a friendship developed between two exceptional individuals.
James Lovell wrote to Abigail Adams—and he assisted her for years—
because beneath the camouflage of male posturing, he was a sensitive and
generous man. He cared enough for Abigail and respected her enough to
surrender an aggressive, sovereign male sexual posture to reveal a devoted, caring, and vulnerable character.

Adams, too, made concessions. She surrendered the proprieties of formal discourse to adopt a candid, witty, and aggressive repartee with a man
she had scarcely met. Her style with Lovell became her most comfortable
expression of herself. Her persistence with Lovell, while initially motivated
by a need for his services, in the end was impelled by other motives. Lovell
resembled men for whom Abigail cared. In fact, Lovell is not dissimilar
from John Adams, but perhaps an impetuous, even crude exaggeration of
John's character. Both men were iconoclasts; both were at war with a world

that was imperfect. Lovell, too, prefigures another unconventional man of whom Abigail became genuinely fond, Royall Tyler, whose engagement to her daughter Abigail Junior was terminated because of his irresponsible behavior—a charming, but incorrigible man.[78] These were men of some genius, of sensibility, men who did not fit their social contexts comfortably but who were outstanding. Each, in a different way, had abandoned a paternalistic stance with Abigail. The terms of discourse initiated by Lovell would never be acceptable to Abigail Adams. They achieved an accommodation only because the disengaged process of letter writing provided a safe medium for him to accede to her terms.[79]

A pattern emerges from the letters, which reveals four stages in the development of this friendship. At first Lovell took an aggressive, dominant, male stance, using the language of flirtation in an effort to force Adams into a submissive female position. She resisted his scheme by using various nondefensive ploys of her own. The second stage occurred when Lovell's letter was intercepted and his posturing with Abigail was undercut by circumstances. He became vulnerable, and she had the advantage. Not shy of exploiting her advantage, in a third stage, Abigail confronted James Lovell and he argued back, defending his service and his honor. Neither responded to the other's accusations from a consciousness of sex. Finally, friendship had developed. The poses of male-female discourse were dropped as Lovell and Adams addressed each other with understanding and sincere regard.

That the status of women in the late eighteenth century was subordinate to men is no revelation. The issue is, given that condition, could women and men be friends? And the answer is affirmative. In this case, James Lovell was capable of friendship, but for some reason—perhaps he was shy—he was not comfortable enough to establish friendship with Abigail at the onset of the correspondence. What the Lovell correspondence reveals in most crass terms is the ultimate resort to which men may turn to ensure a dominant power relationship with women—sexual aggression, in this case with language. Lovell attempted to delineate a dominant stance by using an aggressive sexual posture in the form of flirtation. Abigail resisted the flirtation but persisted in her efforts to gain his assistance.

Friendships did exist between—admittedly extraordinary—men and women, despite the inequality of status, demonstrated amply in surviving correspondence. Mercy Otis Warren corresponded voluminously with leading political figures of her era. The most notable exchange, over nearly a half-century, with John Adams, explored politics, philosophy, and literature. Adams addressed her as "Madam" and she wrote to "Sir." Each signed off with "esteem" and "respect" for over forty years. The allusions to friendship between them are ubiquitous, even though Mercy occasionally deferred to his maleness by commenting on the aberrant nature of a woman writing about politics.[80]

Abigail Adams and Thomas Jefferson corresponded about politics, theater, literature, family life, and gossip from the time she left Paris for
London in 1785 until the breach between her husband and Jefferson, upon
the latter's ascendancy to the presidency. In his first letter to her in 1785,
Jefferson addressed Adams as "Dear Madam," and in contrast to Lovell, he
continued in polite deference: "I have received duly the honor of your
letter, and am now to return you thanks for your condescension in having
taken the first step for settling a correspondence which I so much desired. . . ."[81] Abigail's letter of consolation, upon learning of the death of
Polly Jefferson in 1804, reopened a correspondence that had been severed
by political differences. She ended with the reminder that she was one
"who once took pleasure in subscribing Herself your Friend." Jefferson
responded warmly, writing that "The friendship with which you honored
me has ever been valued and fully reciprocated."[82]

In both cases, the Adams-Warren correspondence and the Jefferson-
Adams correspondence, the letters reflect a continuation of the personal
relationship, based upon compatible interests and an open exchange of
ideas. Unlike the Lovell-Adams correspondence, neither reveals a struggle
over dominance and subordination. Ultimately, Abigail did achieve parity
in the dialogue with James Lovell, the only terms she would tolerate in a
relationship.

But something more can be said of Adams's feelings for Lovell, a final
statement of a woman's consideration of a man. Ultimately she admired
him for the sake of her husband—he served. He served his nation long and
at great sacrifice where others—the sunshine patriots—desisted. He was
". . . the particular Friend and correspondent of him who is dearest to me
and for whose sake alone I should Esteem him . . ." she wrote.[83] Lovell
justified Abigail's own sacrifice of John Adams to public service for so many
years.

The Abigail Adams–James Lovell correspondence represents a small
chapter in the politics of gender in revolutionary America. If equality of
status was difficult to achieve in a correspondence, this imbalance reflected
the ethos, the social behavior of the eighteenth century. Lovell, whose
social discomfort with men revealed itself in abrasiveness, clearly did not
know how to communicate comfortably with Abigail because she was a
woman. He used his familiar devices of sarcasm and wit, in this case,
because she was a woman, masked as flirtation. In the case of Abigail, too,
he had misjudged her character. Abigail would never concede in this kind
of gender power struggle. She worked around his impudence to get from
him what she needed without conceding to his terms.

Abigail Adams maintained the same consistency of integrity and dignity
in this exchange with James Lovell that infused all her relationships and
functions. She took genuine pride in her female role, but with the full
understanding that in her world, women were not the equal of men. "That

your Sex are Naturally Tyrannical is a Truth so thoroughly established as to admit no dispute, but such of you as wish to be happy[,] willingly give up the harsh title of Master for the more tender and endearing one of Friend," she wrote to John Adams as a continuance of her now famous "Remember the Ladies" statement. "Men of Sense in all Ages abhor those customs which treat us only as the vassals of your Sex," she continued to her conclusive statement for the politics of gender. "Regard us then as Beings placed by providence under your protection and in immitation of the Supreem Being make use of that power only for our happiness."[84] Abigail Adams did not consider women to be equal with men, and only occasionally did she chafe at the injustice of her submissive condition. She regarded the earthly hierarchy to be reflective of a divine plan where the "Supreem Being" would use power for the "happiness" of earthly beings.[85] The other side of the equation convinced her that she deserved to be "happy"; to her this meant respect for her dignity as a woman and for the role of woman. She did not consider it a paradox that to be submissive, to be dependent upon men in a world that was harsh even to men, was unfair. She was a woman of her time.

Lovell, with his impertinence and flirtatiousness, had violated the earthly plan which accorded women just treatment by men. Adams resisted his kind of male tyranny with the same force that she encouraged the resistance of men to political tyranny. Lovell, whose behavior had always belied his rhetoric, felt secure in dropping his social facade. In the end the Abigail Adams–James Lovell correspondence represented a virtuous affair. As Abigail saw it, virtue for the man represented patriotism enacted in public service—at the conference table and on the battlefield. Virtue for the woman resonated in a different voice and was enacted in the domestic sphere, preserving the values and principles for which men fought.

5

Gossip

"Father never inculcated any Maxim of Behavior upon his Children, so often as this," recalled Abigail Adams: "Never to speak ill of any Body . . . to make Things rather than Persons the Subjects of Conversation.—These rules, he always impressed upon Us, whenever We were going abroad, if it was but for an Afternoon."[1] What Abigail recalled as her father's most impressive admonition to his children was: "Don't gossip."

That the Reverend Smith made this maxim so central to his children's training—that his daughter remembered his admonitions so vividly—underscores what contemporary social scientists presume about our own time: everyone gossips. Furthermore, evidence from many different sources implies that in every age people have gossiped, and for as long as literature has referenced gossip, its reputation has remained negative. This story will, hopefully, rescue gossip from its maligners by demonstrating ways in which it has operated as a positive force in social relations.

Gossip is defined simply as the telling of tales about a person or persons who are not present.[2] This telling of tales serves manifold functions; it is a universal form of entertainment, a story with a plot and a moral that engages the mind and satisfies the emotions. Moreover, gossip develops a mode of intimacy that reflects not only the social but the psychological bonding of the teller and the listener. And by using the power of this bond, a successful gossip may manipulate opinions to enhance her or his status— or to destroy the status of others.

This potentially malicious use of gossip as a weapon to serve the individual ego has contributed strongly to its negative reputation in philosophy, literature, and religion. The Reverend Smith was merely repeating the dictum voiced in so many different sources—the writings of the Bible, the works of Aristotle, Aquinas, Maimonides, and Shakespeare—that to talk about other people is wicked and that there is a negative moral content to the process.[3] Some ambiguous rules are proposed in the philosophic literature about what constitutes bad gossip: the telling of lies, the disclosure of secrets that one is pledged not to tell, the exercise of conscious malice. Underlying all this discourse is the elementary understanding that language has power, and that the power inherent in the language of gossip derives from its content—those issues that most fascinate human beings— the behavior of other human beings.[4]

However, recent scholarship points to the understanding that the content of gossip is not the subject of gossip and that the telling of tales has an agenda more significant than the mere transmission of information.[5] True gossip circulates news within a small group about other members of the group; it provides, therefore, a means of defining a group; only people who are "in" can tell stories about the behavior of a person who is known to them both. While they analyze the conventions that behavior violates or upholds, they broadcast their group's rules for social behavior. In this regard, gossip can operate as a positive force in social relations, providing a group with a sense of intimacy in the short run, and in the larger sense, with a social orientation. As gossip stores and conveys the unwritten conventions of a circle of people, it is far from idle talk. It is an expression of the rules and values governing behavior in a particular time and place.[6]

This chapter will describe an incident from the late eighteenth century— a romance, a drama, a story of the courtship between Abigail Adams Junior and Royall Tyler as told in letters, memoirs, and histories. By noting some of the uses of gossip in the Adams-Tyler romance, I will suggest that gossip had an informal, though compelling, influence on their courtship, indeed that this influence may be an example of a more universal social process.[7] The conventional wisdom of family history in the last twenty years has emphasized the increased relevance of affection in marriage by the late eighteenth century, when young people could be instrumental in selecting a mate based on mutual attraction. The Adams-Tyler case demonstrates that this is not entirely true; while cruder forms of parental and family influence did not operate, a more subtle mechanism intruded upon free choice. Gossip provided the effective conduit to carry messages about mate suitability within the social group. The gossip that took place among the Adamses' extended family and their friends not only shaped the course of the courtship but also accomplished a great deal of other family business in the process.[8]

On December 23, 1782, Abigail Adams wrote to her husband, then in Paris: "We have in the little circle another gentleman who has opened an office in town—for about nine months past, and boarded in our Cranch family—his father you knew—his name is Tyler. He studied law upon his coming out of college with our Dana." Abigail continued to describe background and character—not just to relate idle information to her absent husband but to advance a delicate agenda. "I am not acquainted with any young gentleman whose attainments in literature are equal to his," she persisted, "who judges with greater accuracy or Discovers a more Delicate and softened taste." Moving from fact to analysis, the first two phases of good gossip, she then proceeded to phase three, judgment: "I have frequently looked upon him with the Idea that you would have taken much pleasure in such a pupil." Finally, Abigail rose to her purpose: "I wish I was as well assured that you would be equally pleased with him in another character for such I apprehend are his hopes."[9] Royall Tyler was courting the Adamses' eldest child and only daughter, Abigail Junior.

Abigail's concerns were not unfounded, for she knew her husband well. Neither had she underestimated the reverberations from Paris: "I don't like the subject at all. My child is too young for such thoughts. . . . I should have thought you had seen enough to be more upon your Guard." John continued his salvo for five paragraphs, before concluding: "This is too serious a subject to equivocate about. I don't like this method of Courting Mothers. There is something too fantastical and affected in all this Business for me." Having finished with Abigail, he added in the tradition of good gossip, "This is all between you and me."[10]

What inspired this outburst was not just John's shock in discovering that his only daughter had a suitor. Royall Tyler's reputation was suspect, and Abigail's letter had reported, in the most diplomatic of terms, the stories that she had heard. It was rumored that Tyler had led a dissolute life while an undergraduate at Harvard. Having inherited a "pretty patrimony," he had "dissipated two or 3 years of his Life and too much of his fortune," owing, Abigail generously allowed, to his "possessing a sprightly fancy, a warm imagination and an agreable person."[11]

This exchange between Abigail and John provides clues to a tale of romance that lasted over two years; despite an abundant trail of evidence, much of it repeated in the form of innuendo or rumor, some aspects of the story remain obscured.

Royall Tyler, as Abigail wrote to John, had arrived in Braintree early in 1782 and opened a law practice. He boarded with Mary and Richard Cranch, sister and brother-in-law of Abigail Adams, and parents of two teenage daughters, Lucy and Betsy. Rather than pursuing a Cranch daughter, Tyler turned his attentions to their sixteen-year-old cousin, Nabby Adams.[12] If his visits to the Adams home were initiated with intent to borrow books from John's library, they were continued because Abigail the mother and young Abigail together found his company delightful. He was literate and literary, a wellborn lawyer with charm and good looks. Further, he seemed smitten with young Abigail, who by all reports was a quiet, reserved, serious, and cerebral young woman.

It is not clear what precise rumors were circulated or how much Abigail knew about Tyler's past. His allies suggest that he was mischievous; more seriously, it was reported that he fathered a child by a housemaid at Harvard. He was rusticated (exiled) for a prank that inadvertently offended a professor. By his own admission, he recklessly spent much of his inheritance; by Abigail's admission, he neglected his studies. Nor was he, it seems, repentant. Tyler was an incorrigible iconoclast, a character of man— his values aside—that appealed to Abigail Adams.[13]

Both young Abigail and Abigail the mother were chastened by John's response, which continued in a barrage of letters from France. In time, John became calmer, more rational, and eventually even resigned to the inevitability of romance. Yet the slow course of his letters across the Atlantic could not keep pace with events at home. While John was conceding to the situation, his daughter was taking his initial admonitions seriously and breaking off her relationship with Tyler. Abigail reported to her husband that their daughter, responding to his disapproval, had gone to stay in Boston for the winter of 1783. Tyler, who remained in Braintree, kept his nose to the grindstone, built his law practice, and generated no unseemly talk. When young Abigail returned from Boston in the spring, however, the romance resumed. Tyler, meanwhile, had excited speculations by purchasing and beginning to renovate the Borland property, a grand, albeit neglected, homestead in Braintree.[14]

All of this activity took place within two larger contexts: the influence of Nabby's extended family and the pressures of her parents' situation. When John was still fulminating in Paris, he had written Abigail, "Your . . . letters concerning Mr. T. are never out of my mind. . . . I don't like the Trait in his Character, his Gaiety. He is but a Prodigal Son, and though a Penetent, has no Right to your Daughter, who deserves a Character without a Spot." Unable to render a decisive opinion from abroad, John counseled Abigail to seek "the advice of our Parents and Brothers and sisters and Uncles and Aunts etc. You must endeavor to know the Opinion of the Family."[15]

The advice was superfluous, for Abigail had already consulted her relations. Her closest confidant in this affair, as in everything, was her sister Mary, who was not only a natural ally but also Tyler's landlady. Abigail also consulted her mother-in-law, who lived next door, her younger sister Elizabeth Shaw in Haverhill, her father in Weymouth, and her maternal uncle Cotton Tufts, whose advice she sought in many of her business affairs. The family consciously took responsibility for the development of the Adams-Tyler union not only to protect their young relative but also to inspect a potential kinsman. In their correspondence, even that which excludes Abigail, and presumably in their conversations as well, they discussed the young couple. Elizabeth noted to Mary that "the dear girl" had surprisingly been more accessible through her heart, "vastly more allarming than if it had been the head."[16] In the goldfish bowl of the Adams extended family, Royall Tyler knew that his behavior was being closely monitored.[17]

An ongoing debate between Abigail and John also shaped the course of the Adams-Tyler romance. With the end of the Revolutionary War and the completion of the peace treaty, Abigail begged John to return home to family life. Yet he wanted a congressional appointment to the ministry at St. James's. As John waited for the decision, he once again felt conflicted between his political ambitions and his family responsibilities, alternately threatening to return if Congress did not choose quickly and pressing Abigail to join him in Europe, a prospect she dreaded.

The family, as a constituency that looked out for the well-being of its members, provided the context that monitored the romance. The Abigail-John negotiation provided the momentum. Young Abigail and Tyler confirmed their commitment to each other, contingent upon the family's—especially John's—approval.

Abigail the mother felt doubly conflicted. She liked Tyler very much for all the qualities that she had described to John, but she feared the reality of the rumors. Furthermore, while she was struggling with her own future, she did not trust her judgment well enough to encourage the romance. She even began to use the issue of her daughter's courtship to leverage her position with John. "I wish most sincerely you was at Home to judge for yourself. I shall never feel safe or happy untill you are. I had rather you should enquire into his conduct and behavior, his success in Business and his attention to it. . . . I believe it is in your power to put a final period to every Idea of the kind, if upon your return you think best."[18]

In the end, John triumphed. By the winter of 1783–84, Abigail had decided that the two problems—her separation from John and her daughter's romance—could best be resolved by taking Nabby with her to Europe. Once this decision was made, events moved quickly. John, sensitive to his daughter's conflict between her suitor and her family, wrote to Abigail that she might allow her daughter to marry and leave the couple behind, if they chose. The young couple, probably reflecting the decision of a dutiful daughter, agreed to part, although they pledged faith to each other. Tyler, meanwhile, possibly to console himself for the separation, wrote to John for permission to marry his daughter. In June 1784, mother and daughter departed on the ship *Active* for the long journey to Europe, leaving behind a bereft suitor. More sadly for Tyler, John Adams's letter of assent to the marriage arrived after the sailing.[19]

The record of the romance is silent for over a year, and events come to light in the retrospective accounts of the various parties involved. Following the reunion of Abigail and her daughter with John and John Quincy, the Adamses lived for ten months in Auteuil, on the outskirts of Paris, then moved to London upon John's confirmation as Minister. Only then does Tyler reappear in the story. Mary Cranch wrote to Abigail, obviously in response to a query about Tyler: "I know very little about him for he is seldom in Braintree and when he is very little at home."[20] In a letter to John Quincy, who had returned to attend Harvard, Abigail quipped that she hoped he would be a more faithful correspondent to his sister than "her L___r." She concluded, "But this is between ourselves."[21] Elizabeth Shaw reported that on her recent trip, "I never saw Mr. T. in the whole course of my Journey—which was to me a matter of speculation—for I suppose *we* were upon good terms."[22]

In fact, Tyler had disappeared after the Abigails' departure; for more than a year, he did not write to any of them, including his fiancée. They did write to him, long letters from Abigail the mother and a steady stream from the benighted fiancée.[23] What transpired with Tyler is a matter of speculation—and gossip. He moved to Boston, where he resided in a boarding-house kept by General Joseph Palmer and his wife, Mary. "He has attended the courts in Boston the last winter and this summer and does not come home till the sessions are over," reported Mary Cranch.[24] His move to Boston is confirmed in the memoir of a young Palmer daughter—the woman whom, interestingly enough, he later married.[25] From the Adamses' point of view, Tyler's actions were most peculiar, a suggestion that he had reverted to his former behavior.

Then abruptly, young Abigail terminated the engagement in the early fall of 1785. Word had reached her from Boston that Tyler was withholding a letter that Nabby had written to a friend and entrusted to him to deliver. More provoking, for some months he had been boastfully showing about personal letters that Nabby had written to him. With this disclosure, young Abigail acted. She spoke with her parents, confessed her distress with Tyler, and expressed her doubts about his "strictest honor." John, characteristically, declared that he would rather see both himself and his daughter in their graves than united with Tyler. Following this conversation, Nabby returned Tyler's miniature and other mementoes and requested that he return her gifts and letters to Uncle Tufts. The family was informed.[26]

With the ensuing outpouring of relief from relatives and friends, more elements of the picture begin to fall into place. "My dear neice has acted with a spirit worthy of her parents," wrote Mary Cranch. "We have been for a long time very anxious for her—Happiness."[27] "Such *neglect* to such *affection* and to *such a person* was what I could not silently nor patiently see," wrote Elizabeth Shaw.[28] John Quincy wrote that "the dissolution of a certain connection . . . afforded me as well as most all our Friends, real consolation. My anxiety was not small before I left but it was greatly augmented after my return home."[29] Uncle Tufts wrote that he would execute his assignment, however painful, to the best of his ability.[30]

Once the family was informed of the broken engagement—a process that took months of exchanging letters carried by ship captains or friends traveling abroad—a fuller picture of Tyler's behavior was revealed. Friends and family disclosed that in the months after the Adamses' departure, Tyler had "showed about" John's letter of assent to his suit, as well as the many letters he had received from Nabby. Pressed by friends to explain this behavior, he responded that he was so proud of them that he wished to show them publicly. He had boasted that he had "never wrote her" but that Nabby had repeatedly written to him. Furthermore, he had withheld letters sent to him that were meant for others, had indeed opened and possibly copied them. In all, the picture that emerged from Tyler's behavior confirmed the family's initial suspicions that he was a disreputable man.[31]

Yet Tyler had charmed many people. Richard Cranch, John's friend long before he was his brother-in-law, had written a letter of commendation. John Quincy wrote: "I have no personal pique against him . . . he behaved to me in the most friendly manner and as a transient acquaintance, I should have considered him as a very agreeable person." The Palmer family, with whom he lived in Boston, became very fond of him and considered him a generous friend. Even Elizabeth Shaw, who had been suspicious of Tyler initially, treated him as a family member during her niece's absence.[32]

At this point, while family and friends were expressing relief to the Adamses, Tyler shifted tactics. He first denied that the engagement was ended, then announced that he would travel to London to set the affair straight, and finally began a campaign of letter writing. He wrote to Abigail. He wrote to John. And he wrote to his erstwhile fiancée—all to no avail.[33] The Adamses, reinforced by the news they were hearing, stood firm in opposition to Tyler. Eventually Tyler sank into a depression that conceded his defeat. At the same time, he constructed his own theory to explain his rejection; the family, all the relatives, he claimed, had mounted a conspiracy against him. They had written lies about him to the Adamses, and behind the campaign was Mary Cranch, who was punishing him for having overlooked her daughters in favor of her niece.[34]

Although the repercussions of this romantic episode continued to affect the Adams family in various ways for many months, the story for our purposes is concluded. In all its aspects, it is replete with the affect and effect of gossip. Gossip shaped Tyler's reputation before his arrival in Braintree, and it followed him there. Once he settled among the Adamses, his behavior was scrutinized and reported upon. Abigail the mother repated rumors as a component of her Tyler profile to John, who in turn embellished the stories with his own reflections. And, in the end, the tales told about Tyler became sufficiently potent to prevent his marriage with Nabby Adams. Most telling, young Abigail took the step of breaking off her engagement after being informed that Tyler had made her the object of gossip. Predicated upon his former reputation, the Adamses matched behavior to gossip and reacted to Tyler.

From its inception, the courtship between Nabby Adams and Royall Tyler was talked about. Romance stirs the imagination in pleasant ways; it invokes memories, good and bad, and inspires wisdom. Elizabeth Shaw wrote sentimental letters to her niece, reminiscing about her own youthful courtships, abstracting wisdom from literature and religious tracts.[35] Gossip distracted family members from the ordinary tasks of daily life, but the stories that circulated, although a diversion, were meant to be serious. On one level they concerned love and courtship; on another, they served to monitor group behavior in the Adams social circle. Gossip has social functions and operates by rules that are rigidly controlled.[36]

As the content of gossip is not its subject, talk about Nabby's romance, and indeed about many other episodes over the years, gave the Adams kin a means to define themselves as a family. When they talked among themselves, in this case when they wrote to each other, they shared private information that encouraged intimacy. By discussing an important private issue, they established a sense of cohesion. The talk about Tyler—an outsider whose reputed behavior deviated from their advertised standards—reminded them that they had common interests and values, that they shared a history and a tradition, that they occupied a special position in the social order. Their telling and retelling of stories, their analyses and judgments, provided an occasion to close ranks as a family, to reassure themselves that they were kin and exclusive. In the process, they announced to Tyler the standards for admission that mirrored their own social position.[37]

The subject of gossip is not the object of gossip in many different, but coincident, ways. Whereas gossip bonded the family together, it also managed admission to that closed group. Gossip advertised the guidelines for membership in the family; it tested applicants, such as Royall Tyler, and punished deviancy from Adams standards. In effect, the group—which included Abigail Junior's parents, brother, aunts, uncles, grandparents, and close friends—used gossip to establish their ties: a common tradition of education, manners, religion, and living styles, as well as economic ties and similar political commitment. In this case, while the subject of Adams gossip was Royall Tyler's behavior, the object was the power of a social group to determine its own composition and to protect its members.[38]

At the outset, Abigail had attempted to establish Tyler in the Adams tradition by explaining his pedigree to John: Tyler had attended Harvard; John had known his father; he had studied with "our Dana," that is, John's friend and colleague at the bar, Francis Dana. This evidence of appropriate social background argued in Tyler's favor, as did his profession. "A lawyer would be my choice," John wrote. Yet Tyler's reputation for deviancy argued a more powerful case against him.[39]

The content of the gossip, the stories that circulated about Tyler's past sins, brought into relief the mores and values of the extended Adams family, traditional Puritan values of hard work, study, thrift, and social consciousness, the cardinal components of virtuous and esteemed character. That Tyler had once dissipated a fortune, had wasted time when he should have studied, and, worst of all, had reputedly fathered an illegitimate son, stirred fear that this man did not fit the established Adams model for a husband to one of their own. Tyler would be forever suspect, for gossip served not only as the articulation of family rules but also as the informal judicial forum and the means of punishment.[40] "That Frivolity of Mind, which breaks out into such Errors in Youth, never gets out of the Man but shews itself in some mean Shape or other through Life," wrote John Adams.[41] Tyler was condemned for life. Although young Abigail was attracted to Tyler and was in all formal senses free to marry after her heart's wishes, she was constrained by her understanding that the family did not wholly approve. Their disapproval was expressed by the circulation of stories that explored the reputation of Tyler, analyzed his behavior, and judged his character; they measured him against their own model.

Their model described an ideal of virtuous manhood, enshrined in myth. Gossip is a carrier of myths.[42] John Adams served as the pivotal figure in this myth, a great patriot, loyal public servant, devoted husband and father. Invented by John, sustained by Abigail, and reinforced within the family at large, this image of the virtuous citizen provided focus to the Adamses' marriage and for male admission to the family.[43]

Conflicting applications of this myth, furthermore, caused much of the tension in the Tyler episode. Abigail the mother attributed to Tyler positive qualities that favored his case, traits that had first attracted her to John. "I feel a regard for him upon an account you will smile at," she wrote to John at the outset. "I fancy I see in him Sentiments opinions and actions which indeared to me the best of all Friends."[44] Her ambivalence during the courtship was caused at first by the gossip and by her husband's powerful opposition, based on the stories about Tyler. In the end, she reluctantly withdrew support because Tyler's behavior seemed to reinforce the stories.

There was no nostalgia on John's part. His reflections were based on the differences between the model of his reputation and Tyler's. He wrote to his daughter: "If I mistake not your Character it is not Gaity and Superficial Accomplishment alone that will make you happy. It must be a Thinking Being, and one who thinks for others good and feels an others woe. . . . One may dance or sing, play or ride without being good for much."[45] Four months later, he expanded his stricture:

Daughter! Get you an honest Man for a Husband, and keep him honest.—No matter whether he is rich, provided he be independent.—Regard the Honour and moral Character of the Man more than all other Circumstances. Think of no other Greatness but that of the Soul, no other Riches but that of the Heart.— An honest, Sensible humane Man, above all the Littleness of Vanity, and Extravagance of Imagination, labouring to do good rather than to make a

Show, living in a modest Simplicity clearly within his Means and free from Debts or Obligations, is really the most respectable Man in Sooth, makes himself and all about him the most happy.[46]

By inference, John was commenting on Tyler; he set standards and implied that the imagined ideal, this mythological projection of himself, was the basis for judging any suitor. John did not indulge in vanity but rather justification. If anything, he needed the myth to guide his own behavior and to rationalize a life devoted to public service rather than to family. Meanwhile, Abigail's fondness for Tyler persisted. "I wish all happines to the Gentleman," she wrote. "He has virtues and amiable qualities and may be much happier connected with many other families than he could ever have been in ours because he has certain habits which would never have acorded with Mr. Adams's sentiments and principles."[47]

Psychologists describe gossip as a manifestation of aggression, an angry attempt at reprisal from a person who feels victimized—a description which easily fit Royall Tyler's behavior after his fiancée's departure.[48] Undoubtedly Tyler was deeply touched by the attacks on his character that had thwarted his pursuit of Nabby Adams and threatened his reputation; yet he was not defenseless. The weapons used against him could be deployed in self-defense. However, if in the short run Tyler succeeded in gaining self-esteem by maligning the Adamses, in the end he lost his claim for entrée to the group. One reason is that gossip about group members is a privilege reserved to the group.[49]

From all accounts, Tyler was distraught after Nabby left. He mourned that all was lost, that he would never see her again. Elizabeth Shaw recorded that he retired to his room in tears. Mary Cranch testified that he became depressed.[50] After this, he disappeared into Boston and very soon took up the behavior that ultimately lost him his case: gossiping about the Adamses, and particularly about Nabby. He first showed off the letter he had received from John Adams, a missive John had considered private. He boasted that he had not responded to the many letters he had received from Nabby, in effect saying to the world that she was more interested in him that he was in her. He kept letters that were not his; he opened them and possibly copied the contents, thus violating the private correspondence of his fiancée. In all of this, he made public that which was meant to be private; in manifold ways he made the Adamses, especially his fiancée, a topic of gossip. Tyler's motive, psychologists would tell us, was founded in his anger, his hostility, and his wish to get even—in this case, by attacking with words. More precisely, by gossiping, Tyler gained a false sense of power.[51]

Furthermore, by publicly degrading other people—in this case, his fiancée or her father—Tyler could gain self-respect. If he could convince people that Nabby was pursuing him, that John wanted him for a son-in-law, then the tales of his dissolute past would be, if not dismissed, at least diminished in light of his current stature among the Adamses. By telling tales, he hoped to gain a constituency among the younger set in Boston. By boasting of his triumphs, by telling stories about himself and the Adamses, he believed he was convincing other people of his success and using the family's reputation to enhance his own. But he did not anticipate the reaction.

For years he had been alienated and defensive, but his hope had been the presence of potential allies in his fiancée and her mother. With their departure, he lost hope; he sought revenge in gossip. Yet the device that the Adamses had used so successfully backfired on him. Mary Cranch observed about this what current theories reinforce, that left to his own devices, Tyler would destroy himself by his own mischief. Tyler failed to regroup because people did not believe him, because he told false stories, because he violated a trust, because his motives did not reflect the values of the constituency he hoped to win. His tales were judged to be tasteless and unfair; as the bearer of bad gossip, he frustrated his own objectives.[52]

From a different perspective, Tyler's behavior illustrates the observation that gossip may signal failure; as a weapon of the excluded, the lower classes, the disenfranchised, it is a mark of weakness.[53] If Tyler believed that the departure of the Abigails signaled the hopelessness of his case, he had nothing to lose. He was desperate and despairing, and he lashed out in an attempt to regain in public stature what he had lost in the private sphere. By denigrating others, he sensed his own public elevation.

Tyler was not the only person to respond to the sting of gossip. Young Abigail, who had puzzled for over a year about her lover, acted only when she learned that she had become an object of gossip. She tolerated neglect, but not attacks on her reputation. Of all the hurt generated by Tyler's past and by his disregard of her after her departure, none was so great as the betrayal of her privacy, when he made her the object of talk.

There are numerous epilogues, postscripts, and morals to this tale, all of which contribute to understanding the effects of gossip. The first observation we can make has to do with the process itself: that the central figure of this episode is a man. Traditionally, gossip is associated with women. One scholar notes, "No one ever says that women gossip *too*."[54] The etiology of the word associates gossip with women; the term derives from female activity, and over time it came to have a negative inference. Dictionary definitions most often associate gossip with women. Literary references make gossip a female activity. The social imagery of the *noun* gossip is female.[55]

In many respects, the Tyler case violates this traditional interpretation. It makes a man the object of gossip in all three meanings of the word, as the bearer, the subject, and the hearer. While a man is central, clearly both men and women gossip in this tale, which is far closer to the reality that we know to be the truth of the issue of "Who gossips?" What we may conclude from the ubiquitous association of gossip with women, therefore, has to do with their status over time. As long as gossip's reputation is negative and as long as gossip is related primarily to women, the equation serves as one more index of the downgraded status of women.

A second observation is that gossip provides a bridge between the public and private spheres, and this happens in several dimensions. Gossip circulates and makes public information that is private. For that reason it is feared; but at the same time it may serve important social functions. Gossip is not merely "idle talk," since the content of gossip is not its only subject. What appears as an idle exchange in fact describes the conventions of a group's social boundaries and its rules; when people gossip, they tell us about their cultural mores and values, as well as more subtly about their social strengths and weaknesses, their *mentalité*, and even their individual psyches. What has been explored in this case for courtship, furthermore, may be demonstrated for many social situations—whether religious, political, or economic—wherever private affairs may affect public attitudes and behavior.[56] Gossip may provide an index for measuring social power. And because gossip bridges the gap between the public and private spheres, it becomes useful to historians as one more source that illuminates the past.

This is not to deny that gossip, whether practiced by men or women, may be damaging. Because reputations, like Royall Tyler's, may be gained and lost by the stories told, and because a successful gossip may manipulate opinions to enhance his status or to destroy the status of others, as Tyler attempted, gossip is perceived as dangerous and is often proscribed, as it was by Abigail's father, the Reverend Smith.

In the case of the Adams-Tyler courtship, however, gossip served a social function that was important and maybe helpful. Although Abigail Adams Junior appeared to be free to choose a mate according to her reason and her affections, in actuality, this was far from true; the opinions, attitudes, and circumstances of her family were a powerful influence. The purveyor of the family message in this case—and in perhaps the majority of similar cases—was gossip.

The continuation of young Abigail's story may more effectively illustrate the point. One year after she ended her connection with Tyler, Abigail Adams Junior was married to William Stephens Smith in London. In 1785 Congress had appointed Smith to serve as John's secretary at the legation in London; unlike Tyler, he came very well recommended. He had been an adjutant to George Washington during the last years of the Revolutionary War; he was from a good family, a graduate of Princeton, a man of appealing carriage and personality. In just a few months young Abigail was swept away in a romance that her mother was helpless to slow down and her father too distracted to protest. Abigail the mother described Smith's greatest qualities in a vocabulary uncharacteristic of her usual evaluations of people. She noted his valor, his good looks, his appearance of integrity and courage—comments more suited to a military recommendation than to her usual review of intelligence, wisdom, learning, industry, and frugality. The marriage, nevertheless, was hastily accomplished, pressed on by the impatience of Smith and his agreeable bride.[57]

The history of this union presents an irony. Smith, who was perhaps well-meaning and sincere, failed at every endeavor he undertook as a civilian. He speculated extravagantly and lost fortunes. When rescued by the Adamses with appointments to public posts, he discredited himself. He used family connections to promote his various business enterprises. As a husband, he was undependable. As a father, he was not a model of integrity. In short, the Adamses got for a son-in-law the very figure they had most feared in Tyler.

There are many possible explanations for this ironic choice of mates. Young Abigail was obviously attracted to Smith on the rebound, and her parents were so sensitive to her previous hurt that they failed to interfere. Smith's military reputation was stellar, and furthermore, he came with appealing credentials.

Another factor may account for the mistaken appraisal of his character. Living in London, far from the protection of their accustomed family and social milieu, the Adamses lacked their traditional mechanisms of surveillance. Young Abigail operated in a social vacuum and was subjected to the pressures of an impatient suitor; her intended was not observed, analyzed, and appraised by the people who had on a previous occasion protected her. In short, there was no family to gossip about William Stephens Smith. The sad result was that Abigail Junior's life with him was at best turbulent, and many were the concerns of her parents and friends, who rescued her family from destitution on several occasions over the years. To her credit, Nabby was always loyal to her husband and suffered her misfortunes with a stoicism that her family respected.

This resolution of young Abigail's story may therefore confirm the recent claims that "romantic" rather than "arranged" or "family monitored" matches became more important between 1780 and 1830. Some historians suggest that increased geographic mobility during this period was responsible for this shift from family monitored matches to romantic marriage. A smaller proportion of brides and grooms were subjected to family scrutiny and gossip, as was the case for Abigail Junior and the man she married, William Stephens Smith. In the end, it appears that the case argued here is consistent with an increase in the proportion of romantic marriages since geographic mobility diminished the importance of family scrutiny.

Tyler, on the other hand, thrived. He left Boston soon after the marriage of young Abigail and settled in New York. There, unpredictably for a lawyer, he wrote a play that was destined to earn him a place in American cultural history. *The Contrast*, performed in New York in 1787, was the first play staged in this country to be written by an American on an American topic. Tyler's reputation as a playwright has far overshadowed his reputation as a profligate.[58] In time he married Mary Palmer and moved to Vermont, where he became a judge, continued to write plays and stories, and fathered eight children.

Were the Adamses mistaken about Tyler? Perhaps his achievements in later life were in part a response to rejection by the Adamses; perhaps had he married young Abigail, the same trajectory of character that emerged when he misused their trust would have prevailed. We will never know. Gossip changed the course of Tyler's life, closing the ranks of the Adams family around its belief system of social values to protect one of its members.

On the eve of her daughter's marriage to Smith, Abigail Adams experienced a strange premonition, which she recorded for her sister. "Some evil Spright sent Mr. T. to visit me in a dream. I really have felt for him."[59] One of the few dreams Abigail Adams ever recorded, it is a surprise. While she submitted to circumstances no longer in her control, her most unconscious self—if we accept dreams as the manifestation of such—protested the content of the gossip that had wielded a far more powerful influence than her own intuition. Her final assessment of Tyler was written to a friend: "I wish the gentleman well. . . . He has good qualities, indeed he has but he ever was his own enemy."[60]

The story is told. The role of gossip as it functioned in the lives of a family group, a social set—as it controlled lives by directing alliances, monitoring, perhaps protecting its members, advertising rules, adjudicating behavior, relieving anger and frustration, building reputations and egos, providing social cohesion—is described. Perhaps, as well, it has provided a bit of entertainment, for such is the intrigue in gossip, talk about the lives of other human beings, even those who lived two hundred years ago.

6

Faithful Are the Wounds
of a Friend

On May 20, 1804, Abigail Adams wrote to Thomas Jefferson to express her grief over the death of his daughter Mary Jefferson Eppes. She described her struggle to write this letter: "Reasons of various kinds withheld my pen," she explained, until her emotions triumphed—"the powerful feelings of my heart, have burst through the restraint"—and compelled her to write to Jefferson.[1]

Abigail's struggle was caused by a four-year estrangement between the Adamses and Jefferson. Since Jefferson had taken the presidential oath and John Adams had departed from the capital in the dawn hours before the inauguration, communications had ceased, but for the previous thirty years Thomas Jefferson and John Adams had been friends. Abigail, who had known Jefferson for only twenty years, called him "one of the choice ones of the earth." These friendships, based upon respect and affection, had survived ideological and political differences; they did not survive Jefferson's ascendance to the presidency.[2]

Abigail had first met Thomas Jefferson in 1784 in Paris. She had recently arrived in Europe, where John and Benjamin Franklin served as American ministers. Jefferson soon joined the Americans in France. For almost a year—until John's appointment as the first American minister to Great Britain—the Adamses remained in France, and Abigail was unsettled. During the first forty years of her life, she had ventured scarcely twenty miles beyond her home in Braintree, and now in addition to the enormity of her voyage and her general displacement, she did not speak the language. The more urbane Jefferson experienced less cultural displacement, but he too suffered from isolation. Abigail and he immediately formed a warm friendship based not just upon alienation and empathy, but upon compatibility of interests and the love of intelligent conversation. Jefferson became a welcome visitor at the Adamses' residence, and together they explored the art, theater, and musical offerings of Paris.[3]

When the Adamses left Paris one year later, Jefferson rode with them to the city limits and soon wrote that "The departure of your family has left me in the dumps—my afternoon hangs heavily upon me." Abigail wrote to Jefferson within days of her arrival in London to say how much she had missed his company at a performance of Handel's *Messiah* at Westminster Abbey. It was during the years in London that Polly, as Mary Jefferson was called, visited Abigail while en route to live with her father in Paris. The timing was significant, for Abigail's daughter had just married and moved to her own residence, leaving Abigail with a sense of loss. Polly, "looking rough as a little sailor," and accompanied by a young servant girl (Sally Hemings), appealed to Abigail enormously, and she set about outfitting the child in a new wardrobe and taming the wild manners she had acquired on ship-board. The lonely mother and the lonely girl learned to love, but within weeks Jefferson sent for Polly and she was gone.[4]

Now almost twenty years later, Polly had died after childbirth, and Abigail broke through the constraints of the Adams-Jefferson political feud to commiserate with her former friend: "It has been some time since that I conceived of any event in this Life, which could call forth, feelings of mutual sympathy," she wrote, but "I know . . . how agonizing the pangs of seperation. I have tasted the bitter cup"; she referred to the death of her son Charles in 1800.

Abigail reminisced about caring for Polly Jefferson: "The attachment which I formed for her when you committed her to my care: upon her arrival in a foreign Land . . . but a child of nine years of age . . . has remained with me to this hour. . . . The tender scene of her seperation from me, rose to my recollection, when she clung around my neck and wet my Bosom with her tears, saying 'O now I have learnt to Love you, why will they tear me from you.' " The power of this memory had overcome the animosity that existed in 1804 and allowed Abigail to communicate with Jefferson.[5]

Following this letter of condolence, a correspondence developed between Abigail Adams and Thomas Jefferson that lasted less than a year, in which the former friends explored the nature of the breach between them. It was a frank exchange, an unusual one given letter-writing conventions of the time, for literary conventions had developed that translated manners to prose; too much candor or informality, especially between a woman and man, would have suggested insolence.[6]

The Adams-Jefferson correspondence initiated by Abigail's letter of condolence violated conventions of polite letter writing. Abigail admitted as much: "I rely upon the Friendship you still profess for me . . . to excuse the freedom of this discussion to which you have led with an unreserve, which has taken off the Shackles I should otherways have found myself embarrassed with."[7] The boldness of their confrontation, their candid accusations—tame as they appear nearly two centuries later—could occur only between eighteenth-century people who had been close friends.

When Jefferson replied to Abigail's condolence letter after a one-month delay, he raised the issue of reestablishing their friendship. Since it was unlike Jefferson to procrastinate in his correspondence with Abigail, the delay may have resulted from many causes—work, grief, the fact that he had forwarded her letter to his bereaved son-in-law. Possibly too, he was considering his strategy, wondering if the timing was appropriate to suggest that the Adamses and he could overcome their animosity. Abigail's response made clear that the breach would not be closed. She had noted at the outset, she pointed out, that her intention had been solely to commiserate; she neither expected nor wished to entertain a correspondence. More important, she confessed, she wrote without John's knowledge. "This letter is written in confidence—no eye but my own has seen what has passed." She was mindful of her husband's intransigence, and she wrote, "Faithfull are the wounds of a Friend."[8]

What were those wounds? In the course of the exchange between Abigail Adams and Thomas Jefferson, three issues surfaced that the former friends acknowledged as causes of the breakdown in their friendship. The three issues, in reality, masked a far more complex set of circumstances, but given their unwillingness or inability to stir up deeper motives, they confined their exchange to the safer, less private sphere of politics.

Two of the three political issues that Adams and Jefferson debated involved judicial reform. In 1801, Congress had passed a judiciary act that removed from members of the Supreme Court the responsibility to sit as judges in the seventeen federal circuit courts. The Judiciary Act of 1801 also reduced the size of the Supreme Court and at the same time remapped and increased the number of federal district courts. The president of the United States was empowered to appoint the district judges. John Adams invoked this power at the end of his term in office, making sixteen appointments to the federal judiciary in the last weeks, days, and even hours of his tenure, when three commissions were signed. The consequence for Jefferson was that he entered office saddled by a judiciary filled with men from the opposition party. It was this circumstance, he claimed, that inspired his anger toward John Adams. "One act of Mr. Adams' life, and one only, ever gave me a moment's personal displeasure," he wrote to Abigail. "I did consider his last appointments to office as personally unkind."[9]

A second grievance grew out of efforts to streamline and centralize the federal judiciary. By custom, since the Constitution had not been specific and Congress had not yet legislated a procedure, local federal commissioners were appointed by district judges. During Jefferson's first year in office, empowered by an act of Congress, he dismissed all state-level federal officers who remained from Adams's administration and replaced them with his own appointments. Unbeknownst to him, John Quincy Adams occupied a minor post in a bankruptcy court in Massachusetts and became a victim of Jefferson's judicial housecleaning. Abigail was doubly wounded by this act which deprived her son of needed income and also appeared to her as a deliberate gesture of disrespect, "and which I could not avoid considering as personal resentment."[10]

The third issue to provoke the Adams-Jefferson breach, acknowledged by Abigail to be the deepest wound, forms the centerpiece of this correspondence. Claiming that she would not have responded had Jefferson's reply "contained no other sentiments and opinions than those which my Letter of condolence could have excited," Abigail reasoned that "you have been pleased to enter upon some subjects which call for a reply." After noting that under other circumstances her candor would be a breach of etiquette, she asserted: "And now Sir I will freely disclose to you what has severed the bonds of former Friendship, and place you in a light very different from what I once viewed you in." The breach had occurred, she admitted, because as one of his first presidential acts Jefferson had freed James Callender, "who was suffering the just punishment of the Law due to his crimes for writing and publishing the basest libel, the lowest and vilest Slander, which malice could invent, or calumny exhibit against the Character and reputation of your predecessor. . . . This Sir I considered as a personal injury. This was the Sword that cut assunder the Gordian knot."[11]

The law to which Abigail referred was the Sedition Act, passed by Congress during the Adams administration. The Sedition Law (among other things) made it a crime to "write, print, utter or publish any false, scandalous, and malicious writing . . . against the government of the United States with the intent to defame." The bill passed by Congress was far milder than the original draft introduced in the Senate, which defined sedition as treason and carried a death penalty. Although John Adams neither initiated nor promoted the passage of this and the companion Alien Acts, he supported its sentiments and signed it into law. Party rivalries, a genuine fear of France's subversive activities after 1798, and fragile egos all contributed to the enactment of this law. Subsequent to its passage during Adams's administration, many of the more vituperative journalist critics of the administration, Callender among them, were fined and imprisoned. Jefferson was the leading Republican opponent of the law and soon after taking office began to dismantle it.[12]

These three issues—John Adams's appointment of the "midnight judges"; the dismissal of John Quincy Adams from his judicial post; and the liberation of James Callender—were the focus of the Adams-Jefferson feud as Abigail Adams and Thomas Jefferson accounted for it in 1804. In the course of many months, the two old friends debated their complaints: both accused and both defended their positions on fundamentally constitutional issues, and both invoked the articulation of constitutional theory as they understood it in 1804. However, in addition to illuminating different approaches to the constitution as well as differences in personal style, education and social position, the discourse between Abigail Adams and Thomas Jefferson expresses a more fundamental difference, that of gender.

By examining the language used by Abigail Adams and Thomas Jefferson, it is possible to observe two different approaches to moral reasoning. The work of psychologists Nancy Chodorow, Carol Gilligan, Jean Baker Miller, and others describes gender difference; they suggest that women are "relational"—that they have been socialized to reason from a stance that makes caring for other people a primary consideration. Men, on the other hand, because of their different social development, are more apt to reason and discourse from abstractions about individual rights.[13] An analysis of this exchange between Abigail Adams and Thomas Jefferson serves as a small forum to explore gender difference. Because the way that people use language is a reflection of their social orientation, this exchange may also provide greater insight into the status of women in republican America.[14]

Since the beginning of the recent women's movement, historians of colonial and republican America have written about qualities of difference in the lives of women and men, and a corpus of historical literature has emerged that chronicles a separate women's world in early America.[15] At the same time a subgenre has emerged that shows a growing tendency to look for ways in which women participated in politics or could be defined as political, much of this incorporated under the rubric of republicanism.

In addition to describing the activities of a few women or searching for the antecedents of nineteenth-century women's political activism, the thrust has been to demonstrate that eighteenth- and early nineteenth-century women had aspirations and were capable of operating in the public sphere; in short that women could be the same as men. The effect of this approach has been to anachronistically exaggerate the political content of their lives, making women of the past mirror men and valorizing their lives by giving them a masculine agenda.[16] Other problems with the approach result from vantage point and emphasis.[17]

While the historical literature primarily describes women's behavior, both public and private, little research has described a separate female *mentalité*.[18] In fact, the topic of different *mentalité* has been the bugbear of feminist scholarship for a decade; no issue has aggravated greater divisiveness among feminists, and with good cause.[19] The recognition of difference carries the risk of substantiating the claims of misogynists. The same language that advocates of difference employ has, under another guise, been used to demean and oppress women.[20] The solution to this paradox, however, is not to deny difference, but rather to reject the masculine definition of difference as hierarchy, to dissent from co-option into the patriarchal camp by denying the pejorative connotations that feminine difference has implied.[21]

In the late eighteenth and early nineteenth centuries, political issues and concerns were not central to women's lives in the same way that they were to the lives of men. Women were not driven to political action as were men. They functioned primarily in the domestic sphere; the ubiquitous activities of childbearing, child rearing, and household management provided their basic occupation, preoccupation, and, therefore, the basic metaphors of their world. Even among educated and privileged women who did consider politics, such as Abigail Adams, her sisters, and Mercy Otis Warren, the approach that they articulated differed from that of men.[22]

Contemporary social scientists provide a method to probe the difference in *mentalité* of eighteenth-century women like Abigail Adams. Although the primary body of research that informs this case comes from psychology, there is a sufficient corpus from anthropology to give this a universal dimension, not only across cultures, but in time. If the same qualities of thought and reasoning can be accounted for in several cultures, it would seem valid to project this validity to the foreign country that is the past.[23]

The work of Nancy Chodorow and Carol Gilligan has been paradigmatic for describing the formation of female personality and morality. Beginning with Freud's concession that he failed to understand women, Chodorow builds a theory to account for different female and male ego development.[24] Babies of both sexes relate most fundamentally to their mothers (or primary caretakers), according to Chodorow, until about the age of three years, when the process of differentiation occurs. At that point boy babies learn that they are not like their mothers, and that they must separate from their mothers and perceive themselves as different and "autonomous." Sons are experienced by their mothers as "a male opposite," and hence mothers encourage differentiation.[25] Little girls, however, since they are like their mothers, do not have to separate. "Because they are the same gender as their daughters, and have been girls, mothers of daughters tend not to experience these infant daughters as separate from them in the same way as do mothers of infant sons."[26]

Because daughters do not experience themselves as different from their mothers, their sense of themselves contains more "flexible or permeable ego boundaries." Sons, on the other hand, learn that they are "other" and will define themselves as "more separate and distinct with a greater sense of rigid ego boundaries and differentiation." The effect, then, is that "the basic feminine sense of self is connected to the world and the basic masculine sense of self is separate."[27] This means that as adults, women experience themselves more relationally, while men "suppress relational capacities" and sense themselves more autonomously. "This does not mean," Chodorow affirms, "that women have *weaker* ego boundaries than men."[28]

Gilligan's work builds on Chodorow's and extends it into the realm of moral development. Starting also from Freud's premise that "for women the level of what is ethically normal is different from what it is in men," and that women "show less sense of justice than men," and the extension of the Freudian premise into contemporary experimental psychology, Gilligan builds her theory of female difference by listening to the unheard female voice.[29]

Given a moral dilemma, to paraphrase Gilligan, women will see it in the context of its meaning to the people who are involved. While Chodorow constructs a theory about "connectedness" in female personality development, Gilligan constructs a theory of moral development based on relationships. Because women have a sense of connectedness to other people, according to Gilligan, they relate to the personal issues of a problem, which, then, appear to women as a conflict of responsibilities "and requires for its resolution a mode of thinking that is contextual and narrative rather than formal and abstract." For men, who experience themselves more autonomously, less in connection to others, "the highest stage of moral development is expressed by abstract considerations of human rights." Gilligan distinguishes between a morality of rights and a morality of responsibilities with "its emphasis on separation rather than connection, in its consideration of the individual rather than the relationship as primary."[30]

A morality of caring and responsibility informs the different voice of women, based upon an underlying psychological logic of relationships; this contrasts with the formal logic of fairness that rises above relationships and informs the justice approach. Gilligan points out the central paradox of female connectedness, that while for women morality is conceived in terms of helping other people, "the very traits that traditionally have defined the 'goodness' of women, their care for and sensitivity to the needs of others, are those that mark them as deficient in moral development."[31]

If the logic of the relation between contemporary feminist psychology with Adams and Jefferson appears strained, Abigail's first words to him on May 20, 1804, provide the connection: "Sir," she began, "Had you been no other than the private inhabitant of Monticello, I should e'er this time have addrest you with that sympathy, which a recent event has awakend in my Bosom. But reasons of various kinds withheld my pen, untill the powerfull feelings of my heart, have burst through the restraint, and called upon me to shed the tear of sorrow over the departed remains of your beloved and deserving daughter, an event which I most sincerely mourn."[32] From the beginning of the correspondence, that touchstone of their breach—the tension between public life and private life—was noted. Had Jefferson been an ordinary person, not president of the United States, she wrote, implying that the political office stood between them as friends, she could easily have written. Nevertheless, her feelings compelled her to break the prevailing silence.

A superficial reading of the next two letters would seem at first to contradict the claims of gender, for in his belated response to her letter of condolence, Jefferson, after an appropriate acknowledgment of her sympathy, immediately extended a warm plea to resume their friendship. By return post, Abigail rejected his effort to be friends, claiming that past political events stood between them, a reversal of the claim for female connectedness and male autonomy.

"[I] am thankful for the occasion furnished me of expressing my regret that circumstances should have arisen which have seemed to draw a line of separation between us," Jefferson wrote in the formal, detached language of proper epistolary style. Then he relaxed: "The friendship with which you honoured me has ever been valued, and fully reciprocated; and altho' events have been passing which might be trying to some minds, I never believed yours to be of that kind, nor felt that my own was." He then rehearsed the history of his friendship with John Adams, which had "accompanied us thro' long and important scenes." Their different opinions, he continued, "were not permitted to lessen mutual esteem, each party being conscious they were the result of an honest conviction in the other." However, the one act of Adams's last appointment of judges did provoke "personal displeasure." "They were among my most ardent political enemies . . . and laid me under the embarrasment of acting thro' men whose views were to defeat mine. . . . It seemed but common justice to leave a successor free to act by instruments of his own choice."

Burdened not only with his role as a public figure, but with the language, Jefferson struggled to express his feelings of regret for the loss of a valued friendship and found a mode: "If my respect for him did not permit me to ascribe the whole blame to the influence of others, it left something for friendship to forgive, and after brooding over it for some little time, and not always resisting the expression of it, I forgave it cordially." In effect, Jefferson allowed that despite his unjust treatment by a trusted friend, he was able to forgive and would return to "the same state of esteem and respect for him which had so long subsisted." He then described the relief that confession afforded him: "I have thus, my dear Madam, opened myself to you without reserve, which I have long wished an opportunity of doing; and, without knowing how it will be received, I feel relief from being unbosomed." Further, he wrote that "tho connected with political events, it has been viewed by me most strongly in it's [sic] unfortunate bearing on my private friendships. The injury these have sustained has been a heavy price for what has never given me equal pleasure."[33]

Jefferson's sensitivity is evident. So is his sincerity. In his efforts to plead his case, he shifted image from public figure to private individual; he changed mode from politics to friendship, from reason to feelings, from duty to pleasure. Abigail's reply, in contrast, was all business.

"Your Letter of June 13th came duly to hand," she wrote. "If it had contained no other sentiments and opinions than those which my Letter of condolence could have excited, and which are expressed in the first page of your reply, our correspondence would have terminated here: but you have been pleased to enter upon some subjects which call for a reply: and as you observe that you have wished for an opportunity to express your senti-ments, I have given to them every weight they claim." With this Abigail turned to the defense of the "midnight appointments."

She explained that she was certain that John Adams had not intended to offend Jefferson by the appointments, or to hurt his feelings. "I think it a duty to explain it so far as I then knew his views of designs," she wrote and listed five reasons for John's action. "The constitution empowers the presi-dent to fill up offices as they become vacant," she began, calling upon the highest law in John's defense; and she persisted by invoking precedent: "This was done by president Washington equally, in the last days of his administration so that not an office remain vacant for his successor to fill upon his comeing into office." Nor was John a bad sport over this, she implied: "No offense was given by it, and no personal unkindness thought of." Thirdly, she reasonably pointed out, it must be the rise of political parties "which have so unhappily divided our Country . . . that had given rise to the Idea, that personal unkindness was intended." So far Abigail had argued quite logically, and she was, perhaps, rather pleased with the terms of her discourse. She was credibly upholding John's position, so far as she then understood "his views and designs."

She continued: "You will please to recollect Sir, that at the time these appointments were made, there was not any certainty that the presidency would devolve upon you, which is an other circumstance to prove that personal unkindness was not meant." With this historical error, her argu-ment began to falter, and it rapidly declined into a discussion of the irrelevant issue of cabinet appointments. "I perfectly agree with you in opinion that those should be Gentlemen in whom the president can repose confidence, possessing opinions, and sentiments corresponding with his own." She continued with this line for a half paragraph.[34]

Abigail had erred in her timing of the election. The tie in the electoral college between Aaron Burr and Jefferson had been broken by the House of Representatives weeks before John Adams appointed the federal district judges.[35] And the question of cabinet appointments was never an issue. On the face of it, Jefferson appears both reasonable and caring while Abigail seems irrational and businesslike. Beneath the logic of literal ex-pression, however, a different logic prevails that expresses the difference in *mentalité* of Abigail Adams and Thomas Jefferson as eighteenth-century persons.

"One act and one act only," Jefferson recalled, had ever provoked his displeasure. So far from accurate was this statement as to represent a rewriting of history. In fact, what Jefferson had overlooked or glossed over in a magnificent case of denial was the decade of growing discord between himself and John Adams that culminated in his opposing Adams for the presidency in 1800. If there had been a period of friendly jousting as the two Founding Fathers discovered their ideological divergence, that fairly ended during Adams's administration when differences of opinion on both foreign and domestic policy led to acrimony. In his statement to Abigail, Jefferson reduced the sum of his own and John Adams's political careers to one hostile act. If in her husband's defense, Abigail was led to fanciful arguments that did not bear on the reality of the situation, Jefferson was no less guilty of the same.[36]

Further, Jefferson concluded, "If my respect for him did not permit me to ascribe the whole blame to the influence of others, it left something for friendship to forgive, and after brooding over it for some little time, and not always resisting the expression of it, I forgave it cordially." Once more Jefferson manipulated reality in order to match the historical situation to the outcome he wished to achieve. Clearly, no one influenced John Adams in his final appointments, so alienated was he from most members of his own party for the ill they had done him by the end of his administration. Jefferson's route out of the insoluble dilemma of his anger was to change the facts, to invent or imagine a villainous third party to absolve John from the blame. Thus the path was cleared for Jefferson to forgive. And what he forgave was not the source of the grievance, but rather an episode that symbolized it. If Abigail had difficulty creating a political and public defense, Jefferson was no better at creating a justification for expressing friendship. The political differences with Adams did matter to him, and in order to recreate his friendship, he had to change the facts.

Abigail, finally, had not presented her own case for John Adams, as she admitted at the outset. She agreed to explain John's behavior, "so far as I then knew his views and designs." She had argued in his words and in his voice, and it did not become her, but she did so in her capacity of caring for him. She tried to recreate his logic, his approach, and she was no more adept than Jefferson in his effort to escape his political persona to make way for friendship. Abigail would find her comfortable mode of expression when she shifted from defending John by John's logic to take the offensive in her own terms. "And now Sir I will freely disclose to you what has severed the bonds of former Friendship, and placed you in a light very different from what I once viewd you in."[37]

To describe Jefferson's sin, Abigail opened fire in language, colored by passion that was undiminished three years after the episode: he had freed Callender, who had maligned and slandered "your predecessor . . . whom you certainly knew incapable of such complicated baseness." Her argument contrasted good and evil, identifying John Adams with virtue and Callender with evil; Jefferson, in turn, she identified with Callender, implying his complicity with vicious conduct. "The remission of Callenders fine was a public approbation of his conduct. . . . If the chief Majestrate of a Nation, whose elevated Station places him in a conspicuous light, and renders his every action a concern of general importance, permits his public conduct to be influenced by private resentment, and so far forgets what is due to his Character as to give countanance to a base Calumniater, is he not answerable for the influence which his example has upon the manners and morals of the cummunity."

Ignoring the conventions of polite literary style, as well as any deference that might be due the office of the presidency, she continued her barrage: "Untill I read Callenders . . . Letter containing your compliment to him as a writer and your reward of 50 dollars, I could not be made to believe, that such measures could have been resorted to," and she rose to new heights of inspiration: "To stab the fair fame and upright intention of one, who . . . was acting from an honest conviction in his own mind that he was right. This Sir I considered as a personal injury." Abigail's system of justice, based upon her vision of Providence, assured her that good would be rewarded as naturally as evil was punished.[38] "The serpent you cherished and warmed, bit the hand that nourished him, and gave you sufficient Specimens of his talents. . . . When such vipers are let lose upon Society, all distinction between virtue and vice are levelled, all respect for Character is lost in the overwhelming deluge of calumny," she persisted, using the biblical metaphor of the serpent to underscore her image of evil.[39]

Abigail's stance in defense of John Adams expresses her domestic position as wife and caretaker. In abandoning the proprieties of social convention to argue about a political event with a former friend who occupied the nation's highest political office, she considered how best to protect Adams. She chose simple and timely metaphors that embraced both the religious and the political convictions of her culture: virtue and vice, both reduced in her mind to their simplest terms, good and evil. John Adams, in her portrait, wore a halo while Jefferson carried Callender's spear.[40]

Her argument, furthermore, resonates with references to relationships, reducing whole systems of thought to personal terms. By remitting Callender's fine, Jefferson had personally endorsed the journalist. "Is not the last restraint of vice," she queried, "a sense of shame, renderd abortive, if abandoned Characters do not excite abhorrence," identifying shame, an emotion, and not law, an abstraction, as the last restraint of vice. She charged Jefferson with political behavior based upon "the influence of private resentment." She argued that Jefferson's conduct, as president, must be exemplary as an influence "upon the manners and morals of the community," thus invoking a familial metaphor.[41]

"When such vipers are let lose upon Society," she continued, "all respect for Character is lost in the overwhelming deluge of calumny—that respect which is a necessary bond in the social union, which gives efficacy to laws, and teaches the subject to obey the magestrate, and the child to submit to the parent." In other words, morality derives from examples of just relationships; the values of the president would be reflected in the people. Respect of the community for the leader—that relationship—represents the basis of the social union. She took Jefferson to task for his relationships—for acting from rivalry and partisanship. From the top to the bottom of social arrangements—from friendship to government, relationships determined moral efficacy, she summed up her statement.

Ironically retreating to higher ground for her finale, Abigail wrote in the first person. "Often have I wished to have seen a different course pursued by you," and perhaps mirroring Jefferson's earlier assertions of forgiveness, she wrote in all seriousness, "I bear no malice I cherish no enmity. I would not retaliate if I could—nay more in the true spirit of christian Charity, I would forgive, as I hope to be forgiven." Jefferson, too, was faced with the image of Christian forgiveness.[42]

In reply, Jefferson did not hesitate over platitudes. Provoked beyond the limits of epistolary chivalry, he wrote that he would answer solely to set the record straight, and then he summarized Abigail's charges. Philosopher that he was, he reduced Abigail's manifold indictments to a convenient but evasive premise, one that he could then argue against: "My charities to Callender are considered as rewards for his calumnies." Having overlooked the richness of Abigail's charges—that personal motives were involved which reflected poorly on a president—Jefferson carefully, as in his previous letter he had done with John Adams, rehearsed the history of Callender. He had first encountered Callender in 1796, after reading and approving his book. He had been moved to offer charity to the journalist, who was destitute and in exile, but he soon came to recognize him for the coarse man he was. "My charities to him," he summed up, "were no more meant as encouragements to his scurrilities than those I give to the beggar at my door are meant as rewards for the vices of his life." Jefferson offered charity, not to individuals, based upon merit, worth, or resources, he claimed, but abstractly, as a matter of principle from one who had fortune, to those who were in need.

He turned then to the Sedition Act itself to explain the liberation of Callender, choosing to respond in the same angry tone that colored Abigail's indictments of him. Once more he rationalized his behavior by abstracting individual behavior into general principles. He noted that he had "discharged every person under punishment or persecution under the Sedition law, because I considered and now consider that law to be a nullity," adding that "to arrest it's [sic] execution in every stage" was his duty. "It was accordingly done in every instance, without asking what the offenders had done, or against whom they had offended, but whether the pains they were suffering were inflicted under the pretended Sedition law." Jefferson's theory of justice incorporated simple notions of right and wrong just as had Adams's, but whereas she looked at good and bad in the individual, to him justice meant theory based on abstract rights. She thought about the hurt inflicted upon John Adams; he considered the constitutionality of the Sedition Act. Further, he noted in expansive contrast to her appeal to the opinions of the community, "I am not afraid to appeal to the nation at large, to posterity, and still less to that being who sees himself our motive."[43]

Abigail was not greatly put off by Jefferson's line of argument. She conceded that his statements about Callender, "and your motives for liberating him, wear a different aspect as explaind by you, from the impression which they had made"—and here Abigail drew the line on compromise—"not only on my mind, but upon the minds of all those, whom I ever heard speak upon the subject." Deference to the opinion of other people provided a recurrent theme in Abigail's argument. Rather than accuse him of obfuscating or concealing facts, Abigail summoned an anonymous audience to serve as a moral barometer. Just as she had earlier buttressed her argument with the word "respect"—"respect as a necessary bond in the social union"—and later would invoke the opinion of Jefferson's "best Friends in Boston" to climax her statements about the dismissal of John Quincy Adams—Abigail looked to personal connectedness as the method for measuring and insuring justice. When Jefferson deferred to opinion, he appealed to abstractions, to "the nation at large, to posterity, and . . . that being who sees himself our motives."

Nor did she intend to pass judgment on the validity of the Sedition Act, Abigail continued, for "different persons entertain different opinions respecting it. It lies not with me to decide upon its validity." Once more arguing for the relative truth of law, and her own inability to set standards beyond her individual experience, she conceded: "That I presume devolved upon the supreem Judges of the Nation," challenging Jefferson on his right to nullify a law. The purpose of government, she argued, was to mediate between opinions. But "if the Chief Magistrate can by his will annul a Law, where is the difference between a republican, and a despotic government?" she reasoned and thereby questioned Jefferson's use of authority.

She persisted, taking a different tack, reducing her theoretical argument once more to the personal: every civilized nation lives by laws, because laws are necessary to control unruly passions. If people don't have laws, won't every man avenge his own wrongs, "as in the late instance, the sword and pistol decide the contest?" She referred to the duel fought between Hamilton and Burr the previous month, in which Hamilton was killed.[44] Law existed to prevent savagery, she continued, explaining that without law, "All the Christian and social virtues will be banished . . . every Mans hand will be against his Neighbor." The negative manifestations of human nature that she observed in her long experience provided sufficient impetus for government and law in Abigail's mind. It reflected not only the suspicion born of her Puritan background, but her vision of the world as a woman. And with the mention of Christian and social virtues, she returned to the theme of her husband and the Sedition Act, noting that Mr. Adams "has never written a line in any News paper to which his Name has not been affixed since he was first elected president of the united States."

She signed off by acknowledging her transgression not only of literary propriety but of friendship. "I have written to you with the freedom and unreserve of former Friendship to which I would gladly return could all causes but mere difference of opinion be removed." The wounds were profoundly faithful.[45]

Again, Jefferson responded, this time without words of friendship, but to set the record straight. And this time he wrote as president and took up the issues of power and the Constitution. "You seem to think it devolved upon the judges to decide on the validity of the Sedition law," he wrote, obviously irritated that she had challenged the president's authority to nullify a law. Jefferson's tone had transformed from one of flexibility, even conciliation, to stern magistry. He was the president of the United States, lecturing her about separation of powers and states' rights. He simplified terms, becoming impersonal, distant, patronizing. "You seem to think" he began, "that the judges should decide on the validity of the sedition law. But nothing in the constitution has given them the right to decide for the executive, more than the Executive to decide for them. Both magestracies are equally independent in the sphere of action assigned to them." He explained that the Constitution established the branches of government to be "checks on each other. But the opinion which gives to the judges the right to decide what laws are constitutional, and what not, not only in their own sphere of action, but for the legislative and executive also in their sphere, would make the judiciary a despotic branch."

Persisting, he sketched constitutional theory as he understood it. The Sedition Act was not unconstitutional because it was a bad law or because it infringed on people's first amendment rights. Rather Jefferson deferred to the tenth amendment: "The power to do that is fully possessed by the several states." He agreed with Abigail that to remove restraints on free speech would unleash an "overwhelming torrent of slander." But the proper jurisdiction for exercising control resided in the states. "While we deny that Congress have a right to controul the freedom of the press, we have ever asserted the right of the states, and their exclusive right, to do so."[46]

Jefferson's response, while it derived from his office as president, from his political stance as a Republican, and from his personal convictions as an eighteenth-century civil libertarian, nevertheless resonates as gendered. He addressed abstract principles; he was detached and high-minded. He rose above issues and personalities. He chose a language and a style that represented public discourse at its best. It might have been directed to an anonymous audience, if not to Abigail.

It was clear to Jefferson that Abigail did not intend to—actually she was not able to—resume their friendship. To conclude he once more expressed his regret about the circumstances that divided them. "I tolerate with the utmost latitude the right of others to differ from me in opinion without imputing to them criminality," he wrote in bitter defense. "I know too well the weakness and uncertainty of human reason to wonder at it's different results. . . . My anxieties on the subject will never carry me beyond the use of fair and honorable means of truth and reason; nor have they ever lessened my esteem for moral worth; nor alienated my affections from a single friend who did not first withdraw himself." The contrast to which he alluded was not lost on Abigail.[47]

When Abigail replied, it was to end the correspondence. "When I first addrest you, I had little thought of entering into a correspondence with you upon political topicks. I will not regret it since it has led to some elucidations and brought on some explanations which place in a more favorable light occurrances which have wounded me." She wished Jefferson well. He did not respond.[48]

Gender difference, however clearly it is revealed, was not the controlling force in the Adams-Jefferson friendship, nor in the breach of friendship. Something else was going on here—an undercurrent that had persisted through the entire exchange between Abigail Adams and Thomas Jefferson. There was a hidden agenda, an offstage voice that controlled the content and direction of the discourse. John Adams was clearly integral to this exchange. Abigail had written surreptitiously to defend his case, but she would never violate his position by conceding to Jefferson. Similarly Jefferson had been appealing to John Adams for the entire time. He cared for Adams, and he wrote to Abigail in hopes that she could mediate their differences, though knowing her loyalty to John. The thrust of his appeal was to John, and in the end, as he attempted to heal the wounds, he returned to the theme of his first letter, the political differences that had caused the breach and the belief that reasonable people could resolve those differences. "Which is right, time and experience will prove." He appealed once more to "truth and reason" and reminded Abigail that he had "ever kept myself open to a return of their justice."[49]

Abigail had struck at the heart of the issue at the start, when she observed to Jefferson: "I have never felt any enmity towards you Sir, for being elected president of the United States"; her next phrase began with "but."[50] It was that "but" that governed the remainder of the correspondence. Jefferson's being president was intolerable to John Adams. Jefferson as anything else would have been acceptable, but Jefferson as president represented the whole of Adams's pain of rejection and sense of failure. "Faithfull are the wounds of a Friend," Abigail had written. The wounds described in this correspondence were small when compared with the magnitude of political and ideological differences experienced by the two Founding Fathers over the course of twenty-five years: the years in France and England, when each was aware of growing ideological disparity; the long years of wrangling when Jefferson was secretary of state and then vice president and Adams was vice president and then president; the split over issues of foreign policy; Jefferson's predilection for France and his frustrations with Adams; Adams's fear of Jefferson's subversion of his foreign policy. They still communicated. Only when Jefferson became president, signalling the retirement of John Adams from public service under a cloud of rejection, did Adams leave the capital, the wound already rankling before the affairs over Callender and John Quincy.[51]

Abigail could not repair, nor had she intended to repair, the friendship, because she knew Adams's intransigence as no other person would. "Faithful [were] the wounds" that she would loyally support. The Adamses' unanimity in opposition to Jefferson was founded on John's need for a single object to serve as the focus of his grievance with the world. The enmity with Jefferson provided that focus.[52] Their estrangement encompassed a multitude of hurts that John Adams could not confront, political and personal: the agonies and frustrations of his presidency, the disloyalty of his supporters, the loneliness of the office, and what he termed the "greatest Grief of my heart and the deepest affliction of my Life," the death, on the same day that Jefferson was elected, of his son Charles from alcoholism.[53]

All of this was encapsulated in John's enmity toward Jefferson.[54] Adams could not permit the friendship to resume, for to do so would mean that he would have to confront his ghosts. (But he spend the rest of his life justifying.) One man and the office summed up Adams's disillusionment. The focus on Jefferson as the enemy protected him from sensing his presumed failure in office and as a father. With John Adams's displaced agenda as the real source of the breach, Abigail was helpless to change. Nor would she try, for in her primary role as caretaker, John Adams earned her first loyalty.[55]

The qualities of caring and loyalty are not gendered; Jefferson cared.[56] The logic and language that express care, however, may be gendered. This exchange between Abigail Adams and Thomas Jefferson reveals the terms by which reasoning about some issues, involving concepts of justice, may be influenced by gender. Furthermore, if gender difference is revealed, a

qualitative hierarchy is not. Neither argument is distinguished by its superiority or its persuasiveness, by expressing more force, more accuracy, or
greater justice. Adams and Jefferson viewed the same world from different
perspectives that colored their reactions differently.

It appeared at the outset of the correspondence that Jefferson cared more
about relationships because he initiated a probe to resume the friendship,
while Abigail Adams seemed more rigid and unforgiving by rejecting him.
In fact, many different issues were at stake here. Jefferson, in order to
justify his approach to the Adamses, had to change historic conditions to
conform to the abstract principles of justice that he advocated. He con-
sented to overlook the "one act" that he identified as John Adams's violation
of justice, but in order to do that he created a false motive for John's
behavior. Further, at every point, Jefferson argued by elevating an individual case into a general principle, thus rationalizing his behavior as philo-
sophically—as well as politically, spiritually, and patriotically—ethical. He
appealed to the nation, to posterity and divine justice.

Abigail appears more petty and vindictive for rejecting Jefferson's
friendly appeal; her system of justice would seem inferior—unreason-
able—based upon feelings of anger and revenge. In fact, hers was a different voice, derived from her own female world of connections. Her public
expressions whether on personal issues of friendship or public issues of
state resonated from her primary experience of bondedness with her family. Whether she spoke awkwardly in John's words or used her own, she
first processed those thoughts—unconsciously—through a system that
fundamentally valued her connectedness to her husband and children.

That Jefferson had even inadvertently dismissed John Quincy from an
office—"I declare to you on my honor that this is the first knowledge I have
ever had that he was so. . . . I thought it . . . proper to enquire, not whom
they had employed, but whom I ought to appoint to fulfil the intentions of
the law"—is consistent with his impartiality.[57] What impressed Abigail was
not the law, but rather that her son had been affected. "I am pleased to find
that, which respected my son, all together unfounded. . . . I will do you
the justice to say at this hour: that I believe that what you then said, you
then meant," she wrote. But she called him on his lofty approach: "With
the public it will remain," and she lectured him on the damage of too great
abstraction. "Sir may I be permitted to pause, and ask you whether in your
ardent zeal, and desire to rectify the mistakes and abuses as you may
consider them . . . you are not led into measures still more fatal to the
constitution, and more derogatory to your honour, and independence of
Character? Pardon me Sir if I say, that I fear you are."[58]

Abigail's dilemma was more complex. She was tangled in relationships
that forced her to choose between love of her family and love of a friend.
"Affection still lingers in the Bosom, even after esteem has taken its flight,"
she admitted to Jefferson.[59] Her dilemma derived from female thinking as

relational and relative—as an eighteenth-century woman, her agenda was governed by issues of to whom she should be responsible. She measured justice by its impact on people, not by abstract principle.

Moreover, her political identity was forged through her relationships as well. She was an unusually intelligent, articulate, well-read, and informed woman, but her stance on the issues that separated the Adamses from Jefferson was informed by a single source of inspiration. Abigail considered political issues by their impact on the people closest to her before any other consideration. More specifically, she was woman before she was republican; the content of being a republican was first processed through her sense of herself as a woman—connected to and caring for other people. She viewed politics as a manifestation of relationships in both the narrow and the grand picture. Her politics supported John Adams's. Her ideology was formed by considering the lives of real people. Her political statements reflected her primary connectedness.

Abigail's and other women's different voices have been heard not as separate but as inferior, both in her own time and in ours. In the era of Constitution building, women were not considered "citizens," because, as John Locke asserted, men and women have "different understandings," and "it therefore being necessary that the last determination—i.e. the rule—should be placed somewhere, it naturally falls to the man's share, as the abler and the stronger."[60] In the late twentieth century it has become popular to confirm the similarities between women and men—especially in the public or political sphere—in order to deny subordinate status.

This analysis of the Adams-Jefferson correspondence proposes a different conclusion. By comprehending the psychological basis of social behavior and by examining language, gender difference—in perspective, in orientation, in approach to reasoning—becomes evident. Abigail Adams argued from a female vision that emphasized the language and metaphors of relationships, while Thomas Jefferson argued from principles abstracted from individual experience. This use of language reflected the cultural lessons and expectations that differentiated female from male in the late eighteenth century.

Neither Abigail Adams nor Thomas Jefferson was the victor. If there was a victor in the end, he was John Adams, and when John was ready, eight years later in 1812, he resumed his friendship through correspondence with Thomas Jefferson. Abigail Adams had been third party to a triangular friendship in which her loyalty to John was primary.[61]

7

The Threefold Cord

Spheres and Connections

"I have a zeal at my Heart, for my Country and her Friends, which I cannot smother or conceal," John wrote to Abigail Adams in the summer of 1774. "This zeal will prove fatal to the Fortune and Felicity of my Family, if it is not regulated by cooler judgment than mine has hitherto been."[1] John described the tension between his heart and his head—between zeal and judgment—that did, in fact, forecast the fortunes of his family. Zeal prevailed over cool judgment, because John was not a man of cool temperament, but, moreover, because he was merely choosing a place in the public sphere in an era that made sharp distinctions. John's connections were divided between his public and private worlds.

Abigail understood John's tension as a moral dilemma, which from one perspective it was, between his commitment to a higher social purpose and his personal responsibility as husband and father. She, having no options outside her positions as wife and mother, experienced no such struggle; her separate and unequal sphere in the late eighteenth century clearly mandated her place, and she did not question its propriety. She also accepted John's struggle as heroic, and as part of the grand design. She dignified his expression of guilt and remorse as a moral dilemma, induced by his dual responsibility to country and family, and she constructed a mythology to justify his abandonment of family life. Encoded in this mythology was her belief that John's unique talent was necessary for the success of the patriotic mission, and that his abandonment of family life represented a personal sacrifice. All of this was built upon the edifice of man's connection to public life.[2]

Abigail's connections to family life defined her destiny, as was the case for other eighteenth-century women, but the implications are more complex. For as often as it complemented the predominant culture, the social message of women's connectedness to the domestic sphere diverged from it. Female connectedness affected the way that Abigail and other eighteenth-century women identified themselves as communal, therefore sustaining a traditional *mentalité* that contrasted with the growing ideology of individualism. Female connectedness also opposed another social current, since the sister bond maintained extended family ties at a time when nuclear households were becoming more common. Connectedness, furthermore, accounted for the strength of Abigail's and other eighteenth-century women's spiritual ties in an increasingly secular world.[3]

Female connectedness, as it was experienced by Abigail, her sisters, and other women, effected a conduit from family life to public life, for at its best its conduct manifested the values that the greater culture advocated. "Virtue" in the republic meant service; it meant sacrifice; it meant working for the good of others, even at a personal cost. "Virtue" was opposed to self-seeking, self-indulgence. It meant industry, economy, sacrifice. Ironically, women were devalued by living the best ideology in the vocabulary of men—those of service and sacrifice. John advocated those principles in the public sphere. Abigail lived them in the family context.[4]

Over and over, as the years passed John remarked that behind every great man was a helpful woman. Sometimes he meant a mother, for in tune with his time, he extolled and thereby advocated that biologically determined role for women. "You are an heroine," he wrote both in gratitude and as encouragement.[5] This vision was too narrow, however, for a different kind of connection supported John's enterprises as a public servant; it operated in a separate and overlooked orbit, that of the sisterhood. Without Abigail's connection to sisters, John would never have been freed, as he was, to exercise his zeal for his country.

For more than seventy years, Abigail Adams and her two sisters, Mary and Elizabeth, helped each other to live. In youth, they grew, played, prayed, worked, and learned together. Later, they meddled in one another's courtships and marriages; they raised daughters and sons according to similar standards; they aged, endured sickness and death of loved ones, and ended their lives, all bonded in what Elizabeth once called the "threefold cord." Each of their personal lives was deeply touched by the others, but in addition, the connections among them had implications for the public sphere. John Adams was enabled to leave home and family in part because Abigail's sisters supported his absence.

The Sisters

After the mother-daughter relationship, "sisters" represents the primary bonding metaphor among women. Yet the implications of this fundamental and profound relationship are rarely examined within the scope of historical or social science literature. The term "sisters" is borrowed from its literal meaning of blood relatives to imply the closeness of female friendships in many senses. Aside from family life, it is used in religious or social contexts, suggesting deep bonding among women. "Sisters" provides a way for women to think of themselves in special and intimate relation to other women.[6]

The power inherent in the reference to "sisters" is taken for granted in a way that "mother-daughter" is not, perhaps because sisters signifies an auspicious relationship. In contrast to the complexity attributed to mothers and daughters, the sisterly relationship is considered more tractable. It is idealized in a way that mother-daughter is not. Because of its strength as a positive metaphor, however, the nature of sisterhood deserves attention. In addition, as a social dynamic, the relationship transcends the idealized metaphoric imagery to describe women's historic place and impact.

The relationship of Abigail Adams to her two sisters may serve as a prototype for the role and its dynamics. Her older sister, Mary, three years her senior, was born in 1741, and her younger sister, Elizabeth, born in 1750, was six years younger. They remained one another's closest friends until they all died in the second decade of the nineteenth century, despite the very different directions their lives took. Unlike Abigail, neither Mary nor Elizabeth is famous two centuries later, but like her, they wrote eloquent letters that reveal the same great intellect and spirit that make Abigail an attractive person in history. They lack fame because, unlike Abigail, their husbands, all deserving and respectable men, did not become Founding Fathers, nor did any of their sons rise so high in public office as John Quincy Adams. Like most women, they are historically anonymous, neither having married a public figure nor performing out of the ordinary. Only as the sisters of Abigail Adams are Mary Smith Cranch and Elizabeth Smith Shaw Peabody rendered accessible.

No portrait of Mary Smith Cranch survives, but she described herself as taller and thinner than Abigail.[7] Nor do records reveal the dynamics of childhood and youth in the Smith household at the parsonage in Weymouth. Some reminiscences from later years provide seductive clues: "You well know what our early education was," Abigail wrote in 1811. "Neither grammar or orthography were taught us. it was not then the fashion for Females to know more than writing, and arithmetic & no Books upon Female Education were then in vogue. no Accademies for Female instruction were then established."[8] Mary's half-century correspondence with family members and friends provides us with her only portrait.

Mary appears the most serious of the sisters, perhaps because in youth she inherited a more responsible position as the eldest of the four children of the Reverend William and Elizabeth Quincy Smith. Whereas the others could be whimsical on occasion, Mary viewed life more soberly; she was neither as romantic as Elizabeth nor as witty as Abigail. Her letters are those of a very busy woman: plain, clear, direct, and written in such haste that the scrawl is at times almost indecipherable. They are also long, the scrawl in this case representing the pen that could not keep pace with the thoughts. Mary was an intelligent and literate woman whose observations about the world and its inhabitants were keen and wise. Nor was she loth to pass judgments or give advice, privileges she earned by her kindness and generosity.[9]

Mary, it was said, lived a religious life from the time she married the pious, good-natured, scholarly ne'er-do-well Richard Cranch. That means she believed in hard work, charity, and training her children to a virtuous life of the same; It means she accepted adversity with resignation and posited her hope for happiness in the hereafter. Her marriage in 1762 preceded that of Abigail by almost three years, thus giving her experience to mentor her closest sister. The timing of the Cranch marriage, like that of the Adams marriage; was concurrent with and subject to the calamities of the revolutionary era; but as ordinary citizens, who did not act on the big stage of revolution making, the Cranches were vulnerable to its social impact in different ways.

A watchmaker by trade, Richard Cranch had migrated from old England to New and was fifteen years Mary's senior.[10] Whether he was a poor businessman or suffered the economic vagaries of war and social change—watchmaking being a luxury trade in hard times—he never earned a satisfactory living. The people of Braintree, however, respected him well enough to elect him to several political offices, and, attesting to his erudition, the board of governors of Harvard College awarded him an honorary degree. Further, Cranch served as a lay leader in his church.

The Cranches moved regularly before settling in Braintree in 1775. As a consequence of her husband's bad fortunes, Mary labored at her wifely duties and carried a large burden for family income as well. For more than forty years, she took in boarders, which entailed providing meals and doing laundry. Relatives were frequent members of her household, and to her shame on occasion she required payment. Mary shouldered her wifely burdens with the same pragmatic fortitude and religious resignation that inspired her sisters.

As the mother of three children, she followed the eighteenth-century pattern of sending her son to Harvard while educating her daughters at home. The quality of her daughters' educations, however, was extraordinary, reflecting her own and her sisters' strong intellectual bent. Like both of her sisters, she fretted about morals and linens when her son left home to attend college.[11] And like her sisters, she watched an adult daughter die of a long debilitating illness and survived the ordeal with religious resignation.

Mary's life never became easy. Her economic struggles lasted for her lifetime. In addition, her children and grandchildren were often her charges as their lives repeated many of the patterns of the parents. Life was serious for Mary, but she knew from her religious background and from her observations that life was harsh. The rewards, she knew as well, came in the hereafter, and thus she did not descend into self-pity or cynicism.

There was pleasure as well as strength in her marriage to Richard Cranch; they expressed love explicitly in letters and implicitly by never criticizing each other. Their companionship was confirmed by their deaths in October 1811, one day apart.[12]

There is a portrait of Elizabeth Smith Shaw Peabody, done by Gilbert Stuart when she was in her sixtieth year, and it remarkably resembles that of Abigail done about the same time:[13] the same delicate, even features set in a heart-shaped face, the same piercing dark eyes, the same alert and knowing expression, the discreet, good quality attire appropriate to women whose stations commanded respect for age and accomplishment. Separated in age from her older sisters by several years—when Mary married, Elizabeth was twelve—she was long regarded as the little sister. Elizabeth was twenty-seven when she married the Reverend John Shaw, unusually late for an eighteenth-century woman.[14]

No explanation survives to tell why Elizabeth waited so long to marry. However, as the youngest of four siblings and the only one remaining at home, Elizabeth was probably designated as caretaker of her aging parents. Only in 1777, after her mother's death, and when her brother's family had moved into the family home to care for her father, was Elizabeth freed to pursue her own life.

Of the sisters, Elizabeth exhibited the most sensitive spirit and least robust health, although none of them possessed physical vigor, in part a reflection of health generally in the late eighteenth century.[15] Abigail repeatedly cautioned Elizabeth, who had inherited their mother's frail constitution, to care for her health.[16] Living so many years in a household with aging parents, where Elizabeth retreated into literature for experience, may account for her romantic nature. She described awakening on a winter morning: "Was anyone Blessed with the descriptive genious of a Thompson, had they the sublimity of a Milton, or the ease and perspicuity of the sweet Bard that Painted the Forests of Windsor and made them harmoniously quiver in his Lines, they could not give you an adequate Idea of the Glorious Scene, that this very moment ravishes my Sight and transports my Soul." It had snowed.[17] The same emotions that left her transported could as easily leave her speechless; she often wrote that words had failed her, that words were inadequate to convey her feelings. "There are affections that can't be expressed in words. Homer represents passion by a deep silence—."[18]

Contrary to that presentation of herself, Elizabeth's letters more typically overflow with sentiment. Like her sisters, she wrote voluminously and over a broad range of topics. Like them, she was a storyteller, repeating diurnal anecdotes in great detail. But she was more meditative, more explicitly spiritual, more poetic.

Twice married, both times to clergymen, she shared a position in life similar to her mother's, which kept her close to the rituals and institutions of the church. As both of her husbands ran academies, she actively participated in student life and teaching. Her liberal philosophy of education, drawn from the prevailing Puritan and Lockean traditions, remained constant over her many decades as a parent and teacher: "I am sensible much is dependent on Education. The Infant Mind, I believe is a blank, that easily receives any impression the hand of Education is pleased to make."[19]

After her marriage to Reverend John Shaw in 1777, Elizabeth moved to Haverhill on the New Hampshire border, a day's journey from her family, and from that time, she saw them at most several times a year. Letter writing, then, became the lifeline of her family tie. Soon after her marriage, she responded to Mary's query about married life—"You say I must give you an account of every thing a *sister* ought to know." She confessed that she was as happy as she could or ought to be: "We spend our time Eating, Drinking, sleeping, getting victuals, cleaning house, Dressing, receiving and returning visits, like other fine folks."[20] The ease of her earliest married days and months, however, belied the rest of a life in which she, like both of her sisters, would labor at domestic chores and then contribute to the livelihood of her family. Her first child, William, was born within a year after marriage, and eventually there followed two daughters, Elizabeth and Abigail.

As a minister's salary could not support a family, Elizabeth was always beset by penury. Her charitable nature flourished in the setting of the parsonage, and domestic chores taxed her energies; she also taught, cared for, and counseled her many students and boarders. Her letters to them after they had departed attest to the scope of her mothering of them all.[21]

In 1794, Reverend Shaw died suddenly at the age of forty-five, leaving Elizabeth a stunned and bereft widow. For some time she struggled alone, and then in late 1795 she married a widower, Reverend Stephen Peabody of nearby Atkinson, New Hampshire, which became her residence for the rest of her life. In 1798 her ailing daughter Elizabeth died, probably of consumption, a blow of enormous proportions to this loving woman.

Like her sisters, Elizabeth knew that life was hard, and in ways unlike theirs, hers was a struggle. Her religious faith, integral to her consciousness, deepened, and with that, her optimism was sustained. To the end of her life she could comment on the beauty of a sunrise, a spring flower, or a snowfall.

The Life Cycle

The complexity of the sister relationship becomes evident when it is examined over the course of the many years of their lives. Because the historic record for their childhoods is typically barren of much specific information, its quality is speculative, but as Mary, Abigail, and Elizabeth grew older and wrote letters that were preserved, a picture of their changing experiences emerges.

The life cycle, one historian has pointed out, is one of the most engaging subjects of history, because it reveals nothing less than "humankind's perception of itself."[22] It has been a topic dear to philosophers, theologians, biographers, and poets but mostly ignored by historians. In the twentieth century its currency has developed primarily in the social sciences, especially among psychologists, and almost universally their models have been male, not different from their historical forebears. The typical life cycle from the Middle Ages forward was described as the "seven stages of Man" and was reduced by the eighteenth century to four stages in order to be more compatible with the natural cycle of the seasons and humor theory. Overall, whether refined into seven or ten stages or contracted into a manageable four, the prevailing masculine imagery has remained: infancy, youth, manhood, and old age.[23] The comparable model for woman, outside of the philosophic or scientific discourse in the realm of popular understanding, depicts her development from daughter to wife, mother, and widow. Man, it appears, grows into an autonomous person while woman ever remains an adjunct, ever defined by her connection to father, husband, and children.

Neither Abigail, her sisters, nor the women she knew would have protested that model. "But as our weak and timid sex is only the Echo of the other," wrote Mercy Otis Warren, who was not known either in her own time or later to possess a weak and timid character, "like some pliant peace of Clock Work the springs of our souls move slow or more Rapidly."[24] Their social self-perception as subsumed by male relatives was reinforced in the home, in the church, and in the economy; only in rare circumstances were they acknowledged by the state, and then merely to confirm the popular image.[25] As is the case with models, however, the abstracted four stages of Woman lacks lustre, depth, energy. A passive model, however, it acquires color, dimension, interest, and importance when viewed from within, from the perspective of women living through their various stages. Defined socially as subordinate, they comprehended their world as relevant and dignified. While John Adams pursued public service, leaving family and sometimes regretting its loss, Abigail sustained family life, regretting his absence and relying upon the connections that existed among sisters.

"Sisterhood" implies a condition of equality and reciprocity of spirit, behavior that belies the dynamics of the bond. In fact, sisterhood is by nature changing and asymmetrical. Age provides one powerful measure of its asymmetry. Younger sisters remain younger, sometimes over the entire life cycle with a multitude of social consequences. All sisters, reported one ethnographic informant, are younger sisters to a brother. Other circumstances create further social gaps. Physical attractiveness, intelligence, charm—personal qualities that are valued—distinguish among sisters, which may result in admiration and deference on the one hand, or jealousy, envy, and competition on the other. In the eighteenth century, as before and after, marriage, the success of one's husband, and children and their talents established the status of a sister. Over time the bonds of sisterhood have proved as volatile and dynamic as those of any other relationship.[26]

In their youth, age first separated Elizabeth from Mary and Abigail. The two older sisters shared space in a parsonage bed chamber, as well as experiences of play, education, church, chores, clothes, and eventually the romance of courtship. It was Mary's betrothed, Richard Cranch, who introduced his friend John Adams to the sisters, and the first letter in the printed volume of the Adams Family Papers is appropriately a joint letter from Richard and John to the sisters. Elizabeth and her brother William, if they were child observers of the courtship, were excluded from the romantic circle of the young adults.[27]

As age first distanced Elizabeth from Mary and Abigail, her lengthy maidenhood further put her at a disadvantage in a setting that reserved respectability for married women.[28] Not only did Elizabeth languish at home with aging parents, but her social isolation at Weymouth stifled her romantic and companionable nature. She complained to John Adams: "Weymouth you know, consists chieffly of Farmers, and has never been distinguished, unless for its Inactivity."[29] To Abigail she described herself as "almost secluded from the Company of [my] own Sex. . . ."[30] Further confined as the caretaker of her parents, Elizabeth carried the responsibility of maintaining the parsonage for her sickly mother rather than engaging in the social life of a young unattached woman. She lamented her seclusion, complaining that her mother's ill health gave her more responsibility than a person her age should have, but acknowledging that duty claimed precedence, she added, "I won't neglect domestic oeconomy . . . it comes before my pleasures."[31] Another time, returning several borrowed books to her cousin Isaac Smith, she wrote wistfully: "What fine times you have at Colledge! *A glorious spirit of Liberty* prevails among you."[32] Her letters to young Isaac, who returned to England, a Tory in the Revolution, mostly reflected her passion for literature and her preoccupation with romance. "I am sensible [love] operates differently, on different Tempors. . . . Yes my cousin, I do hope and really believe, there is such a thing as Virtuous Love."[33] Isolated in Weymouth, Elizabeth longed to be married like her sister to an estimable man. Abigail, she confided to John Adams, had been "highly favored among Women, and perculiarly happy is her Lot in sharing the Confidence, and possessing the Esteem; the tenderest Affection, of a Man in whose Breast the Patriotic Virtues glow with unmitigated Fervour."[34]

An early romance appears to have miscarried, leaving a temporarily embittered Elizabeth to reflect upon "the fickleness of Fortune, the shortness and uncertainty of Life, and the instability of Human Affairs." She addressed pages of disappointment to Abigail, disguising her hurt in abstract reflections about the ephemeral nature of happiness. "By being habituated to Disappointments, we expect them, and by expecting them, we blunt there Edge, and hinder them from so keenly wounding. Whenever I find myself laying Plans of future Felicity, I check the career of my Imagination, and consider that much Tribulation is the inevitable Lot of Humanity." But feelings of regret intruded: "O Heart! . . . Were the seeds of Friendship sown only to inform me, that it would be improper to cultivate them in this promising Soil.—But—," and there follows Elizabeth's characteristic lapse into silence, her code to acknowledge great emotion.[35]

When true romance did come in the form of John Shaw, a student clergyman and boarder for some time at the parsonage, Elizabeth and Abigail began an adversarial sisterly exchange that persisted for nearly three years until after Elizabeth's marriage. Abigail, drawing upon her status as the older married sister, argued forcefully against the developing courtship. She disapproved of Shaw, although it is not known why, and she expressed her distaste in terms that provoked Elizabeth's outrage: "When I received a Bundle a Sabbath Eve, I imagined it contained a Book," she wrote to Abigail, referring to her letter. "On losening the string, something dropt which I supposed to be an Inkhorn, opened it with a Jerk, and stabed the shining Weapon among the veins in my wrist." Emphasizing her resentment, Elizabeth composed a little allegory that described a painful wound. "What thought I, have I done to deserve this fatal Pressent.— Pandora's Box, Lucretia's Poignard, and all the direful Events recorded in History, occasioned by it, rushed with irresistable force into my Mind." This was a mean blow, her allegory concluded, comparing it with "all the direful Events recorded in History."[36]

From Abigail's point of view, her advice, though blunt, was warranted. Candidness was premised as the privilege as well as the duty of an older sister; she considered it her responsibility to protect her younger sister. She strongly disliked Shaw, and she pressed her case with vigor. Elizabeth, in turn, resisted this intrusion with its implication of her own deficient mature judgment.

Denying that a romance existed, an ambivalence that later events would disprove, Elizabeth argued her defense: "Must one who is naturally of a cheerful, and sociable Temper, who lives on the smiles, and pleasant Countenances of Others, be debarred giving the pleasure she receives. . . .

May they not be fond of conversing on what they have read, and on the different Opinions of various Authors, on particular Subjects, without exciting Suspicions in a Family that are dishonourary to both Parties." In other words, she pleaded, she enjoyed merely an intellectual companionship with Shaw. Must she act "the prude," she continued: "No, rather let me, conscious of the innocence of my Heart, and the integrity of my Intentions, glide on in the same uniform Course regulating my Conduct, by the same Principles, governing myself by those divine Laws, which I hope will ever influence every action of my Life." In short, Betsy announced that she, with Divine guidance, would evaluate her intentions and behavior. She further suggested that Abigail attend to her own business, which both by character and in her role as older sister, Abigail could not do.

Betsy's defense persisted: "And can a Sister blame me, who is every Day tasting the calm Pleasure annexed to such a Course of Life?"—perhaps an inadvertent confession of envy. She admitted that Abigail's letter had enraged her, that she had been "plunged in the Gall of Bitterness," that days had passed before she achieved the sense of moderation that permitted her response, one that was "consistent with that *candid, and gentle Treatment* due a Sister." Irony was one of Elizabeth's strongest weapons.

As she had opened with an allegory, Elizabeth concluded her letter with a "legal deposition," signed by herself and (falsely) by her parents and Shaw, that read: "To certify all those whom it does, or may concern, that We John Shaw, and Elizabeth Smith have no such Purpose in Our Hearts, as has been unjustly surmised."

Elizabeth had defined her independence from sisterly control, and she succeeded insofar as she silenced Abigail's outspoken resistance to Shaw. Her attitude did not change; for years, Abigail remained irritated and opposed to Elizabeth's courtship. The source of her distaste for Shaw may be surmised from a statement of John Adams, who in contrast welcomed Shaw into the family. "Tell Betsey I hope She is married," he wrote to Abigail from Philadelphia in February 1777. "My Respects to Mr. S[haw]. Tell him he may be a Calvinist if he will, provided always he preserves his Candour, Charity and Moderation."[37] Perhaps Shaw's strict Calvinist theology and bearing had turned Abigail against him. Her resistance was unremitting. "I cannot do your Message to B[ets]y," she responded, "since the mortification I endure at the mention of it is so great that I have never changd a word with her upon the subject, altho preparations are making for house keeping. The ordination is the 12th of this month. I would not make an exchange with her for the mountains of Mexico and Peru. She has forfeited all her character with me and the world for taste &c. . . . An Idea of 30 years an unmarried is sufficient to make people do very unaccountable things."[38] Frustrated at losing this contest, Abigail exaggerated Elizabeth's age as a last mean blow.

At Elizabeth's marriage, Abigail wrote to John with undisguised ill humor: "The Spirit of Barter and exchange predominates so much here that people dispose of their own Bodies. Matrimony prevails among all orders and Ages; the scarcity of the Commodity enhances the value. Men are a very scarce article to be sure. Among the late marriages which have taken place and are like to, Miss B[ets]y S[mit]h to Mr. S[ha]w last thursday, old Deacon W[eb]b of this Town to a maiden Sister of John Ruggles'es wife, who has lived to the age of 66 unmarried . . ." and she listed several others, not to distinguish her sister's marriage from a host of acquaintances.[39]

No revolution followed upon Elizabeth's notice of independence, but rather a negotiated peace ensued in which neither side conceded: each retreated. Both sisters correctly understood that their relationship would sustain the tension of this exchange, for it was encoded in eighteenth-century family life that sisterhood was indelible, regardless of the degree of strain that existed. While Elizabeth did not resist or protest her parents' demands—nor did she loosen the boundaries of polite correspondence to other family members or friends—sisterhood differed. She felt as free to confront Abigail as Abigail had felt free to provoke her, a liberty embedded even within the hierarchy of sisterhood. Furthermore, in the late eighteenth century, sisterly loyalty prevailed despite tensions that resulted from its asymmetrical arrangement. In this case, affection furnished an additional bond.

Abigail and Elizabeth continued to be friends, and Abigail's attitude towards Shaw improved over the years. She was able to ascribe to him a "sympathetick Soul" and to advise Betsy to "Remember me in affectionate Terms to Mr. S[ha]w."[40] When the time came for Abigail to journey to Europe in 1784, it was the Reverend John Shaw to whom she entrusted her younger sons, both for the care that would be ensured in her sister's household, and for the critical overseeing of their education that would be Shaw's responsibility. She even wrote him friendly personal letters describing her life in London.[41]

A different set of dynamics prevailed between Abigail and Mary. Writing to Mary, whose family had moved from nearby Germantown to Salem in pursuit of business opportunities, Abigail exclaimed: "O my Dear Sister I mourn every day more and more the great distance between us. I think Well now if She was but at Germantown I would run away and see her. I think I could come as often again as I used to."[42] Another time she wrote in brighter spirits: "When ever I receive a Letter from you it seems to give new Springs to my nerves, and a brisker circulation to my Blood, tis a kind of pleasing pain that I feel and . . . I feel so glad that I can scarcly help feeling sorry. These seem to be odd, tho I believe they are very natural Sensations."[43]

From her new home in Salem, Mary's response echoed Abigail: "Indeed my dear Sister the Winter never seem'd so tedious to me in the World. I daily count the days between this and the time I may probably see you. . . . I would give a great deal only to know I was within Ten Miles of you if I could not see you."[44] Nearly twenty years later, after Abigail had departed for Europe, Mary's words repeat a similar theme: "This winter has been a solitary one to me—there never has been a time since I lived in Braintree when I should have missed your company so much."[45] A number of factors account for the close bond that existed between Abigail and Mary. Age was primary, for only three years separated them.

Still, there persisted a subtle sense in which Mary remained the older sister. "Indeed my Sister I cannot bear the thought of staying here so far from all my Friends," she wrote, qualifying her loneliness by submerging her sister within a crowd of "Friends."[46] Mary had doubtlessly helped to raise her younger siblings wherein she had developed a sense of responsibility, a matriarchal posture towards them from which there was no recovery. Lacking Abigail's spontaneity, which represented perhaps a difference in style, her greater reserve created a distance between her and her sisters that elicited respect from Abigail and deference from Elizabeth. In many ways, Abigail's relationship with Mary reflected her bond with her mother, an eighteenth-century connection that included identification, affection, trust, and dependence. It differed from a maternal bond in that Mary's needs, as a sister, were reciprocal.

In contrast to Shaw, Abigail always admired Richard Cranch. "To our dear and venerable Brother Cranch do I owe my early taste for Letters," she reminisced in later years, accounting for her lifelong attachment to him. "He it was who taught me to Love the poets and put into my hands, Milton, Pope, and Thompson, and Shakespeare. he it was who taught me to realish and distinguish their merits and to him I was indebted for the works of Richardson; then just published. . . . whatever I possess of delicacy of sentiment, or refinement, taste, in my early and juvenile days, I ascribe to the perusal of those Books."[47] These reflections from old age serve as no small testament to the impact of Richard Cranch on Abigail and explain their lasting compatibility. It is not surprising, then, that Cranch had first introduced his friend John Adams to the Smith household, an event that John recorded in his diary by noting: "Polly and Nabby are Wits," addressing Mary and Abigail by their nicknames, and identifying them both as clever women.[48]

Just as they had courted simultaneously and married but three years apart, the Cranches and Adamses lived as neighbors for several years until Richard Cranch moved his family to Salem. By this time, each family had one small daughter, who figured largely in the correspondence between the sisters. Much as they expressed their own affection, they displaced that bond onto their children. "Nabby sends her Love to her cousin Betsy and would be very glad of her company, to tend Miss Doll, who is a very great favorite of theirs," wrote Abigail.[49] Or "my Dear Betsy, what would I give to hear her prattle to her Cousin Nabby, to see them put their little arms round one an others necks, and hug each other, it would really be a very pleasing Sight to me."[50] And Mary returned: "Betsy Dear creature longs to see her cousen."[51]

Conscious that tales about children bored adults, Abigail freely disclosed her maternal feelings to an understanding sister. "How every word and action of these little creature, twines round ones heart? All their little pranks which would seem ridiculous to relate, are pleasing to a parent. How vex'd have I felt before now upon hearing parents relate the chitt chat of little Miss, and Master said or did such and such a queer thing—and this I have heard done by persons whose good Sense in other instances has not been doubted. This tho really a weakness I can now more easily forgive, but hope in company I shall not fall into the same error."[52] The constraints that limited her public discussion of children did not prevail among sisters, and the topic of children figured in their lifelong correspondence. "Nabby . . . Poor Rogue . . . has been very poorly these 3 or 4 Days, cutting teeth I believe. Her cough too is bad again," she informed Mary.[53] The sisters also exchanged practical items: "I send my little Betsy some worsted for a pair of Stockings to go to meeting in." And, "I should be obliged if you would Lend me that quilted contrivance Mrs. Fuller made for Betsy. Nabby Bruses her forehead sadly she is fat as a porpouse and falls heavey."[54]

The Cranches returned to Braintree in 1775. From that time Abigail and Mary were neighbors, except for the years when the Adamses lived abroad or in the nation's capitals. During the crucial years of John's absence, during the Revolutionary War, Abigail lived near Mary. In values, in religion, in politics, the older sisters mirrored one another, resulting in endless and easy communications. Even the social gap that developed as Abigail's husband gained public stature, while Richard Cranch's fortunes declined, did not strain that connection, in part because Mary's generous nature and religious acceptance afforded her the fortitude to surmount pettiness of spirit. And when Mary died in 1811, seven years before her own death, Abigail's demonstrations of grief exceeded only those she had expressed at her mother's death more than a quarter-century before. Her distress in both cases signified a fundamental loss in her sense of well-being.

Kinkeepers

For a time after 1781, John Adams's position—though not his loyalty—became ambiguous; his public zeal was challenged and once more outmatched his concern for his family's fortunes. With the British defeat at Yorktown in October, the campaign had shifted from the battlefields to the negotiating rooms of Paris, and John would be a principal figure. Indeed this had been his whole purpose in traveling to Europe in 1779, but political complications within the peace mission and in Congress resulted in a delay of his instructions; distance further complicated the situation. So while John impatiently awaited the arrival of his commission, he negotiated with Abigail.

She wished him to return home: "Permit me, my Dearest Friend to renew that Companionship—my heart sighs for it—I cannot O! I cannot be reconciled to living as I have for 8 years past."[55] Typically weighing his "zeal for his country" against his private ties, John responded: "If it were only an Affair of myself and my family I would not accept a commission if sent. But I consider it a public point of Honour."[56] For two years the Adamses negotiated. "Come to me with your daughter," he suggested. But as months passed and no word arrived from Congress, he shifted: "I am determined not to wait . . . but to come home," he announced, adding, "provided it does not arrive in a reasonable Time."[57] By the fall of 1783, their positions could not have been further apart. Abigail wrote, "if Congress should think proper to make you another appointment, I beg you not to accept it."[58] Almost simultaneously John was writing, "My life is sweetened with the hope of Embracing you in Europe. Pray, embark as soon as prudent."[59]

Abigail's reservations about traveling to Europe were manifold. She expressed not only her apprehensions about the hardships and dangers of sea travel, but other concerns as well: "I think if you were abroad in a private character," she wrote, "I should not hesitate so much at coming to you, but a mere Armenian as I am, unacquainted with the etiquette of courts, taught to say the things I mean, and wear my heart on my countenance, I am sure I would make an awkward figure, and then it would mortify my pride if I should be thought to disgrace you."[60]

Several issues at home further complicated her thinking. Her daughter's courtship with Royall Tyler had become serious, and without John's approval, she was reluctant to confirm their betrothal. In addition, there was the issue of what to do with her younger sons. Charles, who was 12 years old in 1782, had previously traveled with John and John Quincy to Europe in 1779 and, overwhelmed by loneliness, had made a hazardous return journey alone. Clearly it would be folly to uproot Charles once again, particularly as his education was reaching the critical stage in preparation for college. Thomas, two years younger, had never consciously known his father, but to take him would isolate Charles once more, as well as disrupt Thomas's schooling. To solve this dilemma, Abigail turned to her sister.

By 1782 Elizabeth had become the mother of a son and baby daughter whose care overwhelmed her. She complained to Mary: "If Ideas present themselves to my Mind, it is too much like the good seed sown among Thorns. they are soon crazed and swallowed up . . . by the wants and noise of my Family and Children. . . . The bad writing," she continued, "you must impute to my rocking the Cradle."[61] Elizabeth's responsibilities further extended to managing the parsonage and caring for Reverend Shaw's pupils. Some time that year, Abigail began to explore the possibility of placing Charles and Thomas with the Shaws in the event of her going to Europe. Abigail's choice of the harried Elizabeth as caretaker for her sons had to do with her trusting not only Elizabeth, but ironically, the Reverend John Shaw as well.

Elizabeth, responding as amanuensis for her husband to Abigail's request that he serve as "Preceptor" to "my dear nephews," cited at length the advantages of their boarding with the Shaws. It was common in other circumstances, she noted, for student boarders to be "sent into the Kitchen to herd among themselves. By this method their whole subsequent Lives have a tincture of awkwardness which the politeness of a Court could not eradicate." She noted that they could consequently develop "a low opinion of themselves. . . . feel conscious of a wrong that depresses their spirits and make them dread of going into polite company." Elizabeth's direful speculations about the effects of the kitchen on the psyche were intended to confirm Abigail's selection of herself as caretaker. She further established that her charges would have a "sufficient supply of Beef, pork, corn, rice, butter, milk." They would be given a good chamber with a good bed and bedding and would lodge together. Further, she would have a desk made for them.[62]

Elizabeth's exhortations betrayed her eagerness to receive her Adams nephews; their coming to her was a way of affirming her relationship with Abigail and of legitimating Shaw's position in the family. Her nephews, she reassured Abigail, "would have the watchfulness of parents" of "tender parental affection" within the Shaw household. Elizabeth tended always to oversell herself with her older sisters, never quite confident of her status among them.

At the same time, this would be a business arrangement, and the sisters carried on this enterprise in a straightforward manner. "If the children live with us we must be sole arbitors of their company and playmates," Elizabeth stipulated. The terms were "$2 per week for each child including teaching." The high price was necessary, she noted, because of "the high costs of everything these days," and payments could be quarterly.[63]

Abigail's many family dilemmas were solved by her decision to travel to Europe with her daughter. She would be reunited with John and become reacquainted with her eldest son who had grown into manhood during the five years since she had seen him. The separation would further test the strength of Nabby's affections for Royall Tyler. The one great wrench for Abigail was leaving her young sons. "Our two Sons go on Monday . . . to Haverhill; there to be under the care and tuition of Mr. Shaw. I have done the best I could with them," she wrote to John before her departure.[64] Elizabeth witnessed her sister's painful departure. "Ah! My sister," she wrote to Mary, "My spirit was witness to the Parting Scene . . . I saw the struggle in the Parents Br—st—the absolute necessity—." Elizabeth noted deep emotions by silence.[65]

Charles and Thomas lived with the Shaws until they both entered Harvard, and a tradition was initiated in which Elizabeth and her husbands—Shaw in his lifetime and later Stephen Peabody—boarded her nephews and prepared them for Harvard. John Quincy Adams, after he returned to America in 1785, lived with the Shaws for almost a year until he was accepted for advanced standing at Harvard. A generation later his sons, George and John, boarded with the Peabodys at Atkinson, New Hampshire, while John Quincy and his wife, Louisa Catherine, lived in St. Petersburg during John Quincy's service as American minister to the Russian court. Elizabeth's household, furthermore, became the preparatory school for generations of nephews. Mary's grandsons, both Nortons and Cranches, came to Atkinson for preparation, as did Abigail's grandsons, William and John Smith, Nabby's sons. The attraction was certainly that the children would receive excellent training in Greek, Latin, and mathematics—but overriding that issue were kinship and the confidence and respect that generations of her relatives had for Elizabeth.[66]

The term "kinkeeping" has been used to describe the pivotal role of women in holding together and exercising guardianship for an extended family.[67] As eighteenth-century families became mobile and separated, and as ties among family members became tenuous, it was women who exercised the functions that kept alive extended family bonds, not just because of loyalty or for ceremonial purposes, but because the support that family members provided for each other was indispensable. Mary, Abigail, and Elizabeth supported each other's families in different ways; each was a kin keeper to the other. As sisters, their caretaking was reciprocal, though often asymmetrically across generations. Elizabeth became the surrogate parent to generations of her family's sons who were sent to be educated in her husbands' academies.

"I take the same prudent care of [Charles and Thomas] that I think you would," Elizabeth wrote to reassure Abigail after her departure.[68] "Thomas is a very good child," she wrote later. "[H]e does not want for fondling over because you are absent, he has many a fine stroke and kiss upon that account." Again, she wrote, "Cousin Charles has outgrown all his [clothes] and Thomas must have them. I have made them both winter coats."[69] Her pride when Charles was accepted at Harvard was expressed in an anecdote. When he and Reverend Shaw returned from Cambridge after his examination, "they put on long faces and attempted to look very *trist* when they rode into the yard, but I could easily discern by their countenances . . . that joy and satisfaction played sweetly at their hearts."[70] Elizabeth was intrigued by John Quincy when he arrived, commenting that "there never was a youth that bore a greater resemblance to both parents."[71] The next spring she wrote to Abigail, "Should I my Dear Sister, too much alarm the Heart of an affectionate Mother . . . if I were to say plainly—That I wish Mr. JQA had never left Europe—that he had never come into our Family . . . Then we should not have had this occasion of sorrow—His leaving it— Indeed my Sister our House looks gloomy now he has left it. Mr. Shaw & I feel the loss of him more than of any Pupil that has ever lived with us."[72] Abigail had correctly judged that her children would be loved and cared for as well as educated in Elizabeth Shaw's home.

Twenty-five years later, Abigail sent her grandsons to Elizabeth. "George and John I must commit to your care. they have not been kept so regular this summer, as they ought to have been."[73] Originally John Quincy and Louisa Catherine had left their older two sons to board with the Cranches, but because of Mary Cranch's illness and the many stresses within the Adamses' household, Abigail decided to send them to Elizabeth. "I hope they will not give you any unnecessary trouble. . . . English Grammar for John before he commences Lattin. George will pursue his studies in Lattin and greek . . . there entrance money will be sent with them. and we shall expect to pay the same as others."[74]

As the Shaws educated the Adams sons, the Cranch home had become the gathering place for them during their Harvard vacations. "Our children are so happy together that I can scarce forbear a sigh," Mary wrote to Abigail. She also visited them at Harvard where her son William roomed with John Quincy for a time. "I was at Cambridge sometimes in the Vacancy to see Cousin JQA. he was well and quite a gallant among the Ladies. Cousin Thomas is a great favorite. . . . Cousin Charles is a lovely creature. He is so amiable and so attentive that he will be beloved wherever he sets his Foot."[75] Mary's misfortunes embarrassed her: "My dear sister I have been obliged to do what give me great pain. The troublesome times into which we have fallen have deprived Mr. Cranch of the possibility of getting one shilling from the publick of what is due to him for his service . . . by which means I find it impossible to provide Food for our Family during the vacancys without taking something for the Board of my dear Nephews. It has given me more disagreeable feelings than I can express . . . I have charged 10 shillings a week for each of them."[76]

Kinkeeping operated differently among the young daughters of Mary, Elizabeth, and Abigail. It was common for girls to visit, indeed live with, relatives for extended periods. Elizabeth thanked Mary for news of little Betsy Shaw who was staying with her aunt, admitting, "She never lodged out of her house before, and I feel that her absence touched some maternal strings, that never before were in motion." Elizabeth missed her little daughter.[77] The following August, Lucy Cranch visited at Haverhill.[78] Betsy Smith, daughter of the derelict brother William Smith, lived for many years with Elizabeth, who confessed, "She is like a daughter to me"; her sister Louisa became a lifelong member of Abigail's household. "My neice I must send to her mother," Abigail wrote before departing for Europe.[79]

Strong ties, both emotional and intellectual, existed between aunts and nieces, attested to in their correspondence. Writing to Nabby, Elizabeth observed that she could not agree with Rousseau's appraisal of women: "For he asserts that all women are naturally Coquettes—which if allowed . . . all women must have a considerable share of Vanity and Presumption." Indignantly, she concluded that all of his ideas were "Chimeral and scemes."[80] After her daughter's marriage, Abigail in London felt lonely: "I wish I had my little neice here. I should find an amusement which I really want."[81] She wrote lengthy letters to her nieces, Elizabeth and Lucy Cranch, describing life abroad, advising them on manners and literature as an expression of her affection. Elizabeth returned: "I think of your cheerful fireside—which used to afford me great pleasure—but I think of it now with tears. Variety and pleasure have now flown."[82] Kinkeeping functioned in different dimensions among the sisters. Because she lived in the neighborhood, Mary became a caretaker of the Adams household. "Your things at your cottage are in as good a situation as I could expect," she wrote to Abigail in London. "Everything is done we could to preserve everything from the moths. Your cloth and carpet are both safe."[83]

During the vice presidential and presidential years, Abigail traveled back and forth from Braintree to Philadelphia and New York, and for one season, to the new capital city of Washington. Mary, during those years, served many roles to Abigail. "You must write me every week," Abigail wrote repeatedly, requesting Mary's attention.[84]

Abigail in turn could disclose her misfortunes and pleasures and receive sympathy. She confessed grief over Charles's alcoholism and her daughter's difficult marriage, as well as her pride in John Quincy, the delight of Thomas's dancing party in the presidential house. Mary became her alter ego as one woman empathizing with the trials of another—in a way that John Adams could not, because he was more connected to public service. From Philadelphia she described for Mary an incident with her husband, the president: "I yesterday about 11 oclock went into the Presidents Room to see if John had returned from the post office. My good Gentleman was soberly standing at the fire with your Letter open and very gravely reading it. I scolded and very soon carried it of." He had invaded their private realm, innocently, perhaps in curiosity or envy, and she evicted him.[85]

Because there was no need to affect manners among sisters, Abigail's instructions to Mary were direct. As she had many years earlier eschewed polite form in her ill-advised warnings to Elizabeth against Shaw, she hardly disguised her orders to Mary: "I want to hear from you again. . . . I will thank you to get from the table draw [*sic*] in the parlour some Annetts [dill] and give it to Mrs. Burrel. . . . In my best chamber closset I left a white Bonnet. Be so kind as to take it and give it for me to Mrs. Norton. In a small wooden Box is a new crape cap which I designd to have sent. . . . In my Bathing machine you will find a peice of canvass which will cover the Box. You will have it addrest & give it into Mr. Smiths care who will send it to me."[86]

Abigail was not alone either meddling in private affairs or expressing herself directly. "You never can live in that house when you return," Mary wrote, advising Abigail to purchase a grander home than the Braintree cottage. "It is not large enough for you. You cannot crowd your sons into a little bed by the side of yours now." She continued to press her case: "Mr. Adams will be employed in public business. . . . That house will not be large enough for you."[87] The sisterly prose style signified trust and intimacy. They were kin keeping. Within the scope of connections, sisterhood was as vital as motherhood and wifehood.

Among the sisters, only Abigail rose to a privileged social position, a status that they each acknowledged differently. All were impressed. In various ways they struggled to suppress the differences that would separate them. Elizabeth, who was more isolated by distance and by age, struggled to cancel the differences. "I believe there never were three Sisters more generally alike in the Opinions of Things than we," she wrote in her effort to identify with the others.[88] A few years later she capitulated to the change, and nostalgia pervaded her confession to Mary after Abigail departed for New York: "I fear she will always be moving from us—She is so connected in public Life, & must have so large a Sphere to act in that it is not likely we shall ever have that sweet enjoyment in still domestic Life which we used to experience in the private Circle of dear Friends—."[89] Whereas Elizabeth's diffidence towards Abigail was reinforced by her fame, Mary's position as the eldest and maternal sister was secured by tradition. Abigail turned to her for reassurance from her new and lofty position as wife of the first vice president of the constitutional nation: "If at any time [you] perceive any alteration in me . . . arising . . . from my situation in Life, I beg [you] would with the utmost freedom acquaint me with it. I do not feel within myself the least disposition of the kind, but I know mankind are prone to deceive themselves."[90]

Over the years Abigail used her status—both public and economic—to assist her sisters. Elizabeth was always paid for taking care of nephews, though none of them considered taking nieces as an economic exchange. Abigail purchased Elizabeth's portion of their parents' Medford estate after their father's death, perhaps providing financial assistance to Elizabeth. She directly gave money to Mary, responding to her protests: "Do not talk of oblagations. Reverse the matter & think yourself if you would not do as much for me?"[91] A decade later, she repeated the same message for some kindness performed: "You estimate much too highly the little services I am able to render . . . and you depreciate the value of your own."[92] And for many years, both Elizabeth's and Mary's sons received political favors because of the Adams connection. Young William Shaw became John's secretary during his presidency, and for years afterwards, Abigail looked after his well-being during his infirmities in Boston.

The fortunes of Mary's son William Cranch were for many years in jeopardy, and it was Abigail who repeatedly came to his rescue.[93] Ultimately, young William became one of the three midnight judge appointments made by John Adams during the last hours of his presidency, a position that William held with distinction for half a century. Kinkeeping among sisters operated reciprocally through several generations.

Ironically, within this women's network, the female offspring benefited less materially from kinkeeping after their marriages. Because women functioned within the private sphere, aunts, like mothers, were better able to administer domestic than effective economic assistance, reinforcing women's dependence upon the men they married. Abigail provided a fund of small personal gifts as well as gifts of charity to her nieces, sending items of clothing as well as cash. Her dresses frequently were handed down to her nieces. Abigail could no more provide for the impoverished Lucy Cranch Norton in her worst distress, than she could rescue her own daughter from financial disasters.[94] The limitation of women's world to the domestic sphere circumscribed the assistance they could give to each other. Since women could give away to other women only that which they owned—which in the late eighteenth century did not include property or public power—they gave of themselves.

Kin Work

The function of kinkeeping operated within the scope of women's social world as a mechanism of important mutual assistance; it also gave identity, dignity, and even power to women's work of caretaking. Kin work, as opposed to kinkeeping, refers to the ritual aspects of maintaining extended family ties, work performed mostly by women.[95]

Letter writing was the primary means by which the sisters maintained their ties when they lived apart. They visited and they sent messages by travelers, but in their letters they described the texture of their lives on a regular basis. "What, no Letters from Quincy," Abigail wrote in dismay from Philadelphia. "You can hardly judge how impatient I feel if I do not hear once a week."[96] And again, "You must write to me once a week certainly, no matter whether you have a subject of more concequence than our mere domestick affairs." And she suggested a topic, "How does the building go on? Have you seen it lately?"[97] Elizabeth, too, pressed Mary for letters: "You cannot think how anxious I have been to hear from my Sister Adams and You," she wrote.[98]

The sisters' correspondence rarely conformed to Abigail's ideal of once a week, especially during the early years when all were preoccupied with babies and housekeeping; most of the letters that survive were written between Abigail and Mary, perhaps reflecting their closer relationship, or perhaps the typical attrition of letters over centuries. Their letters substituted for their conversations: "How often I have wished to be near you that we might mutually comfort and assist each other," Elizabeth lamented to Mary.[99] When they wrote to a sister, their worlds took on reality and importance. Primarily they wrote about ordinary experiences and concerns that made up their daily lives, but they also wrote—apologetically because it violated some female code of propriety—with depth and wisdom about politics and the economy.

Gossip in all its forms provided a major focus of their correspondence over the years. By writing about people, they recreated the context of their daily lives and achieved a kind of intimacy that comes from telling stories. They gossiped about their families, about their friends and neighbors, about the nation's leaders, and about each other. They also wrote about literature and politics, farms and travel, their thoughts and feelings, but mostly they wrote about what affected their lives as women—which was other people.[100]

Whenever Abigail was away, Mary kept her informed: "Mr. Bordon is married to Mrs. Arnold and is gone to live in her house. Mrs. Arnold's eldest son is married to Deacon Adams eldest daughter and lives in the house that Mr. Bass sold."[101] An analysis is a component of good gossip, they judged: "We live in an age of discovery—one of our acquaintances has discovered that a full-grown fine child may be produced in less than five months as well as in nine."[102] A favorite butt of their gossip for many decades was their local minister: "Parson Wibird visits me every other day. He still lives in that vile house. I told him the other day that nobody but he could live in it. . . . That house is so scandalous that in Boston the selectmen would tear it down."[103]

Elizabeth described the texture of country life: Polly Harrod, her "near neighbor and very intimate friend" in Haverhill had "wasted many years" waiting for her lover, who had experienced an "unhappy part in public affairs." Despite her many other suitors, "she mourned like a turtle dove her absent mate. . . . And what a Brute must he have been not to have received her with grateful and extended Arms—," but eventually they were reunited and happy. Thus, Elizabeth concluded with a moral: "the sacrifices she had made were fully compensated by the happiness she was then in possession of."[104] Whether Mary had ever met or knew of Polly Harrod was irrelevant, since Elizabeth's motive was to describe what was important about her life and acquaintances to a sister who was thoroughly interested.

None of the sisters, of course, could match Abigail for gossip. Compared with the Wibirds and the Arnolds, her sources were spectacular, but her purpose for reporting was the same; she needed to explain her experience and be understood. Presented to the Queen of England, Abigail reported to Mary that Charlotte was "not well shaped or handsome," and "as to the ladies of the Court, rank and title may compensate for want of personal charm; but they are in general, very plain, ill-shaped and ugly." She added, "Don't you tell any body I say so."[105] In contrast, Abigail was charmed by Martha Washington: "She received me with great ease & politeness. She is plain in her dress, but that plainness is the best of every article. . . . Her hair is white, her Teeth beautifull, her person rather short than otherways, hardly so large as my Ladyship, and if I was to speak sincerly, I think she is a much better figure. Her manners are modest and unassuming, dignified and femenine, not the Tincture of Ha'ture about her."[106]

Their letters to each other substituted for conversations in which they confessed their most intimate concerns, and in return they received encouragement. "My dear Sister some parts of your Letter made me melancholy," Abigail responded to Mary. "I know very well that a small Farm must afford you a scanty support . . . but I know your prudence & occonomy has carried you along, tho not in affluence, yet with decency and comfort, and I hope you will still be able to live so. . . . Do not look upon the gloomy side only."[107] She continued to cheer Mary by reminding her of the many blessings in life and concluded with an offer of a loan.

Family ties were maintained by correspondence. In letters the sisters recreated the landscape of their lives, so that despite the distances they traveled from each other or the years that separated them between visits, they remained familiar and familial. Their stories described the world as they encountered it and as they wished it to be viewed by those closest to them. Their responses reinforced the validity of their stories, which, after all, comprises one function of family life, the sharing of a belief system that derived from an historic connection to each other.

Spheres and Connections

Abigail and her sisters had been connected to politics since childhood. Their maternal grandfather Quincy had devoted his life to public service; indeed, their Quincy family was immersed in the world of politics.[108] Mary and Abigail had married men who practiced politics professionally. All of them had learned an ideology and rhetoric of politics, and as especially articulate women, they entered the proscribed arena, knowing that to talk and write about politics was daring. "Excuse my being so busy in [politics] but I am so connected with them that I cannot avoid being much interested," Abigail wrote from London.[109] "These are dull subjects for one lady to write another upon," Mary apologized for writing about local politics to Abigail, "but our country is so much interested in these affairs that you must excuse me for troubling with them."[110] The affairs that Mary described would affect the Cranches and the Adamses differently.

During the late summer of 1786, news of popular discontent in western Massachusetts began to reach the Adamses, who were living in London. "People will not pay taxes nor debts of any kind," Mary Cranch complained to Abigail. "Mr. Cranch has been working for the public for three years and never received any salary." He was owed some three hundred pounds, she admitted, but where there were no taxes, there was no treasury. She feared poverty. "Mr. Cranch thinks of coming home to mend watches and farm."[111] What Mary was describing to Abigail was the prelude to Shays' Rebellion, an uprising that would occur in the winter of 1786–1787 in western Massachusetts, led by Revolutionary War veteran Daniel Shays, to protest the depressed conditions that western farmers especially experienced, but which prevailed generally at the conclusion of the war. To citizens of the eastern part of the state, like the Cranches and the Shaws, it appeared that a second rebellion of the dimensions of the Revolution might develop. During the last months of 1786 and the new year, Abigail's sisters provided her with a major fund of information about economic and political conditions at home, as well as their appraisals of the ominous situation.[112]

She would make no apologies for writing to Abigail about politics, Mary continued, because as wives of a minister and a senator, they shared an interest in events. Furthermore, as her family had become impoverished as result of her husband's unremunerated public service—Cranch had been elected to the state Senate from Braintree—she was angry. Inspired by anger, she entered the political arena by writing to Abigail.

Mary had a novel idea: "Let no one say that the Ladies are of no importance in the affairs of the nation. Perswaide them to renounce all their Luxirys and it would be found that they are—and believe me there is not a more affectual way to do it than to make them acquainted with the causes of the distresses of their country—we do not want spirit. we only want to have it properly directed."[113] Mary's idea was novel not because the issue of a boycott was new or because she had not previously boycotted tea. The novelty stemmed from Mary's expression of so radical a position—that women could be organized to exercise power—that within the scope of the domestic world, the means of exercising economic and thus political power existed. For Mary this acknowledgment represented a bold step. She did not, however, write, speak, or organize publicly, for she was constrained by her vision of women's place in the private sphere. Her radicalism was confined to writing to her sisters.

Months later, reacting to the uprising of some two thousand farmers and its easy suppression by the state militia, Mary commented: "Shays and his party are a poor deluded people. They have given much trouble and put themselves and us to much expence and have greatly added to the difficulties they complain of."[114] Elizabeth concurred, and she too voiced her opinion that the rebellion had been "dictated by Fear, Ignorance, Malice,

Envy and Self-interest the most powerful of all. . . . No one is willing to believe themselfs the Cause of any Evil they feel," she persisted, "but attribute it to the weakness and perfidy of government." And she expressed her sympathy for "those who head the government." Elizabeth, not attached to politics by marriage, was less secure about the legitimacy of her commentary: "But I will quit politics and leave them to the Gentlemen who I presume give you a much more particular account."[115]

Elizabeth's modesty reflected the common litany of amends that marked women's venture into the male domain. Abigail repeatedly expressed the same reservations in her early correspondence, but less frequently, and, one suspects, with less conviction over the years. Her reflections about Shays contained no apologies: "An unprincipled mob is the worst of all tyrannies," she responded to Elizabeth. "Shame to our citizens that they wish to curtail the salary of our governor. do they want to make him a man of straw?"[116] And to Mary she wrote that she wished to return "and share the fate of our country—whether she stand like Mt. Atlas. Tis treason to harbour an idea that she will fall. Trip and stumble I fear . . . she shall not fall."[117]

Abigail and her sisters were unanimous in their understanding that politics belonged to the public sphere. Like their gossiping about other people, they entered a world where they did not belong, their exchanges satisfying their need to analyze and sealing a bond among them. As their gossip revealed something about their world and their place in it, so did their political exchanges. Elizabeth, who was least attached to politics, commented the least. Mary wrote for two reasons: to inform Abigail about events that developed in her absence, but primarily to describe the way that events touched her life. Her most eloquent statements grew out of her own hardships in consequence to political issue—political developments as she experienced them firsthand. And Abigail, most prolific of all on the topic of politics, described the effect of her sharing John Adams's world.[118]

Abigail's ideology was partisan, reflecting the politics of her husband, and later those of her son. She became their best ally and exponent, which meant that, as caretaker, she entered their worlds not only domestically but intellectually as well. While she contested some of their ambitions and offices, she never contradicted their political positions. This, in turn, meant that she was frequently defensive—explaining, complaining, and comforting. Her audience was narrow; among her women friends, only one, Mercy Otis Warren, shared her political consciousness.[119] To her sisters, however, and especially to Mary, she wrote openly about what was happening in John's world.

Mary, in fact, received up-to-date accounts on events as they developed—classified information, so to speak—because Abigail needed to describe her world to her sisters. Her disclosures were embedded in a context of social activities, gossip, requests for items or favors, and reports about her health. Politics did not take precedence; they were part of the fabric of her life because she was married to a statesman and because she shared her whole life's activities and thoughts with her sisters.

"I am sorry to learn that Cousin Betsy has a Cough," she wrote from Philadelphia in 1798. "I expect your next Letter will bear me the melancholy tidings of Suky Warners death. . . . Tell Cousin Betsy if her cough does not soon mend, to lose a few ounces of Blood." The next paragraph continued: "I cannot say what Congress mean to do. The dispatches are but just decypherd. Whether the President will think proper to make any further communications is more than he himself can yet determine, but it must strike every Body, that every thing which might endanger our Envoys, who are still in Paris, for any thing to the contrary . . . must and will be kept Private, clamour who will." Mary was given the insider's view of developments as they occurred during the XYZ Affair.[120] Abigail's letter continued to berate the press for its nasty attacks on her husband, with news about Nabby, and inquiries about various other family members and friends.

Towards the end of her life, Abigail still wrote impassioned political commentary. During President Madison's administration, the nation was once more at war with Britain, and the people were divided in its support. The Adamses supported Mr. Madison's War. Elizabeth, it appears, was opposed. Abigail justified the war in religious terms, perhaps because she was more religiously expressive in her old age, or because she was addressing Elizabeth. In elaborate metaphors, she explained why this war was ordained by God.

Good, Abigail explained a paradox, often appeared as evil. In the sale of Joseph into Egypt by his wicked brothers, "they meant it unto him for evil but God meant it for good." She continued, "I am one of those who believe in the rightness and justice of the present war with Great Britain. it was become necessary to preserve that independence and to defend it. as the former War. was to obtain it." She lamented the "invasion of Canady," but the means must justify the end. "I do sincerely pray for Peace," she concluded, reaching her compelling point, "and great indeed would be my joy if my Dear son may be an instrument in the hand of providence for accomplishing it" (which indeed he was). In her old age as in her youth, Abigail offered a familiar vindication for writing about politics: "And now my dear sister to quit a subject in which I am personally so much interested. I will say a few words upon domestic concerns."[121]

Political action belonged to the public sphere of men, and to talk about politics breached social convention for late eighteenth-century women. Otherwise, Abigail and her sisters would not have needed to apologize, especially to each other, for indulging in political commentary. Abigail, furthermore, would have written more freely to other women on this topic. They understood that their connection to politics was indirectly derived through their relationships to men, and while they breached convention, they did not usually complain about this restriction to their sex.[122] They did not envy men, because they respected themselves and considered domestic work as great a contribution from their own sphere. Religion, perhaps, offered them the best explanation for the existence of two spheres, each separate and necessary to the functioning of this world. "Men nor women were not made to think alike—it cannot be," wrote Mercy Otis Warren to Abigail.[123] Among a community of sisters, this was a source of pride.

In the end, despite the differences that developed among them owing to age, marriages, children, war, travel, death, poverty, fame, and work, Abigail saw herself bound to sisters by history, tradition, experience, trust, interests, loyalty, identity, need, generosity, and love. When Mary died in 1811, she grieved in every letter she wrote, and Elizabeth mourned, "My dearly beloved and only sister . . . the threefold *silken cord is broken.*"[124] Abigail outlived Elizabeth to claim herself as the "only Sister," the "last bond of union, of the ancient Stock; the last ligament which bound her to Earth."[125] Abigail lived for three years more.

The Elements of Sisterhood

Sisterhood represented a special kind of connection for Abigail, Elizabeth, and Mary. In their correspondence, the protocols of epistolary style were absent, but other social barriers were absent as well. The intimacy of the bond afforded freedom in ways that few other relationships permitted. Because their family history bestowed upon them a shared identity, they could be critical, argumentative, or uncomplimentary without giving lasting offense. They expected favors from each other that would have been extraordinary impositions in contexts outside the family. They confessed to conditions about themselves—their health and their feelings—that would have been inappropriate elsewhere. They gossiped abundantly and without inhibitions. They cared for each other's well-being and as an extension the well-being of each other's children. They appreciated each other's triumphs and celebrated life's transitions. Always, they were each other's most trusted allies in a world that they understood could be hostile. Neither geographical distance nor social class, when it separated them, dissipated the bond of being born sisters. This is the metaphor in its best sense, as it was experienced by Abigail and her sisters. This represents the ideal that is projected by the concept of "sisterhood."

At a time when she was feeling lonely and separated from her sisters, Elizabeth confessed to Mary: "There is really something so pleasing, so tender in a sisters care and pity, as stills the nerves as cannot be described by anything, but by what we experienced from our mother's affectionate Tenderness."[126] Elizabeth identified the essence of sisterhood. Only among her sisters, she claimed, did she sense a return to that most elementary of bonds, that with her mother. The concept of "sisters" carries an automatic reference to those feelings best remembered from infancy and childhood—"tender" or nurturant qualities that suggest connection—dependency, trust, caring, and even identity. From her experience, Elizabeth discerned and described the nature of her relationship with her sisters as resembling that which she remembered with her mother.

The term "sisters" is used in contemporary literature as a metaphor for caring relationships; analytically, it more often describes a code of behavior among women friends.[127] Feminist scholars concur that connections among women grew strong in a society that clearly differentiated between female and male worlds, that the development of female friendships flourished within women's separate world and served as a validating subculture for women.[128] Elizabeth Smith Shaw's observation takes the issue a step further by suggesting the essential nature of the relationship.

By summoning a memory of her mother's love to describe how she and her sisters felt about each other, Elizabeth too invoked an ideal.[129] Yet memory of a mother's tenderness can hardly be separated from the issue of a mother's authority. Elizabeth selectively remembered her mother's affection, while suppressing another memory, the years that she sacrificed her own happiness to care for her aging parents. That suppressed memory bears witness to the power gap in the parent-child relationship. Motherhood implies authority as much as it implies affection.[130] Sisterhood is freed from the memory of authority. Elizabeth, by restricting her memory to "tender affection," could describe what she needed from sisterhood—an ideal of caring and care-taking that was reciprocal. Her ideal was still drawn from a powerful memory, that of maternal nurturance.

The contemporary concept of "sisterhood" is premised on the same ideal of a caring relationship that is reciprocal, but it differs in several respects from kinship born in blood. Sisters as kin are durable in a way that "sisters" as friends are not.[131] One way to understand that difference is to appeal to some general rules that anthropologists use to distinguish between kin and non-kin.

There are mechanisms and processes that define the family domain that are "irreducible and indispensable credentials" for kinship, suggests one theorist; they are "assumed everywhere to be axiomatically binding."[132]

Mankind [sic] consists of relatives and strangers. . . . Relatives should interact quite frequently and at least in times of crises and on the occasion of one another's rites of passage. Transactions among them should be carried out in a spirit devoid of commerciality—preferably consisting of sharing, non-reciprocal giving, and bequeathing among closest relatives, or of lending, among more distantly related ones. Among themselves relatives should feel and express emotions of affection or at least amity.[133]

Fundamental to kinship, then, is the notion that "transactions among them should be carried out in a spirit devoid of commerciality," or to restate the premise: "Market behavior and kinship behavior are incompatible." In other words, kin caring is done voluntarily, nonreciprocally, and automatically.

The case for friendship differs. Caring among non-kin is "jural" or contractual as opposed to voluntary. It becomes mandatory for friends to return a favor for a favor received.

> The notion of friendship is founded upon sentiment, but at the same time, the sentiments of the participants must be mutual, for it is a particularistic relationship, not a general attitude. . . . There must be reciprocity in friendship, for failure to reciprocate in action is a denial of reciprocity of sentiment. . . . By definition all friendship must be both sentimental in inspiration and instrumental in effects since there is no other way to demonstrate one's sentiments than through those actions which speak.[134]

This means that friendship is contractual—albeit an unconscious or unwritten contract—that it is premised on mutual exchange of caring, and that it survives only so long as the exchange is complementary and reinforced. Friendship does not survive when one only person is the "one-caring."[135]

Kinship, on the other hand, is freely given. Reciprocity is voluntary; no exchange is mandated or expected. However, since kinship is voluntary, and thus a moral stance, it incorporates the paradox that reciprocity will inherently operate. Moral people return favors because not to do so would cancel their goodness. With kin, reciprocity, furthermore, may function asymmetrically across generations, since kinship endures over time. The model relation of kinship, it is suggested, is one of unity and solidarity—not necessarily affection—but "internal rivalries actual or potential" will be offset by external solidarity. "We do not have to love our kinfolk, but we expect to be able to trust them in ways that are not automatically possible with non-kinfolk."[136]

The point of this as it relates to sisters, such as Abigail, Mary, and Elizabeth, and to the modern concept of "sisterhood" is that kinship is indelible. Despite the differences that exist among sisters, which derive from order of age or social roles, the relationship persists. Because they are based upon sentiment and contract, relationships among friends must continually be reinforced, and they are at risk when confronted with conflict and rivalry. The ideals implied by sisterhood, and by "sisterhood"—equality, trust, caring, and identity—remain ideals, perhaps masking a meaner reality, but also establishing goals that conform to the best utopian visions.

When Elizabeth Shaw wrote to Mary Cranch that "There is something so pleasing, so tender in a sisters care . . . as cannot be described by anything but by what we experienced from our mother," she articulated a deep truth about women. She described an ideal that has permanence in female consciousness, the quest for maternal nurturance. She also glossed the complexity of sisterhood in a way that has persisted as well. That continuity from her experience to the present makes it possible to look at the lives of the three sisters, Abigail, Mary, and Elizabeth for insights into the complexity of sisterhood.

8

Mother and Citizen

In her pioneering analysis of the role of mothering, the poet Adrienne Rich distinguishes between motherhood as an institution and motherhood as experience. The "institution" of motherhood, she explains, is culturally determined, ideologically based, and often distinct to a period of time or a place. It is opposed to the "experience" of motherhood, which represents the concrete, lived, material reality of women as mothers. Separate though they are, the "institution" and the "experience" are nevertheless everywhere interrelated, because experience operates within the institutional parameters that determine the boundaries of behavior. Yet experience remains discrete, worked out differently for every woman, depending upon, among other factors, social conditions and temperament.[1] Still, Rich continues, one historical fact has remained constant: in every culture in recorded time, the "institution" of motherhood has been patriarchally defined and regulated.[2] Institutional motherhood, the ideology and the rules, then, are determined by men.

By patriarchy, Rich, as well as most feminists, means a system in which men are dominant and women are subordinate. It is a "familial-social, ideological, political system" in which men retain power "by force, direct pressure, or through ritual, tradition, law and language, custom, etiquette, education, and the division of labor . . . in which the female is everywhere subsumed under the male."[3] This does not foreclose the use of certain powers by women, but these are delegated and often honorific and serve a conservative function by impressing "patriarchal values" on future generations.[4]

A corollary to this sexual hierarchy is its characteristic idealization of women, the "pedestal" complex, so to speak, the honorific role that professes women's moral superiority. Nowhere has this concept been more prevalent or useful than in its idealization of motherhood. Women as mothers fulfill their "nature" through nurturance and self-sacrifice, which represent the finest intrinsic human moral qualities and values. Within this mystique of motherhood, children become the emblems of success or failure, not just socially, but to the women themselves.

Borrowing Rich's model, which distinguishes between motherhood as institution and experience, and especially its idealization of motherhood, it is possible to shed new light on women's role in early America. In the last decade and a half, the concept of the Republican Mother has gained hegemonic currency as the descriptor of the lives of women in the early American republic. The term lives almost autonomously, sans substance, sans qualifiers. It has become synonymous with "women," used as the self-evident rubric that universally defines and justifies the place of women in the post-revolutionary period. It has in fact become a cipher—a slippery, elusive term that bears historiographic examination.

Originating in the work of Linda Kerber, the appearance of the term in the mid-1970s filled a gap in the intellectual and social history of women for the revolutionary period. As historians of women groped for ways to describe the changes in the quality of women's lives during the upheaval that transformed America from colony to independence, where most men achieved citizenship and agency, it set forth a place for women in an otherwise barren female landscape. It answered the question, What gains did the Revolution achieve for women? Eschewing the negative claim that the Revolution did nothing to change women's lives, the concept of Republican Mother established a case for the limited political agency of women as a consequence of independence.[5]

Surveying the literature of the Enlightenment that provided the theoretical framework of revolutionary and constitutional rhetoric, Kerber's landmark article, "The Republican Mother: Women and the Enlightenment—An American Perspective," concluded that the men, and a few women, of the Enlightenment had no positive role to offer women. Therfore, "In the face of a denial that women might properly participate in the political community at all, there was invented a definition of women's relationship to the state that sought to fill the inadequacies of inherited political theory." In other words, some Americans invented an ideology that "included—hesitantly—a political role for women." It used the "classical formulation of the Spartan Mother who raised sons prepared to sacrifice themselves to the good of the *polis*. It provided an apparent integration of domestic and political behavior, in a formula that masked political purpose by promise of domestic service."[6] The key to the concept of Republican Mother was, as Rich indicated by the idealization of motherhood, the creation of a son who would serve the state.

Given that women were not allowed to vote or hold office, Kerber's argument continued, and that American intellectuals shrank from the option of creating a "vehicle by which women might demonstrate their political competence," some theorists proposed an alternative model by the 1790s. These theorists were Judith Sargent Murray, Susannah Rowson, and Benjamin Rush. They argued for "self-reliance on the part of women," literacy, contempt for the "frivolities of fashion," political responsibility. In short, Kerber concluded, "The model republican woman was a mother." Her life, Kerber continued, "was dedicated to the service of civic virtue; she educated her sons for it; she condemned and corrected her husband's lapses from it."[7] The model describes ideally what Rich has called the "institution" of motherhood, a social formulation for maternal behavior.

Since the mid-1970s, the Republican Mother model has been absorbed into the historical canon on American women, receiving along the way numerous cosmetic elaborations and amplifications. It has been expanded to Republican Wife, probed for its origins, discoverd in novels, promoted in biographies.[8] Still, in its original sense it persists as a merging of the domestic into the political, the private into the public, the personal into the communal—in all, a means of legitimizing women's past by, however limited the scope, elevating the domestic role of women into the masculine political sphere. Republican Mother describes the "institution" of motherhood in the early republic.

The "experience" of motherhood, Rich acknowledged, may be different for every case. Nevertheless, this concept provides a material basis for understanding lives. In this case, the famous mother, Abigail Adams, of a famous statesman, John Quincy Adams, provides an opportunity for the subjective exploration of the mother/son experience over time and even generations. Because a vast and unique correspondence between them exists over the period from the Revolution well into the republican era, the Adamses are well-documented, as well as intriguing, subjects. But also because so much material survives, two periods from their correspondence will serve for the whole: a sequence of years during the Revolution and then later, in the second decade of the nineteenth century. During both of these periods, Abigail and John Quincy were separated by an ocean, and in both cases Abigail wrote motherly advice to her son.

John Adams had traveled to Philadelphia in 1774 as a Massachusetts delegate to the Continental Congress, leaving at home in Braintree Abigail, their four young children, and his two law clerks. Committed to the political protest, and optimistic of its quick and successful outcome, Abigail wrote cheerful letters to John, describing conditions on the home front and her activities. "I have taken a very great fondness for reading Rollin's ancient History since you left me," she wrote, "I find great pleasure and entertainment from it, and I have perswaided Johnny to read me a page or two every day, and hope he will from his desire to oblige me entertain a fondness for it."[9] The substance of Adams's child rearing is told in this statement. At the age of seven, John Quincy was already reading the classics. More to the point was Abigail's approach to teaching her son. She persuaded him to read to her, considering that from his "desire to oblige me," he would be indirectly attracted to history. She counted on the transference from one kind of obligation to another; Abigail expected that Johnny's already keen sense of duty would carry her message about reading history.[10]

Central to eighteenth-century relationships, such as the Adamses, was a legacy of the Puritan family style, a concept of hierarchy and of duties, a family system that Edmund Morgan has described as both tribal and corporate.[11] Permeating the culture, and deriving from the religion, were the principles of place and reciprocal obligations. Every person was positioned in a social space that determined not only privileges but also social dues. Abigail invoked the Puritan notion of "duty" when she plotted the transference of learning from her young son's "desire to oblige me."

The concept of "duty," as Philip Greven has pointed out, was the "dominant theme," the significant motif of "the moderate temperament and religious experience." Children grew up with an intense sense of duty, " a word that implied subordination, deference, and respect, the obligations of inferior persons to superior persons both within the family and the community at large." Duty further described the "sense of connection and of relationships that shaped . . . consciousness"; it ensured that "each set of relationships would be governed by rules of decorum and obedience while also sustaining a sense of reciprocity. Duty symbolized the maintenance of position and place within the familial order by asserting both the obligations of obedience and the limitations upon the exercise of authority and power."[12] Abigail Adams *unconsciously* depended upon duty as the medium of her child-rearing practice because she had *consciously* trained her children from earliest infancy to a sense of duty.

Therefore when she encouraged her eldest son at the age of eleven to accompany John to Europe in 1778, and again in 1779, it was because she believed it to be her duty to provide him with a unique educational opportunity.[13] "It is a very dificult task my dear son for a tender parent to bring their mind to part with a child of your years into a distant Land [but] You have arrived at years capable of improving under advantages you will be like to have if you do but properly attend to them," she wrote after his departure in 1778. "You are in possession of a natural good understanding and of spirits unbroken by adversity, and untamed with care," she candidly catalogued his talents, before reminding him of the obligations this entailed: "Improve your understanding for acquiring usefull knowledge and virtue, such as will render you an ornament to society, an Honour to your Country, and a Blessing to your parents."

Thus, in one grand swoop, Abigail organized John Quincy's obligations:

to society at large, to his country, and to his parents. Its overarching source resonated in her admonition to "Adhere to those religious Sentiments and principals which were early instilled into your mind and remember that you are accountable to your Maker for all your words and actions." She concluded with a finale that, while it registered Abigail's deep religious conviction, may appear harsh to twentieth-century sensibilities: "I had much rather you should have found your Grave in the ocean you have crossd, or any untimely death crop you in your Infant years, rather than see you an immoral profligate or a Graceless child."[14] Thus Abigail explained reciprocal duties, hers to send him abroad and advise him, and his to fulfill his talents, to become useful in the social, civic, and familial spheres.

It was never easy for Abigail to part with her children. To a friend she wrote: "And now cannot you imagine me seated by my fire side Bereft of my better Half and added to that a Limb lopt of to heighten the anquish. In vain have I summoned philosiphy, its aid is vain. Come then Religion thy force can alone support the mind under the severest trials and hardest conflicts humane Nature is subject to."[15] Still she sent her sons abroad once more in 1779, again because of the educational opportunities of European travel, but again too, because in the long run education would enable them to best discharge their social obligations. "If I had thought your reluctance arose from proper deliberation, or that you was capable of judgeing what was most for your own benifit, I should not have urged you to have accompanied your Father and Brother when you appeared so averse to the voyage," Abigail wrote John Quincy, carrying on the debate after his departure, still justifying her role. "You however readily submitted to my advice, and I hope will never have occasion yourself, nor give me reason to Lament it." Then she persisted at length to outline the advantages of learning languages and of travel. "These are times in which a Genious would wish to live," she perceptively observed, and went on to cite as models Cicero and Mark Antony.[16]

Abigail went to further lengths to explain to John Quincy his obligation to reap the advantages of his journey. Referring to the harrowing sea voyage that carried their little ship to the coast of Spain—barely—instead of France, she wrote: "You have seen how inadequate the aid of Man would have been, if the winds and seas had not been under the particular goverment of that Being who streached out the Heavens as a span, who holdeth the ocean in the hollow of his hand, and rideth upon the wings of the wind." And she continued: "If you have a due sense of your preservation, your next consideration will be, for what purpose you are continued in Life?—"

Then having set herself up to answer her own question, citing duties owed for privileges given, Abigail persisted to provide a concise but forceful formula for his life: "[E]very new Mercy you receive is a New Debt upon you, a new *obligation* to a diligent discharge of the various relations in which you stand connected; in the first place to your Great Preserver, in the next to Society in General, in particular to your Country, to your parents and to yourself." Abigail proceeded, then, to the exegesis of her own advice. "The only sure and permanant foundation of virtue is Religion. Let this important truth be engraven upon your Heart, and that the foundation of Religion is Belief of the one only God, and a just sense of his attrubutes as a Being infinately wise, just, and good, to whom you *owe* the highest Reverence," after which she explained to her young son that the way to discharge his obligations was in the "performance of certain duties which tend to the happiness and welfare of Society" expressed in one short sentence: "Thou shalt Love thy Neighbour as thyself."[17] In the short run, then, John Quincy could show his gratitude for having survived the dreadful sea voyage by diligently developing himself so that as a man he could repay his obligations through public service.

"Justice, humanity and Benevolence are the duties you owe to society in general." But Abigail went further: "To your Country the same duties are incumbent upon you with the additional obligation of sacrificeing ease, pleasure, wealth and life itself for its defence and security." Abigail—operating from within a religiously prescribed social/familial tradition—was teaching civic responsibility before there was a republic. She went further still: "To your parent you owe Love, reverence and obedience to all just and Equitable commands." And finally in her list of duties—"To yourself—here indeed is a wide Field to expatiate upon. To become what you ought to be and, what a fond Mother wishes to see you, attend to some precepts and instructions from the pen of one who can have no motive but your welfare and happiness, and who wishes in this way to supply to you, the personal watchfulness and care which a seperation from you, deprives you of at a period of Life when habits are easiest acquired. . . ." The vigilant mother continued to issue injunctions, analyses, and predictions, citing the dangers of self-deception, self-love, and passions. She called upon reason to control nature. "Virtue alone is happiness below," she stated, meaning on earth. And she concluded: "I will not over burden your mind at this time." Her conclusion extended, while she confessed that she meant to continue the subject of "Self-knowledge" at some other time and "give you my Sentiments upon your future conduct in life."[18]

Abigail's letters are replete with advice to her son: "Be dutifull my dear Son, be thoughtfull, be serious, do not gather the Thorns and the Thistles, but collect Such a Garland of flowers as will flourish in your native climate, and Bloom upon your Brows with an unfading verdure."[19] She was anxious lest he be as easily corrupted as educated. "This will rejoice the Heart and compensate for [my] continual anxiety." She begged for reassurance. John Quincy wrote faithfully, describing his observations, his schools, his studies. Always he ended by sending his "duty" to his mother, to his grandfather—and his love to his siblings, an eighteenth-century convention that reflected the social hierarchy and derived from the Fifth Commandment.

The powerful legacy of Puritan New England culture survived into the late eighteenth century, governing the values, attitudes, and behavior of families such as the Adamses.[20] They believed in hierarchical relationships among family members, premised on duty owed reciprocally all along the line. These social obligations translated easily into civic obligations. Education entailed the understanding that its purpose involved not only individual gain, but obligations to the community as well. The religious basis of all of these values retained primacy among people who read the Bible as the ultimate source of all human order and retained a providential understanding of human progress.

On June 30, 1811, John Quincy Adams, United States Minister to the Court at St. Petersburg, wrote a typically long letter to his mother, then aged and retired to her home in Quincy. This letter was especially concerned about local politics in Massachusetts. At the end, not skipping a beat, he wrote, "Let me turn to your letter—The President [he meant James Madison] had informed me of that which you had written to him. . . . The consequence was that on the 4th day of January last I received his commission communicated to me by the then Secretary of State to return home."[21]

Abigail Adams, without consulting her son, had written to President Madison during the summer of 1810, requesting John Quincy's recall from his diplomatic station. Citing the personal hardships that his family endured, which she had learned about from letter after letter from both John Quincy and his wife, Louisa Catherine, and totally empathetic from her own experiences at diplomatic stations abroad, Abigail had been moved to request his recall. Madison immediately complied, writing both to Abigail and to John Quincy.[22]

Responding to this turn of events with remarkable equanimity, John Quincy explained at length to his mother why it would be impossible for him to return. "From the 4th of January it was for more than five months physically impossible for me to embark for America," and he explained that while the ice of the river had broken up "rather earlier in the season than usual," it was not until mid-June that a vessel bound for the United States had sailed. But by this time, another factor had arisen to prevent their sailing, "which might continue untill it would be too late to embark during this year's navigable season and which if so would detain us untill June 1812." He continued, "I suppose you know why I say it might detain us and why I yet say it may detain us untill that time. We were and are looking forward to an uncertain period—it may be longer or shorter—It may even now still terminate in time to make it possible for us to embark this year . . ." and John Quincy continued to cryptically encode the information that his wife was pregnant.[23] His ambivalence about the certainty of her pregnancy was doubtlessly due to her having suffered numerous miscarriages over the years. Thus did private issues intrude into the public life of the American minister at St Petersburg.

The issue did not end here, however. Abigail Adams, separated from her son not only by distance, but by the three to six months and more that it took for letters to be exchanged, took it for granted that her letter to the president had done the job, that the issue was resolved.[24] "I write to you by every opportunity although I hope you will have left St. Petersburgh before this can reach you," she informed John Quincy in mid-June.[25] Another time she advised him to bring home "your Beds, and linnen, both sheeting and table Linnen and any other furniture you have suitable for this Country."[26] But by this time, another turn of events had developed. Upon the death of Justice Cushing, President Madison offered and the Senate confirmed the appointment of John Quincy Adams to a seat on the Supreme Court of the United States.

Abigail was ecstatic. "I will not impose my judgement as a Law upon you," she wrote with perhaps false restraint, "but I will say I consider it as a call of providence to you. I hold it in higher estimation than the place of First Magestrate"—she meant the presidency—"because the duties of it are not so arduous—the responsibility of a different kind. tho both founded upon the same principles of immutable justice and integrity. The rule of the judges duty is uniform, and invariable, having nothing to consult but the Law."

She continued: "I believe you can be more extensively usefull to your Country in this than in any other employment. certainly you can be of more benefit to your Children by being able to superintend to their Education," she wrote, invoking familial duties, and here Abigail reached her full crescendo, "should the lives of your parents be prolonged a few more years, your presence will prolong and heighten the few remaining pleasures and comforts which remain to advanced Age." She rested her case for duty: "I will take it for granted that after mature reflection you will resign yourself to the call of your Country and hold the scales of Justice with an honest heart and a steady hand."[27]

Abigail's case here is reminiscent of an earlier exchange between herself and John Quincy. In September 1800, she had written to him at his diplomatic post as minister in Berlin, requesting his return. "The 17 of the present month will compleat six years since you left your native Country. as I then advised you to go. I now advise you to return. Six years is a period full long enough for a man at your age to remain seperated from all those with whom he is hereafter to take a part. . . . it is too long to be parted from those who have but a short leise of Life remaining to them. and to whom you are very dear."

Abigail then argued her case: "Services renderd to a Country in a diplomatic line can be known only to a few. If they are important and become conspicuous they rather excite envy than gratitude," she wrote bitterly, the wounds from John's experiences still rankling. "[B]ut at present it is my opinion that you may serve your country to more advantage at home than abroad. You have tallents which cannot fail of being brought into action let who will hold the Helm; I have no great allurements to hold up to you if you serve your Country. you must do it from motives as disinterested as your Father has done before you; and very like. meet with as much abuse and calumny."

Abigail continued: "you must endure envy, jealousy and mortifications of various kind's. you will find those who have grown rich and prosperous under a wise and just administration of Government, rising up to throw that system of political wisdom which has raised them to their present oppulence." She persisted, mixing her motives: "I still request you to return to the Bosom of your parents and make some establishment for yourself; it is high time that you were settled and in some regular course of busines—tho a return to the Bar may be [irksome?] to you after a lapse of years." The one persistent theme in her rambling petition to John Quincy was her imploring him to return. Her argument continued to shift channels; he should return to public service at home; it was time to settle down into private law practice.

But her overarching theme was that he should return to the "bosom" of aging parents who needed him. In this case, she meant herself as parent. Life in September 1800 was bleak for Abigail Adams—just as it would be in 1811. John's political position as president was critical; he faced an election with his administration in disarray and most members aligned against him. The prospects of his reelection were grim, nor would he concede defeat and retire. More pressing and closer to her soul were the conditions within the family. Charles Adams, her second son, who had accompanied John and John Quincy to Europe in 1779 and then returned home alone after one year because he was homesick, was dying of alcoholism at the age of thirty.

"To think of again seeing you. a wise and virtuous man is a cordial to my Heart and mitigates in some measure the pressure of sorrow which weighs it down from an other source—" Abigail's letter to John Quincy admitted. "[B]y one from which I have not a hope of change. habits are so rooted. the temper so [sound?] the whole man so changed that ruin and destruction have swallowd him up, and his affairs are become desperate." Charles's wife and infant had returned to her mother, while Abigail took the child Susan home to Quincy. "All is lost—poor poor unhappy wretched man. all remonstrances have been lost upon him. God knows what is to become of him." Abigail continued to pour out her heartache to John Quincy in Berlin. "His Father has renounced him—but I will not my dear Child afflict you. I bless God that I have dear and worthy children. who serve to comfort and support me under so trying a calamity."[28]

Such were some of the circumstances that afflicted Abigail's life in September 1800 when she begged John Quincy to return "to the Bosom of his parents." There was more. Her daughter's life, too, was in disarray, her husband, William Stephens Smith having disappeared, leaving Abigail Junior alone and destitute with her children on a farm in upstate New York.[29]

Nor were the circumstances of Abigail's life better in 1811 when she plotted John Quincy's return from St. Petersburg. "I have been in great distress for this fortnight for my dear Sister Cranch whose valuable Life has for more than a week been despaird of from a plurisy fever reduced to the very brink of the Grave," and she went on to explain that should his Aunt Mary die, his uncle "could not many days survive her."[30] In addition, her niece Elizabeth Norton, whom she loved "next to my own Children," had just died, leaving behind eight young children.[31]

Moreover, Abigail confessed to a more terrifying prospect: "My anxiety is great also for my dear and only Daughter. I have not mentioned it before. . . . She is apprehensive of a cancer in her breast. I have besought her to come on to Boston and take advice. . . . I cannot yet prevail upon her. she thinks that she cannot leave home. . . . I believe she thinks the physicians would urge the knife. which she says, the very thoughts of would be death to her. Heaven knows what is proper for our trials in Life. I pray that I may be resigned and submissive. what ever I may be calld to endure."[32]

As Abigail had written to President Madison, requesting John Quincy's recall from St. Petersburg, she continued to justify her position to her son: "I believe you can be more extensively usefull to your Country in this than any other employment."

In both of these episodes, in 1800 and again in 1811, when Abigail Adams lobbied for her eldest son's return from his diplomatic post abroad, she argued many cases. She protested that service abroad was a waste of time, personally and publicly, and that diplomatic service carried few rewards; nor did it accomplish much. Moreover, she reiterated that much more could be done with his talents at home. Occasionally, she even suggested a return to private law practice, which she knew to be anathema to John Quincy. In all these cases, something else was at stake.

Life was painful for Abigail in 1800. She was embittered by the political machinations that were destroying her husband's public career, but she was distraught over the terrible death of Charles, her charming and beloved middle son, and the bleak circumstances of her daughter's life. And in 1811, disease and death were claiming those who were closest to her at home. When Abigail Adams wrote to John Quincy to return home "to the Bosom of his parents," she buttressed her arguments with patriotic or political rhetoric. No small part of her motive was her personal need to have her son with her, to see him, to derive comfort from the presence of

John Quincy. Among the duties and obligations she knew he respected, she still laid claim to filial duty. The "institution" of motherhood, in this case expressed by the rhetoric of public service, provided the justification for her private motives.[33] Thus, in the "experience" of Abigail Adams were merged the claims of private and public life.

As the legacy of the Puritan past promoted an ideology of community service that has been translated into "Republican Motherhood," it sanctioned as well a role for the father in child rearing. When Abigail agreed to allow eleven-year-old John Quincy to travel to France in 1778, she confessed, "nor could I have acquiesced in such a seperation under any other care than that of the most Excellent parent and Guardian who accompanied you." She added: "Let me injoin it upon you to attend constantly and steadfastly to the precepts and instructions of your Father as you valued the happiness of your Mother and your own welfare. His care and attention to you render many things unnecessary for me to write which I might otherways do, but the inadvertency and Heedlessness of youth, requires line upon line and precept upon precept, and when inforced by the joint efforts of both parents will I hope have a due influence upon your Conduct."[34] Another time she wrote, underscoring the importance of both parents: "Ever remember that your parents are your disinterested friends . . . and that they would not direct you, but to promote your own happiness. Be thankful to kind Providence who has hitherto spared your parents lives the natural guardians of your youthful years."[35] She complained to her friend Mercy Otis Warren during John Adams's long absence: "I find myself . . . not only doubled in Wedlock but multiplied in cares to which I know myself unequel, in the Education of my little flock I stand in need of constant assistance of my Better Half."[36]

A refrain in her petition to John to return from Europe repeated her feelings of inadequacy as a parent. "I have hitherto been able to obtain their Love, their confidence and obedience," she wrote, "but I feel unequal to the task of guiding them alone."[37] Acknowledging his parental responsibility, John, in a moment of great loneliness, frustration, or guilt, lamented: "Much better should I have been employed in schooling my children, in teaching them to write, cypher, Latin, French, Greek."[38] And he continually advised Abigail from a distance: "The education of our Children is never out of my mind. Train them to Virtue, habituate them to industry, activity and spirit. Make them consider every Vice, as shameful and unmanly; fire them with ambition to be useful—make them disdain to be destitute of any ornamental Knowledge or Accomplishment. Fix their ambition upon great and solid objects, and their contempt upon little, frivolous and useless ones."[39]

During the years that John was in charge of John Quincy in Europe, he closely supervised his education: "Making latin, construing Cicero, Erasmus . . . Phaedrus, are all Exercises proper for Acquisition of the Latin Tongue. . . . The Greek Grammar and the Racines I would not have you omit, upon any Consideration," and he added, "As to Geography, Geometry and Fractions I hope your Master will not insist upon your spending much Time upon them . . . my wish at present is that your principal Attention should be directed to the Latin and Greek Tongues, leaving the other studies to be hereafter attained, in your own Country. I hope soon to hear that you are in Virgil and Tully's orations, or Ovid or Horace or all of them. I am, my dear Child, your affectionate Father . . ." and as a postscript: "The next Time you write to me, I hope you will take more care to write well. Cant you keep a steadier Hand?"[40]

So proficient were his Latin and Greek that John Quincy, to the great joy of his father, gained entry to the celebrated University of Leiden in 1780. From there he wrote long reports to John, describing primarily his studies: "I have finish'd Phaedrus's fables and the lives of Miltiades, Themistocles, Aristedes, Pausanias, Cimon and Lysander; and Am going next upon Alcibiades. . . . I translate and learn also a Greek verb through the Active, Passive and Medium Voices every day."[41] He also described sight-seeing excursions and entertainment: "I should be glad to have a pair of Scates they are of various prices from 3 Guilders to 3 Dukats those of a Ducat are as good as need to be but I should like to know whether you would chuse to have me give so much," he wrote breathlessly in one long run-on sentence, perhaps reflecting his nervousness over the nature of his request. John assented to the skates, but after reflecting for a few days, he returned to the subject: "The Ice is so universal now that I suppose you spend some Time in Skaiting every day. It is a fine Exercise for young Persons, and therefore I am willing to indulge you in it, provided you confine yourself to proper Hours, and to strict Moderation." Conscious of his fatherly responsibility to hold out some long-range social benefit to all activity, John was also haunted by specters of laziness, frivolity, wasted time: "Skaiting is a fine Art. It is not Simple Velocity or Agility that constitutes the Perfection of it but Grace. There is an Elegance of Motion, which is charming to the sight, and is useful to acquire, because it obliges you to restrain that impetuous Ardour and violent Acitivity, into which the Agitation of Spirits occasioned by this Exercise is apt to hurry you, and which is inconsistent both with your Health and Pleasure." John went on at length, making strained references to the art of skating and describing people he had seen skate, both in Amsterdam and in Boston. He discussed skating's relation to "Hogarth's Principles of Beauty," and finally, he made his point: "Do not conclude from this, that I advise you to spend much of your Time or Thought upon these Exercises and Diversions. In Truth I care very little about any of them. They should never be taken but as Exercise and Relaxation of Business and study. . . . They should all be arranged in subordination, to the great Plan of Happiness, and Utility."[42] John Adams regarded and performed his responsibility as father with seriousness.

Thirty years and one generation later, John Quincy's letters from Russia restated a familiar theme. When they sailed for Europe in 1809, John Quincy and Louisa Catherine left behind their two eldest sons, George and John, under the supervision of his parents, taking the infant Charles Francis with them to Russia. Echoing his mother's early admonitions to him, John Quincy wrote to George of his hopes that both sons "will prove useful citizens to their country, respectable members of society, and a real blessing to their parents," then he offered a batch of advice about achieving these goals.[43] He wrote to his mother as well: "You mention in your last letter, that George is getting awkward tricks and habits, which gives me some concern. . . . It is upon the Ladies that I almost entirely depend for giving this sort of polish to my boys, and I rely much upon your goodness in this respect to the two that are with you. I am not . . . under the idea of being entirely useless to their education—I should in no case take much share in the formation of their *manners*. But their *morals* are of my concern." Therefore, John Quincy continued, he planned to write a series of letters to his sons; if they could not understand them, he asked Abigail to interpret "everything that [they] may find to hard."[44] Having assigned Abigail to teach manners, he then took it upon himself to write about morals, the purpose being, as he had written earlier, to make them useful citizens and members of society.

In fact, John Quincy was good to his word. Over the next several years he wrote a number of letters—addressed to George, as elder son, but probably intended for all of his children—explicating his thoughts about reading the Bible. "I have myself many years made it a practice to read through the Bible once every year. I have always endeavored to read it with the same spirit and temper of mind which I now recommend to you," he introduced the subject. "That is, with the intention and desire that it may contribute to my advancement in wisdom and virtue. . . . My custom is to read four or five chapters of the Bible every morning immediately after rising from bed. It employs about an hour of my time, and seems to me the most suitable manner of beginning the day."[45] As John Quincy had learned piety as a youth, he now impressed upon his own children that the formula for becoming a virtuous person, if not citizen, rested on religious foundations.

Another time the minister at St. Petersburg wrote to his mother: "Charles has just the instant left me—I gave him this morning La Fontaine's Fables with wooden cuts to each Fable; and he has been standing this hour by the side of my table spelling out the titles of the Fables, and looking for the animals in the cuts—appealing every now and then to me to help him out, and so immoveable from his stand that I could neither get rid of him, nor continue writing . . . as it has always been one of my hobby horses to teach my children something myself, I enjoy it with him by instructing him in his A.B.C."[46] Charles, at age four, he admitted, was literate only in French.

The fact that John Quincy had left his sons under the supervision of his parents was an endorsement of their approach to child rearing.[47] He expected them to demand high standards, and he predicted accurately. His father wrote to young George at school in Hingham: "Your Progress in the New Testament in Greek, and in Virgil, is Satisfactory, but I am not Satisfied with your Arithmetick. Of all your Studies I wish you to be a Mathematician, next to Morality and Religion because those Sciences make Youth Studious." But Abigail invoked her grandsons' education as an inducement to urge her son to return. He should return to teach his sons, she urged, noting that George especially didn't write well. John Quincy must come to teach his sons, she emphasized.[48]

If there was an "institutional" construct to encourage mothers to raise good citizens, so there existed a similar injunction to fathers. Dictated by a long tradition, the paternal obligations of parenting were derived from Puritanism, in which the authoritarian father was defined as teacher and held up as a model to his sons, and in which he was patriarch to the entire family. That Puritan legacy survived the Revolution into the early nineteenth century; religion served as the arbiter of social convention and children were not yet free of the Fifth Commandment. Perhaps more powerfully, the father served as role model to sons, especially in a culture where, as in early nineteenth-century America, economic exigencies dictated social continuity over generations.[49] Furthermore, the rules that had prevailed for one generation were inherited by the next. The father role, for citizens like the Adamses over two generations, was central. For them the obligations of parenting were religiously ordained, socially prescribed, and economically expedient. If mothers raised sons for citizenship, so did the men who, as citizens, controlled the republic.

Ideology, social scientists tell us, "is an attempt to *sell* history, to sell an interpretation of the time and place in which men and women live their lives to those same men and women." It is, furthermore, an effort to universalize the interests of the dominant group by making their interests appear normal. Ideology, by this definition, "succeeds when those to whom it is directed assume that it is normal, natural, definitive, and thus destined to endure."[50] Ideology, in this sense, becomes midwife to the institution of motherhood, insuring and reassuring that women will preserve patriarchal structures and values.

When we think of an institution, Adrienne Rich points out, we imagine something concrete, like a building or an organization. But "institution" also refers to a system of power and is sustained by ideology. An institution, Rich writes, is the way in which "power is maintained and transferred . . . the invisible understanding which guarantees that [power] shall reside

in certain hands but not in others." She searches for some "visible embodi-
ment" of the institution of motherhood—what comes to mind is "the
home"—and she writes, "we like to believe that the home is a private
place."[51] It is not. Politics, the exercise of power, enters the private arena
through the agency of ideology, therefore confirming the feminist claim
that everything is political.

Abigail Adams operated fully within the social constructs and the ideology of her time in raising her children. Her first source was her liberal
religion which told her that life on earth would be difficult and that all
events were providential, that rewards and punishment for human behavior would be administered in the hereafter by a benign God whose
motives remained inscrutable to human reason. She knew from her religion that there was a distinction between good and evil, that much of the
message about living well was accessible in the Bible. She knew that the
purpose for worldly life was to do good and that every person was responsible to contribute to the good of the larger community.[52] As she had
inherited an understanding of religion that explained reality, she taught her
children the same lessons. Her methods for teaching were inherited as
well, tempered over time and generations, but fundamentally she saw
herself as a teacher, responsible for the souls of her children as well as their
physical well-being.

When Abigail Adams sent her eldest son abroad, she worried that once
out of her control, he would be subject to corrupting ideas, so she lectured
him bountifully in her letters—the only method then available to her. She
advised him repeatedly that as he possessed gifts and privileges, he inherited the obligation to serve "the various relations in which you stand
connected; in the first place to your Great Preserver, in the next to Society
in General, in particular to your Country, to your parents and to yourself."
She specifically defined her case that "Justice, humanity and Benevolence
are the duties you owe to society in general," and that "To your Country the
same duties are incumbent upon you with the additional obligation of
sacrificeing ease, pleasure, wealth and life itself for its defence and security." Her words to John Quincy echo from within the tradition of Puritan
New England. They are in turn mirrored in the lessons that John Quincy
would impress upon his own children.

Abigail's message to John Quincy was didactic, but it served her in
another forum as well. It justified the ten-year absence of her husband.
Indeed it served for almost a lifetime of sacrifice of family life, since John
Adams had left home in 1774 and remained in public service for most of the
quarter of a century that followed. The ideology of patriotism provided the
rationale for many years of solitary hard work and loneliness.

In many ways Abigail used the prevailing ideologies, not just because
they were expedient, but because she believed them. As she had justified
her husband's absence for many years because his unique talents were

necessary for the state, she justified asking her son to return home from his foreign diplomatic posts. Her deepest personal motives included seeing this son before she died, but she constructed elaborate idealized arguments to present her case.[53] Nor was she the only mother during the age of the Revolution and early republic to do so.

Mercy Otis Warren, of distinguished patriotic lineage, struggled as the mother of five sons to consider the impending sacrifice at the outset of the war. For all the "solicitude" she felt for her country, she wrote to Abigail, "Shall I own to you that the Woman and the Mother daily arouse my fears and fill my Heart with anxious Concern for the decision of the Mighty Controversy between Great Britain and the Colonnies. . . . Methinks I see no less than five sons who must Buckle on the Harness." Mercy, for all her patriotic fervor, confessed a mother's private fear for the lives of her sons. Twenty-five years later, Mercy, too, became involved in her grown son's life, asking her friend John Adams, as president, to make her son a federal appointment.[54]

Looking at the institution of motherhood in late eighteenth- and early nineteenth-century America presents an opportunity to see still another aspect of male/female relationships. In a period of patriarchal dominance, there existed one oasis where the prevailing hierarchy did not operate effectively—namely that of mother and son. In an era when religion still had the force of ideology as well as of law, the Fifth Commandment wielded authority. John Quincy Adams reacted calmly to Abigail's interference in his life as an adult, not only because he loved and respected her, but because she was his mother. Between mothers and sons, the patriarchal lines of power were reversed in childhood, but they did not ever recover. Motherhood commanded the "duty" of respect, if not deference. If John Quincy was patriarch to his own wife and children, even to the nation, he was son to Abigail.[55]

The bond between Abigail and her adult son was confirmed in manifold ways. The range of topics about which they wrote to each other reflected similar interests: books, travel, politics, gossip. They wrote honestly about their feelings. Just as Abigail poured out her anguish over Charles's alcoholism and death, John Quincy in return described grieving for his daughter: "Two Years have nearly gone by since my only daughter was taken from me and to this hour I cannot meet in the street an infant of her age in its mothers arms, but it cuts me to the heart."[56] They wrote affectionately. Sending New Year's greetings to his mother in 1811, John Quincy reflected on the unpredictability of his life, adding, "Wherever we may be, at least one thing will be unchangeable as long as the pulse of life shall beat at my heart—it is the dutiful affection of your Son."[57] Several years later, Abigail described meeting a man who had recently returned from St. Petersburg: "As I enterd the room, he said this Lady is the Mother of Mr JQ Adams. I bowed assent. Your Son Madam is very fond of you. he talked much of you. indeed he is very fond of you—I replied that the attachment was reciprocated. this he said not in a cold formal manner, but with a warmth and ardour as tho he enjoyd what he described—and you may be sure it was a cordial balm to the Heart of an affectionate parent."[58]

The experience of motherhood has much to tell us about the institution of motherhood, about the narrowness and determinism of the political ideology of motherhood. The experience reveals those qualities that are personal, continuous, perhaps not subject to reasoning. It illuminates as well the cracks in the ideology, the places where it is necessary to administer control, because there exists danger from a different set of rules.[59] It shows the extent to which theory may mask reality, as the role of fathers was central in some children's upbringing. Above all it erases the false distinction that mothering, parenting, family life were ever exempted from politics. Ideologies have shifted with circumstances, but the use of ideology to create institutional power has moved in a single straight line. In a period and in a culture where men were dominant and women were subordinate, reinforced by an ideology shared by both women and men, a democratic revolution did not change that fact.

9

My Closest Companion

For the second time in two years, Abigail Adams Smith traveled the three hundred miles from her upstate New York home to Quincy, where her parents lived. She had made the previous trip in July 1811 to consult physicians in Boston. This time, July 1813, she was coming home to die. Abigail was accompanied by her eighteen-year-old daughter Caroline, her son John, a lawyer, and her sister-in-law. The arduous and painful trip took fifteen days by stagecoach and carriage with a brief stopover at Balston Spa to take the waters. They proceeded then at an easy pace so as to least distress the invalid.[1]

In Quincy, Abigail and John Adams met the party at their gate. Abigail Junior was taken from her coach and carried in a chair to her room, and physicians were summoned to consult on what everyone knew to be a hopeless case. Abigail Smith, at the age of forty-nine, had cancer, and so wasted was her body at this late date that the best remedy that doctors could offer was opium to ease her pain. When the spasms that racked her body abated, she was content, even cheerful. She chatted with family members and close friends who visited. She consoled her parents. To her mother, Abigail, she was in every way a model patient, just as she had been, in Abigail's opinion, a model daughter, wife, and mother.[2]

Abigail the mother faced this ordeal with outward resignation and inward horror. She had first learned of her daughter's recurrent cancer during the previous winter, when letters arrived from Lebanon, New York, advising her that Abigail Junior was suffering from severe rheumatism.[3] Then came the news that the cancer, which they all believed to have been excised by her operation eighteen months previous, had developed in the other breast, indeed had spread through her whole body. Suspecting the worst, Abigail wrote of her fear to John Quincy, then in Russia: "Of your dear and only Sister, I can only say that she has been and still is a patient sufferer under Severe and afflicting pain. So much reduced that she cannot either write or walk."

"My Heart bleeds," she continued, "I cannot get to her. nor she to me. I am too infirm myself to take such a journey." And in resignation, she wrote, "Unto the will and disposal of our heavenly Father—I commit her."[4] Throughout this ordeal and after, religion offered not only consolation but also the providential explanation for cruel circumstance. "My only source of satisfaction—and it is a never failing one, is my firm persuasion that every thing—and our oversights and mistakes among the rest are parts of the grand plan. in which everything will in time appear to have been ordered and conducted in the best manner."

Abigail was sixty-eight years old, and she considered herself ancient. Always fragile, she had experienced exceptionally poor health during the last decade, although between bouts of illness her activities were undiminished.[5] She governed over an expansive household that included family and endless numbers of visitors. Her daughter-in-law Sally Adams, widow of Charles, and Sally's daughters Susan and Abby lived much of the time with the Adamses, including that summer of 1813. Abigail was frequently called upon to nurse Sally, who was sickly, possibly afflicted with stomach ulcers. She was responsible for servants, such as the Brieslers, who had resided in the Adams household for thirty years and were treated as kin. Thomas and his growing family lived nearby, so that young grandchildren came and went. Extending outward from her household, Abigail cared for a multitude of neighbors and friends, offering charity in several forms, sometimes small donations, sometimes personal ministrations. A steady stream of visitors appeared to converse with the former president, and Abigail was noted as a gracious hostess. Her nephew Josiah Quincy recalled her handsome dress, "her rich silks and laces," appropriate to her "position," as well as her "generous hospitality."[6]

Nor had Abigail's interest in the world diminished in her ancient years. She continued to read broadly and to reflect upon her readings, often suggesting books to her grandchildren as well as quoting maxims of wisdom that had impressed her. Conscious that the admonitions "which may fall from the pen of her aged grandmother" might seem tedious, she protested that "She still remembers that she once was young."[7] Close to her heart, as well as to her mind, was national politics, in which Abigail, perhaps as much as John, served the role of elder states-person. The understanding of over a half-century of political engagement informed her judgment. The sacrifices she had made to her country were reflected in her commentary. She had risen above local politics during the years since the Revolution and her husband's presidency to become a strong partisan of the national system. So while local citizens, including her sister's family, protested the current war with England, Abigail's politics followed from her personal investment in the larger scene of national affairs.[8] Moreover, her son now served as minister at St. Petersburg. Wishing to spend their final years near him, Abigail and his father had urged John Quincy to come home.[9] Typical of the sweep of events that dominated her past life, all of these activities and issues engaged Abigail at the time of her daughter's final illness.

Abigail's bond with her daughter was deeply felt. "She has always been my closest companion and associate, and I have no other daughter to supply her place—" she wrote after Nabby's marriage to William Stephens Smith.[10] That marriage, which had culminated a romantic London courtship, was performed by the Bishop of St. Asaph's in June 1786. "In what a world do we live and how strange are the events which take place!" Abigail wrote to Mary Cranch. "Who would have told your neice two years ago that she should marry a gentleman who she had never seen in England too, and be married by a Bishop—who of us would have believed it."[11] The marriage—a fairy-tale match, so to speak, between the daughter of the American minister and Lady at the Court of St. James's to a handsome, high-ranking military officer, former adjutant to George Washington, and secretary to the American legation in London—augured a bountiful future. If there were signs that the fairy tale would collapse, they were suppressed even by Abigail the mother.

Within one year a son was born, baptized William after his father and Steuben after the Revolutionary War hero under whom Smith had served for a time. Within another year the entire family sailed for home, the Smiths separately to New York, and the Adamses to Braintree. The English idyll ended. In New York, Abigail Junior settled into the Smith household at Jamaica, Long Island, where she met her in-laws, the widowed Mrs. Margaret Smith and the nine sisters and brothers of her husband, who warmly welcomed her.

If Abigail the mother had aspirations for retirement at Braintree, they were short-lived; within months of their return, the Adamses learned of John's selection as vice president of the United States, a challenge and an opportunity he would not resist. The only advantage that Abigail perceived in yet one more public sacrifice at the expense of a comfortable existence within a familiar neighborhood was its proximity to her daughter. In fact, she preceded John to New York, the capital city, in the fall of 1788 to be present at the birth of the Smiths' second son, John Adams Smith.[12]

The fairy tale that began in London persisted in New York for a time. The vice-presidential mansion, called Richmond Hill, was a delightful house, situated on the heights overlooking the Hudson in what is now Greenwich Village, and Abigail's greatest problem was finding a sober cook. "I cannot find a cook in the whole city, but what will get drunk," she wrote Mary.[13]

Her household, she explained, consisted of eighteen, ten of whom were her family. The Smiths, with two infants and expecting a third child, as well as Charles Adams, lived with their parents; John Quincy and Thomas spent vacations in New York. It was a gay time, a political honeymoon for the new president and vice president, and a testing of the new government. New York suited Abigail primarily because her daughter and family lived with her, sharing the daily round of work and social activities.

This interlude ended when the capital was moved to Philadelphia, which Abigail dreaded, not only because of its climate, but because she would be leaving her daughter. "At present you have your Family with and near you," she lamented to Mary, "but it is my destiny to have mine scatered and scarcly to keep one with us. My separation from Mrs. Smith is painfull to me on many accounts."[14] In the weeks before the move, she became ill and was nursed by her daughter, who herself had recently given birth. Abigail recovered sufficiently to travel to Philadelphia in late 1790 to a house called Bush Hill, which she did not like. "The House had not been inhabited for four years & being Brick you may judge the state of it," she complained.[15]

Then, William Stephens Smith disappeared. Unannounced, he sailed suddenly for England in late December on a mysterious mission, having to do, he claimed, with some personal business. Smith's peremptory behavior, it would turn out, represented a pattern, one that had surfaced in England and would be repeated several times in the course of the next decade. The Adamses, if they privately comprehended this pattern, did not acknowledge it.

The first of Smith's peculiar flights had occurred soon after his arrival in England. Having requested a one-month leave to tour the Continent, he disappeared for four. "Where is Smith?" the Adamses queried friends as well as each other. He reappeared in Paris after three months, where Thomas Jefferson was charmed: "I congratulate you," he wrote, "on the extreme worth of his character."[16] The Adamses welcomed his return to London. Soon after the birth of his son, Smith disappeared during a diplomatic mission to Portugal. His prolonged absence was considered odd but was overlooked by the Adamses. Indulged because of his charm in the short run, Smith was tolerated in the long run for his wife's sake.

While the Adamses were baffled by Smith's impulsive journey in 1790, they were also distracted by their own move to Philadelphia. "I have a source of anxiety added to my portion on my dear daughters account, Col. Smith having saild last week for England. His going was sudden and unexpected to us," Abigail explained. "She, poor Girl, is calld to quite a different trial from any she has before experienced, for tho the Col. was once absent, she was in her Fathers House. Now she writes that she feels as if unprotected, as if alone in the wide world."[17] Smith returned in the summer of 1791 to a government office supplied by President Washington, but the appointment was short-lived. In early 1792, the Colonel took his entire family to England, this time, he claimed, to pursue business opportunities. The Abigails were again separated, much to the distress of the mother. "This you may be sure is a heavy stroke to me. . . . Mrs. Smith is in circumstances which will make me more anxious for her, but my Family are destined to be scatterd I think."[18]

By the time the Smiths returned to New York early the following year, Abigail Adams had retreated to Quincy, where she would remain during the next five years of the Washington administration. Only after John became president did she return to her post in the nation's capital. During that five-year period, however, she visited her daughter once in New York after the birth of her granddaughter, Caroline Amelia, observing personally what John had found most vexing. William Smith had assumed a gentlemanly mode, living in such ostentatious style that John expressed scorn and Abigail alarm. They both feared that Smith was living beyond his means, and the fear was soon substantiated.[19]

By the spring of 1797, Smith's fortunes had collapsed. En route to Philadelphia to assume her work as First Lady, Abigail visited her daughter at the Smith farm in upstate New York; there she discovered the dismal reality of the lapsed fairy tale. Smith was gone again. Her daughter was desolate, abandoned on a remote farm with few adult contacts. "My reflections upon prospects there, took from me all appetite to food, and deprest my spirits, before too low. The Col. gone a journey, I knew not where, I could not converse with her. I saw her Heart too full. Such is the folly and madness of speculation and extravagance. To her no blame is due. Educated in different Habits, she never enjoyd a life of dissipation."[20]

Abigail continued her journey to Philadelphia, where she began her duties as First Lady. "Yesterday being Monday, from 12 to half past two, I received visits, 32 Ladies and near as many Gentlemen. I shall have the same ceremony to pass through to day, and the rest part of the week."[21] She continued to worry about her daughter, who by the following November had received a letter from Smith, but no Smith. One month later, Abigail informed Mary that her daughter "lives without a Human being to call upon her from one week to an other, buoyd up with an expectation of the Col's return, which however I have very little faith in."[22] Abigail was now persuaded that the Colonel had abandoned his family. When he finally did show up, Abigail was relieved for her daughter's sake. "At any rate I am glad he had returnd. It really seemd to me at times, as if Mrs. Smith would lose herself," Abigail admitted to Mary. "She has sometimes written me that existance was a burden to her; and that she was little short of distraction. I have been more distrest for her than I have been ready to own. You know she always kept every thing to herself that she could, but she writes in better spirits, and is at least relieved from that worst of States, I think, a constant anxious expectation, and anticipation."[23]

The contradictions in Abigail's life were accurately described in her own words as "splendid misery."[24] On the surface, she performed the duties of First Lady, a persistent round of social events and parties that she tolerated but never loved. Privately, she lived with her husband's mounting stresses as the problems that would lead to his political defeat after one administration compounded. And her most intimate self was distressed by her growing awareness that the lives of two of her children were unraveling.[25]

Her providential religion strengthened her. "I [receive] pleasure and assurance from the source of inspration. that not a swallow falleth without notice."[26] The religion that comforted also reminded her of her blessings; she was satisfied that John Quincy thrived in his new post as minister at Berlin, and Thomas, despite his illnesses, had promise. Yet Abigail herself was ill much of the time, chronically afflicted with rheumatism and with what she called her "intermittent fever." She frequently mentioned not sleeping well and may have been an insomniac.[27] No small part of her physical pain may have been a manifestation of the pain in her soul. When she grieved the most, she wrote: "My heart bleeds at every pore," employing a physical metaphor to describe emotional pain, a metaphor replete with suggestion.[28] While she was forced to present a stoic facade to the public, she wept privately, on the inside. She may literally have felt hurt in her heart, the center of her being. The heart is associated with love and with life. She felt that her most intimate part was injured, bleeding, wounded. Abigail seems not to have become desensitized to adversity over time. She did possess the resources to cope despite adversity. Her husband, as beleaguered president, knew this well, for her acuity of mind was undiminished as she participated wholeheartedly in his political life.

Smith reappeared in February 1798 from the Northwest Territory, where he had been pursuing yet one more speculative fantasy. The Adamses were dispirited, but in an effort to stabilize their daughter's life, John acquired a military appointment for his son-in-law—not without administering a lecture about industry and frugality—and the Smith household carried on.[29] Smith did not get into real trouble again until 1805. By that time he was serving as inspector and supervisor of customs in New York, another of John's appointments, when he foolishly became involved with an ideologue, Francisco Miranda, whom he helped to mount a liberating expedition to the former's homeland of Venezuela. The upshot of that episode was that William Steuben Smith, eldest grandchild of the Adamses, who had been lured into this folly, ended up in prison in Caracas. William Smith, the father, faced a trial in the Supreme Court, and although he was acquitted, he was thoroughly discredited and dismissed by Jefferson. The Smiths retired to their farm in Lebanon, New York.[30]

Abigail Adams commended her daughter for her loyalty to this incorrigible man, reconciled herself to the misalliance, and placed hope in their children. She had early on sent young William and John to her sister

Elizabeth for their schooling, hoping at least to insure their education to steadier habits. Her fondness for her granddaughter Caroline was second only to her bond with her daughter. A strand of that bond with her daughter was composed of guilt. Writing of her daughter's troubles, Abigail once reported: "No station in Life was ever designed by Providence to be free from trouble and anxiety. The portion I believe is much more equally distributed that we imagine." She then wrote, obliquely: "Guilt of conscience is the work of our own Hands and not to be classed with the inevitable evils of Humane Life."[31] If Abigail felt guilt about her daughter's situation, it was a fault of circumstances rather than design.

Abigail Junior by all reports differed from her mother in many ways. Physically she tended to the Adams corpulence rather than the leanness of her mother's family, which is evident in pictures as well as in Abigail's descriptions: "Mrs. Smith grows very fleshy, as much so I think as before she first went abroad, tho being older and more moulded into the form of woman, she does not look so burden'd."[32] Her face resembled John's. She is described as quieter, "reserved," though sweet-tempered, and always "patient." Her letters reveal a good mind, not given to her parents' wit, but with the full force of the Adams erudition. She was extraordinarily well educated for an eighteenth-century woman, which must indeed have clashed with William Smith's superficiality. Intelligence and reverence for books aside, the one way she did resemble her mother was in her persistent loyalty to her husband, despite Smith's transgressions, and in her devotion to her children. These qualities she learned from her mother, but also from observing her mother's experiences.

Abigail Junior had been nine years old when her father left home to serve his nation. She was nineteen when she and her mother journeyed to Europe to be reunited with John. During the intervening ten years she had lived in a mother-centered household as her mother's "closest companion"; observing her mother during those years, young Abigail learned that when men abandoned women, whether the cause was public service, as in John's case or self-serving in the Colonel's, women's only option was acceptance. Abigail Junior knew firsthand that men went away, sometimes for very long times during which there were no communications, and that women suffered and survived. She was, as a consequence, unusually well equipped to tolerate a husband such as William Stephens Smith. Abigail Adams's understanding of that dark irony may explain her statement about guilt. The noble sacrifice of the mother's experience was sadly mirrored in her daughter's unsuitable marriage. That knowledge confirmed one more strand of the bond between mother and daughter.

"Your sister and Caroline have made me a charming visit this summer," Abigail wrote to John Quincy Adams on September 25, 1811. "They will leave me next month."[33] Abigail Junior had journeyed to Quincy early in

July to consult with physicians in Boston. Her mother's casual statement, near the end of a letter containing a litany of sad news about Mary Cranch's declining health and the illnesses and deaths of other family members, concealed many truths, partly as a deliberate ploy to protect her son and family from alarming information, partly as an unconscious act of self-deception to protect herself, and partly because the whole picture had not yet, on September 25, been revealed to her. The next day, the letter would arrive from Dr. Benjamin Rush that strongly advised radical surgery to excise the tumor that Abigail Junior had discovered in her breast. One day later, Abigail wrote to her son-in-law, at home in New York State, to advise him that the operation was imminent and that he should travel to Quincy to be with his wife.

Abigail's suppression of the whole story in her letter to John Quincy characterizes the mystification and complexity of events during the summer and fall of 1811. Little information exists about the operation in which Mrs. Smith's entire breast was amputated, following a diagnosis of malignant cancer. The precise date of the operation is unknown, although it probably took place within the first two weeks of October 1811. Nor is there information about the location or procedures of the surgery. Abigail was unusually reticent about this episode; many reasons may be suggested for her silence.

First, she spoke with her most intimate correspondents, John Adams of course, but also Mary, who lived in the same village and was herself dying of consumption. Elizabeth visited Quincy during this period, and their correspondence after her return to Atkinson focused upon Mary's illness. Abigail's primary correspondent within the family circle was John Quincy in St. Petersburg; Abigail wanted to protect him and especially her grandson, William Steuben Smith, John Quincy's secretary, from unwarranted alarm.

Moreover, the nature of Abigail Smith's illness constituted a forbidden area of discourse for an eighteenth-century correspondent. Public reference to female anatomy was proscribed by social convention, so that even as enlightened and profuse a letter-writer as Abigail was loth to discuss sexuality in writing. These topics she reserved for private, intimate discussions among women. She did not, for instance, describe pregnancy—"in circumstances" she termed it—childbirth, menstruation, or menopause, although she cryptically coded messages to her correspondents.[34]

At the same time, breast cancer carried significant meaning in a culture where women's role of bearing and nurturing children represented their primary purpose and identity. The breast as metaphor signified women's sexuality, fecundity, social role in a culture which made clear distinctions in gender spheres. It was an age, as well, where dress design had become more daring, exposing more breast than Abigail approved of. She had commented on it with displeasure in England, and she expressed high disapproval when she observed it in her own executive mansion.[35] Abigail, prudish by some standards, expressed eighteenth-century New England values with regard to sexuality. That is, she distinguished between private and public matters and believed that sexuality belonged in the realm of the private.

Silence about breast cancer, moreover, persisted into the twentieth century, as several commentators have noted. The poet Audre Lorde described her painful feelings of isolation as resembling the caste of "untouchable." "You can die from that specialness, of the cold, the isolation."[36] Susan Sontag wrote that cancer "is felt to be obscene—in the original meaning of the word: ill-omened, abominable, repugnant to the senses."[37] That Abigail Adams, an eighteenth-century woman, censored her commentary about this most devastating experience reflects a continuing distancing from the horror associated with the most dreaded disease of woman, breast cancer with all its social implications about womanhood.

Even had she been able to breach the conventional cloak of secrecy surrounding this disease, another factor restricted Abigail from fully disclosing the nature of her daughter's illness. Abigail, it appears, was hiding its reality from herself before all others. So painful was the contemplation of its full implications that Abigail coped by consciously repudiating its existence. Therefore, even though she had known about Abigail Smith's breast tumor for nearly a year, she wrote to John Quincy that "Your sister and Caroline have made me a charming visit." With that statement she recreated the world she preferred to the reality of a breast cancer. The depth of her fear was attested to by her uncharacteristic disclaimer.

Circumstances at home abetted her fiction. Her daughter-in-law Sally Adams lay critically ill in the Adams home, and her sister Mary, afflicted with "a pleurisy" in May, now appeared to have developed consumption. John Adams further contributed to the scenes of malady by injuring himself: "He went out in the dark to view the comet, and struck his leg against a sharp stick & cut it so much as to lay him [up]."[38] Most of Abigail's energy was taxed by ministering to the critically ill, and all of her fears focused on Mary. By September 1811, at the same time that she wrote about the "charming visit" to John Quincy, she acknowledged that Mary was dying. So ubiquitous were illness, death, and injury that summer that the entire family's emotional and physical resources were concentrated upon the sick. Elizabeth's daughter, Abbe, came from Atkinson to assist in nursing. Louisa Smith, Abigail's niece, nursed primarily in the Cranch household, assisting Mary's daughter Lucy Greenleaf. Abigail traveled back and forth between her home and the Cranch home. Then, the volatile situation was further destabilized when Richard Cranch suddenly suffered a stroke and perished within three days. Mary survived one more day. Abigail was inconsolable for months. If she had reason to grieve in the loss of her closest sister, that grief could embody as well her fear for her daughter. It was against this context of disease and death that the saga of Abigail Smith's breast cancer unfolded. Abigail Adams was so distracted by the immediate demands of the ill and dying that her attention to her daughter—whether deliberate or unconscious—was suppressed.

By the early nineteenth century, breast cancer had a long history, although its diagnosis and remedies had not significantly changed in the two thousand years of its written record. Hippocrates in the fourth century B.C. and Galen seven centuries later established the formulas that prevailed until modern medicine transformed scientific understanding about the nature and cure of disease. Hippocrates associated breast cancer with menopause, and for different reasons, Galen concurred. Galen's pathology, based on humoralism, attributed tumors—he distinguished between benign (scirrhus) and malignant (carcinoma)—to a congestion of black bile. For both he recommended conservative treatment—diet, fasting, medication—unless a tumor was too far advanced, in which case, surgery was advised. Several permutations of Galenic theory persisted through the eighteenth century to the time of the Enlightenment, but essentially the same diagnostic and remedial treatment continued.[39]

The written record of breast cancer and its remedies is amplified by artifacts and art, extending the chronology backwards to the second and third millennia B.C. Early Greek votive statues exist, substantiating the claim of medical historians that where science failed to provide solutions, supernatural or spiritual appeals prevailed. Etchings from the third century show St. Agatha, patron saint of breast cancer, martyred by the amputation of both breasts. Drawings and etchings from later centuries depict surgical instruments especially designed for breast amputations. Still other paintings graphically illustrate scenes of doctors, surgeons, family members, and perhaps even a little dog surrounding a patient.[40]

By the early nineteenth century when Abigail Smith discovered her tumor, the theory, diagnosis, and prescription available to her in New England were as advanced as those in Europe. Generations of American physicians and surgeons, Benjamin Rush among them, had trained at Edinburgh, London or Paris. They, in turn, brought advanced medical techniques to America. Evidence from several letters of family members indicate that the advice and treatment available to Abigail Smith in Boston was congruent with contemporary approaches in Paris and London.[41]

Following Mrs. Smith's early consultations in Boston, her mother and husband corresponded as a means of keeping Col. Smith, at home in Lebanon, New York, informed. Clearly Smith had been reading current medical literature on cancer. He cited Dr. Stoerck, a leading surgeon of Vienna who had completed a textbook on cancer. He cited Dr. Nicholson of Barwick, another exponent of "the Cicuta," a derivative of hemlock, along with arsenic, two medications then in use. "You say that [the Dr.] does not pronounce it to be a cancer, tho he cannot say, but it *may* terminate in one," the Colonel responded to Abigail Adams. "But knowing as I do that hemlock is the principal medicine recommended in Cases of Cancer. . . . I have no doubt in my mind, but he conceives this to be the disorder. Mrs. Smith in her letter of the 11th of July says the doctors opinion is that it is an obstructed Gland," Smith continued. "But what is a cancer? it is a hard indolent tumour seated in some of the Glands; as the breast, arm pits etc. If the tumour becomes loose unequal, of a livid, blackish or leaden colour attended with violent pain, it is plainly called an occult cancer. When the skin is broken and . . . [illegible] is discharged it is plainly called an open or ulcerated cancer."

Smith, after a lengthy lecture about different types of cancer and different types of therapy, proposed his own approach: "I am an advocate for prompt and decisive experiments to ascertain the nature of the complaint, and its decided character, this was to me the primary essential object of the visit. I hesitated to take it as a cancer . . . but if it is a cancer, let it promptly be cured—If it is simply a swelling of the breast common to females from 40 to 50 years of age," he hoped that the visit to her mother would be an effective palliative.[42]

Smith's letter then led abruptly into a different sensitive area of discussion. Given the Adamses' age, he wrote, given Abigail's desire to have her daughter nearby, "I will wave the rights to claim the performance of duty enforced upon a wife, *vis* that she shall quit father and mother and cleave unto her husband. . . . I will leave my mother and family and cleave unto my Wife, thus reversing the obligation connected with a marriage Contract." Whether Smith's offer to move to Quincy was inspired by generosity or represented an opportunity for him to move once more into the Adams political arena, the offer was not well received.

Summoning the skills she had learned in a lifetime of public service, Abigail responded: "Your proposition to remove near to me would of all things be agreeable to me," she wrote, "but I would not require such a sacrifice as you must make to gratify my desire of having my dear daughter near me."[43] The sacrifice, indeed, was Abigail's, and probably reflected John's antipathy to Smith, as well as her own.[44] Smith was in exile.

Another two weeks passed before Smith meekly responded: "I may have expressd myself with too much solicitude and given my opinion too decidedly in opposition to the professional men," he conceded. It would be best "having advised with Surgeons and Physicians to follow their advise—I shall never hazard an opinion on the subject again," and he admitted, "I am totally ignorant of the case." Further, he wrote, taking command where he could: "With respect to my proposition to reside near you I conceived it a duty I owed you, and Mrs. Smith. that duty being paid, I rest satisfied with your answer." And he requested that "Mrs. Smith and Caroline would be in motion homeward as soon as agreeable to them."[45]

Smith's wishes would be disappointed, however, for events moved quickly in a different direction. Throughout the summer of 1811, against the backdrop of family illnesses and injuries, Abigail Smith had weighed the opinions of several physicians, whose diagnoses of the nature of her tumor varied.[46]

John Adams, all this while, acting in the role of elder statesman, carried on a rich correspondence with several distant political allies. With great intensity that summer, he and Benjamin Rush reexamined the Revolution, recast their roles, and measured the effects of old age. How it came about that his daughter decided to seek Rush's opinion about her cancer is not clear. She noted that reading Rush's treatise on cancer inspired her letter, so in early September 1811, Abigail Adams Smith wrote to Dr. Benjamin Rush.[47]

This letter to Rush may be the only surviving example in her own hand from this period, for among the documents that exist, Abigail Junior's voice is otherwise mute. The voice that projects from this one letter, however, is distinct and resonant.[48] It begins as a model of self-restraint, perhaps reflecting the conventional epistolary style of the period and not just the deference of a sick woman for a man of professional authority. "You will I hope pardon the Liberty I have taken to address myself to you Sir upon a subject which has become very interesting to myself." Her salutation complete, the letter continues to describe her illness with the clinical detachment and descriptive detail of a medical case history. It had been in May 1810 that

> I first perceived a hardness in my right Breast just above the nipple which occasioned me an uneasy sensation—like a burning sometimes an itching—& at times a deep darting pain through the Breast—but without any dis-colouration at all. it has continued to Contract and the Breast has become much smaller than it was.—the tumour appears now about the size of a [Cap] and does not appear to adhere but to be loose—

Abigail Smith's remarkably explicit statement notes the essential facts, locating the tumor in place and time and tracing its transformation. She continued to describe her treatment: "I applied to a Physician and he recommended me to apply a Plaister of the circuta," which she did, but not experiencing relief, she discontinued this therapy. She had also "taken a considerable of the circuta in Pills," but the hemlock derivative had caused "a heaviness in my head," so she had stopped taking them too. Currently, she admitted, she used no medication. Her general health—the tumor aside—appeared good, she continued, but she was concerned, because the tumor was "becoming harder and a little redness at times on the skin." Smith probably knew from her own research that as cancer advanced, it often erupted or ulcerated on the surface of the skin. The lucid report of her disease reflects Smith's careful repetition of her tale, probably told many times before to doctors or family members. It reflects as well common medical procedure, for until the middle of the nineteenth century, it was unusual for physicians to examine their patients, particularly female patients. A meticulous, though subjective, statement was considered an adequate source of diagnostic data until the development of clinical procedure in the nineteenth century.[49] Smith, however, had been examined, for she wrote to Rush that "Dr. Warren who has seen it told me that in its present state he would not advise me to do anything for it." He had also warned that if it "should enflame," he would recommend surgery.

For the first time, then, Smith asserted her opinion, claiming "this is a remedy that I don't know in any Event I could consent to submit to." As if hearing protests, echoing from memories of previous discussions, she continued: "certainly I should wish to try every other possible expedient first." Culminating with the expression of her worst fear, Smith rested her case before Rush. She was asking for a reprieve.

Rush did not respond to Abigail Smith. He wrote instead to John Adams: "I prefer giving my Opinions & advice in her case in this way. You and Mrs. Adams may communicate it gradually . . ." and Rush advised the most dread therapy. He first cited his experience—fifty years of practice; he cited evidence—nineteen out of twenty cases of this sort. He diagnosed on the basis of Abigail Smith's description. "From her account . . . the tumour is now in a proper situation." The remedy, he sentenced, "is the knife."[50] Not known as a physician of conservative temperament, Rush had gained a reputation as an interventionist practitioner over the years, which had led to controversy.[51] His advice, in this case, however, fell within the scope of conventional cancer therapy. Surgery was radical therapy, but it was medically sound. The terrifying aspect, for any victim of surgery in that age before anesthesia, was the prospect of pain.[52]

Rush attempted to console Smith on this account. "The pain of the operation is much less than her fears represent it to be," he wrote. He personally had undergone surgery recently for a tumor, "perhaps a larger size," cut out of his neck, and the operation was concluded before he realized it. "I was surprised when the Doctor's assistant told me the operation was finished," he wrote, and he had exclaimed, "Is this all." What Rush dissembled, Smith comprehended; the operation would be painful. "I repeat again," he concluded, "let there be no delay in flying to the knife."

Rush's counsel proved decisive. Abigail Smith delayed for several days, but in the end agreed—probably in the face of overwhelming pressure—to submit to the surgery. Current medical wisdom, which advocated voluntary submission to cruel pain in order to live, prevailed, even in her own mind.

Less than two months after writing of her daughter's "charming visit," Abigail wrote a different tale to John Quincy. "There has been an operation upon your sister," she admitted and told the full story: that Abigail Smith had arrived in July with Caroline to consult with doctors about a tumor in her breast, that the doctors "had pronounced a tumor," and that in their opinion "there was no chance for her Life, but by an immediate operation." The surgery over, "she is doing as well as could be expected after an operation in which the whole Breast was taken off."[53]

Abigail's brief report once more suppressed as much as it confessed. At the end of a letter which informed John Quincy of the deaths of Mary and Richard Cranch, she also had the onerous duty to convey news of the death of Louisa Catherine Adams's mother. "My own Bosom has been so lacerated with repeated stories of woe that I can mingle, tear for tear, with [my] affected daughter," she wrote. "God grant that it may be good for me that I have been afflicted."[54]

Abigail Smith's surgery had occurred within days of the deaths of the Cranches. Abigail's presentation of the operation reflected her ambivalence. While she acknowledged the serious nature of her daughter's disease, her brief description comes at the very end of the letter, and she introduced it by forecasting its success: "Shall I fill my paper with Dirges? let me sing of mercies as well as judgments." She described the outcome of her daughter's operation as a mercy. She already had declared the operation a success; her life had been saved. "Every affected part was removed," she declared. "We have every prospect of her perfect recovery to heatlh and usefulness again."

Abigail reported only general information about the operation, however, in contrast to her earlier descriptions to John Quincy of the morbid details of other afflictions. Mary Cranch's "feet have swelld, and a voilent Cough daily wastes her," she had written. Sally Adams "was seized with a puking of Blood to a very allarming degree."[55] Abigail's reticence in the case of her daughter's operation, whether the consequence of social or emotional constraint, leaves a cloak of silence and secrecy about the mastectomy.

Less than two centuries after Abigail Adams did not fully describe Abigail Smith's mastectomy, I, a storyteller, wonder how to describe it. I have a dilemma. While there exists no evidence to reconstruct the history of Abigail Junior's operation, there does exist a detailed report of a mastectomy that occurred within days of hers. Fanny Burney, the English novelist, was operated on in Paris on September 30, 1811. Her entire breast was removed. Several months later Burney wrote a letter to her sister, Esther, telling in great detail—in Gothic detail—about her operation, about the discovery, the diagnosis, and the sentence to surgery. She wrote of her repugnance, her resistance, her courage. The work of a famous novelist, Burney's letter has the narrative drive of fiction in its attention to detail, character portrayal, imagery, and emotional impact.

Should I use this letter? If so, how can I use it? My story, after all, concerns the Adamses. Burney's story is sensational, horrible, repellent. Does her tale inform the story of Abigail Adams Smith? Does it contribute to the history of women? Is it history? I search for motives that justify its use—that this is medical history, that it relates medical history from the patient's viewpoint, from a female patient's viewpoint. It tells a story of women's courage in the face of pain, as numerous war stories have recounted male courage.

Moreover, this story enters the private, secret realm of female sexuality; it addresses the breast as an object of narration. The breast is hidden, obscuring the mysteries of female sexuality—of procreation and nurturance, emblematic of power that is at once awesome and terrifying. To lose a breast symbolizes failure and impotence. To lose a breast implies mortality.

I have decided to use portions of Fanny Burney's mastectomy narrative as a way of expressing the experience of Abigail Smith, but also because it addresses the history of women. It is the tale about many women's experiences that warrants telling.

Like Abigail Smith, Fanny Burney discovered her tumor in mid-1810. Both women described pain that increased; their language is similar. Both delayed appealing to physicians, submitted to medical examinations, resisted operations. Both lost right breasts, implying helplessness as right-handed women, which Burney admitted and Smith probably was. Both experienced humiliation before male physicians. Both were misled by doctors in the interests of their own well-being. Both deferred to the authority of professionals. Both protected their husbands by arranging their operations in their absence.

There were differences as well. Burney lived for thirty years and Smith died two years later. Burney wrote her story, to allay the fears of her sister but also to expunge its memory by recreating it in words. In the process, she recreated the story of other women as well.[56]

Burney's narrative begins with her discovery of the tumor. "About August 1810 I began to be annoyed by a small pain in my breast, which went on augmenting from week to week, yet being rather heavy than acute." Burney's husband, the Baron d'Arblay, urged her to see physicians; she resisted until he mobilized several of her friends to persuade her. "I was . . . rebellious to the first visit of this famous anatomist . . . so odious to me was this sort of process; however I was obliged to submit." After consultations with leading doctors, "I was condemned to an operation by all Three." They discussed pain: "*Vous Souffrirez—vous souffrirez beaucoup!*" came the response. They agreed not to set a date but rather to announce the operation spontaneously to ease her anxiety. Burney requested four hours' advance notice in order to banish her husband from the house.

The announcement came on the morning of September 30, 1811. She dressed. "I finished my breakfast, &—not with much appetite, you will believe! forced down a crust of bread." For the next few hours Burney was occupied with arrangements: "I had a bed, Curtains, & heaven knows what to prepare—but business was good for my nerves." Then, preparations complete, she had to wait. "This, indeed, was a dreadful interval. I had no longer anything to do—I had only to think—TWO HOURS thus spent seemed never-ending." She paced the room until she became "torpid,— without sentiment or consciousness."

At 3:00 the doctors began to arrive, "7 men in black." She was given a wine cordial. One doctor ordered the rearrangement of the room. "These arranged to his liking, he desired me to mount the Bedstead. I stood suspended, for a moment . . . I felt desperate—but it was only for a moment, my reason then took the command." M. Dubois, chief surgeon, issued commands "*en militaire,*" but again she resisted. "I was compelled, however, to submit to taking off my long *robe de Chambre,* which I had meant to retain—Ah, then, how did I think of My Sisters!—not one, at so dreadful an instant, at hand to protect—adjust—guard me."[57]

A handkerchief was placed over her eyes, but it was transparent. "I refused to be held; but when, Bright through the cambric, I saw the glitter of polished Steel—I closed my Eyes . . . a silence the most profound ensued, which lasted for some minutes." In those minutes the surgeons signalled to each other, making the sign of a cross with a circle, indicating that the whole breast must come off.

"The dreadful steel was plunged into the breast—cutting through veins-arteries-flesh-nerves . . . I began a scream that lasted unintermittingly during the whole time of the incision—& I marvel that It rings not in my Ears still! so excruciating was the agony." The wound was made and the knife withdrawn, only to be returned, "describing a curve—cutting against the grain, if I may say so, while the flesh resisted." Several times the surgeon, Dr. Larrey, stopped to rest his hand, to shift hands, to cut in the other direction. Several times Burney lost consciousness, revived by the pain. She felt the knife "[rank]ling against the breast bone—scraping it! . . . I heard the Voice of M. Larrey . . . in a tone nearly tragic, desire everyone present to pronounce if any thing more remained to be done." The response was "yes." The scraping continued until every "atom" was removed to the satisfaction of everyone. Finally came the treatment with salve and the bandaging.

"I bore it with all the courage I could exert, & never moved, nor stopt them, nor resisted, nor remonstrated, nor spoke," Burney wrote, "except once or twice during the dressings, to say '*Ah Messieurs! que je vous plain'* " (I pity you). This she addressed mainly to the kind-hearted Larrey whose whole face spoke grief to her.

The following day, October 1, 1811, a medical student who had been present at the surgery wrote its medical case history. The operation, which took twenty minutes, he reported, "was very painful and tolerated with great courage." He described the tumor as scirrhous (hardened), and wrote that it "showed the beginnings of a cancerous degeneration in its center," but that all parts were removed and the operation appeared a success. He described post-operative spasms and nausea, but the patient had two hours of peaceful sleep. By 10:00 the next morning, "the patient was surprised at the well-being she felt."[58] The physicians prescribed a diet of boiled rice pudding, meat jelly, chicken broth, and a portion of barley "gummed and acidified with lemon."

Abigail Smith remained in Quincy through the winter and spring after her mastectomy, recuperating steadily under the care of her mother. "My dear Mrs. Smith is upon the recovery from a most dangerous and what must have proved fatal disease," Abigail wrote in late November.[59] Weeks later she wrote to John Quincy: "Your sister is recovering fast but time only can be expected to restore after such an operation."[60] By late December, she had regained some use of her arm, and in the new year of 1812, there was general acknowledgment that the operation was a success.[61] Benjamin Rush wrote to John Adams to express sincere pleasure "in the successful issue of the operation upon Mrs. Smith's breast."[62] Finally, Abigail declared to John Quincy: "Your sister Smith . . . has recovered from the operation . . . and does not experience any inconvenience but a weakness in her arm."[63]

That year after the mastectomy and the deaths of the Cranches was a time of recuperation for Abigail Adams as well as for Abigail Smith. "My Bosom has indeed been lacerated with wound upon wound," she wrote to her daughter-in-law Louisa Catherine, choosing a metaphor that identified herself with her daughter's condition. "I can scarcely trust my pen to describe them," she persisted, but, nevertheless, she recounted the details of her wounds—that in addition to the surgery and deaths, Mrs. Charles Adams "has recovered from a puking of Blood in large quantities which endangered her life" for many months.[64] She reiterated her woes to John Quincy, adding that "about the same Time Your Father received a wound in one of his Legs which became so serious to oblige him to keep it up for two months and have it daily attended by a surgeon."

"Amidst this complicated scene of distress, grief and sorrow, I am alive to relate it. Spared Sustaind Supported beyond what I could conceive." Once more choosing the metaphor that identified her ordeal with her daughter, she continued: "The only balm to heal the wounded Bosom, is to be found in the Christian Religion which teaches us Submission and resignation to the all wise all merciful Sovereign of the Universe."[65] In fact, while Abigail derived spiritual comfort from religion, she was consoled consciously by the presence of her daughter and beloved granddaughter Caroline. Elizabeth wrote to her nephew that "I rejoice that your Sister Smith and daughter are with your Parents during this long cold winter to cheer their gloomy Hours."[66]

Believing her recovery complete, Abigail Junior and Caroline Smith returned to New York State in the early summer of 1812, leaving behind aged parents who were saddened. "It has been a relief to us to hear that you are well, and that your dear Mother bore her journey so well," Abigail wrote to Caroline. But she confessed that their absense left "my spirits at a very low ebb."[67]

Abigail Smith's reprieve from illness was short-lived, for by the following December, she was suffering once more from what everyone described as "rheumatism." "Mrs. Smith has been much troubled this winter with the rheumatism both in her Limbs and back," Abigail Adams wrote to a friend, noting at the same time that the latest news reported her condition improved. Furthermore, she explained with some pride, Colonel Smith had been elected to Congress from his district in New York, "by a large majority of votes."[68]

As Abigail Smith's health declined over the winter, suspicion mounted among family members that the diagnosis of rheumatism disguised the reality of recurrent cancer. Mother and daughter in a series of letters began to discuss the possibility of one or the other visiting: "I have urged her to come and pass the time with me during the col.s absence in Congress and she had determined to do so if she should recover so as to make such a journey."[69] Abigail did not feel strong enough for the journey, nor did she wish to leave John.

By June of 1813, it was accepted that Mrs. Smith's cancer had returned; her other breast was clearly affected, and the disease had probably metastasized internally. "When you first mentioned her having the Rheumatism I was apprehensive her disease was of a diffrent nature," admitted Elizabeth.[70] Mercy Otis Warren wrote to inquire: "It was reported to me yesterday that my beloved Mrs. Smith was again attacked by a dreadful malady which she had once surmounted; and that apprehensive of its fatal and speedy termination she has sent for her mother. Please answer. . . ."[71] Finally, Abigail acknowledged the terrible truth that she had resisted: "Of your dear and only Sister," she wrote to John Quincy, "I can only say that she has been and still is a patient sufferer under severe and afflicting Pain. . . . Heaven only knows to what sufferings she may yet be reserved. My heart bleeds—I cannot get to her. nor she to me. I am too infirm myself to undertake such a journey."[72]

So powerful was the desire to be with her mother that Abigail Smith did return to Quincy to die. "Mrs. Smith [arrived] here Yesterday about ten o clock," Abigail wrote to her niece Lucy Cranch Greenleaf. "She is indeed a very sick woman. spasms draw her up. cannot take food. everything oppresses her. . . . how she got here is a marvel to me."[73] Elizabeth commented: "O What a solace to be folded to a fond Mothers Bosom."[74] Abigail wrote to John Quincy that "I fear I shall have one of the most distressing and trying scenes of my Life to go through."[75]

Abigail Smith lived for three weeks, nursed by her mother and daughter, cared for by her father, son, relatives, and friends. William Stephens Smith arrived from Washington one week before his wife's death. By all reports, Mrs. Smith died peacefully. "After a few struggles her spirit was released to join those of your dear parents and many others of the just made perfect," Abigail wrote to her niece.[76]

Following Abigail Smith's death, Abigail Adams's resistance to writing about her daughter's condition collapsed. She became voluble and glib, writing obsessively about Mrs. Smith, repeating, mantra-like, the story of her cancer, the operation, the outcome. In letter after letter for months, she wrote about her daughter's virtues, her goodness, and her certain passage to a better life. She described her own grief, her struggle to accept this blow as an act of providence, her acceptance and resignation, but again, her grief. She wrote to John Quincy; to Louisa Catherine; to Mercy Otis Warren; to Lucy Greenleaf; to Thomas Jefferson; to Francis Vanderkemp; to Julia Rush—and doubtless more letters that did not survive. "I have lost, O what have I not lost in . . . my only daughter, one endowed with every virtue, consummate prudence industery frugality patience resignation and submission to her lot and portion in Life and in Death."[77] For month after month, in letter after letter Abigail poured out her pain. She could no longer deny circumstances by silence. The death of her daughter opened the floodgates of emotion, and Abigail wrote about her grief.

"To me the loss is irreparable," she wrote to John Quincy.[78] For the first time in her life, Abigail expressed loss of hope. No event, no issue had ever conquered her belief in her own recovery. She had always known that time would heal her wounds; she had always advocated patience. The death of her daughter was a crisis of a different magnitude: "The wound which has lacerated my Bosom cannot be healed."[79] A fire had dimmed in her soul.

Something else changed. Over the years, Abigail's religious beliefs had been increasingly liberal. She had believed in one God who worked in mysterious but benign ways. But after her daughter's death she wrote: "My own loss is not to be estimated by words and can only be alleviated by the consoling belief that my Dear Child is partaking of the Life and immortality brought to Light by him who endured the cross and is gone before to prepare a place for those who Love him and express his commandments."[80] The rhetoric of the Trinity had entered into the language of this eighteenth-century woman who had rejected Calvinism as too harsh, Catholicism as she observed it in France as too heathen, and the Anglicanism of England as too intolerant; who had read and conversed with Richard Price and Joseph Priestley, whose spiritual leaning was towards Unitarianism. So convulsive was the blow of her daughter's death, that Abigail reverted to Trinitarian doctrine that contained the consoling assurance of a hereafter for her "pure," "blameless," "virtuous", and, therefore, saved daughter.

The mother-daughter bond is most often described from the perspective of the daughter; from birth to death, the empathic approach is that of younger to older, from infant bonding, separation, tension, to resolution.[81] The death of the Mother is described, as is the daughter's struggle to adjust. In her letters, Abigail Adams told a different story, that of a mother's bond and love for her daughter. From the time she was separated from Abigail Junior by marriage and wrote: "She has always been my closest companion," to her old age, she described the deep connection she experienced with her daughter. "I feel grateful for having it thus in my power to hold converse with you, my dear and beloved daughter, separated as we are by circumstances which we cannot control, and to which we are necessitated to submit. When my mind is sometimes prone to rebel and rise indignant against those who have been the cause of our painful separation, I hush each mummuring sigh by the consideration, that it is one of those trials assigned me by Providence, not only to wean me from the world, but to teach me submission, and make me humble."[82] Puritan rationale crept into Abigail's vision of separation.

By declaring that she would not recover, that the loss was irreparable, Abigail was claiming that a part of her had died. She identified with her daughter in life; that bond broken in death, a part of her had died. She consoled herself: "O my Full Heart, shall I wish for life for her who is releived from pain and sufferings."[83]

Abigail's correspondence during this two-year ordeal describes her method of coping with her daughter's mortality. She could not confront the cancer and the operation by writing about it; instead, she focused her attention on the several other demands of her world. She substituted the illness and death of others as the source of her pain. Once the operation was completed, she immediately declared the mastectomy a success. The strength of her connection with her daughter was revealed by identifying her emotional condition with Mrs. Smith's physical condition; she wrote about the "laceration" of her own "Bosom." Finally, after Abigail Smith's death, the floodgates of emotion were opened, and she released her grief. Letter after letter intoned the same message, making it real to herself that Abigail Smith had died.

Abigail Adams viewed herself differently after her daughter's death. She began to advise people that she had changed: the "years have stamped with indelible furros your Mothers visage," she warned John Quincy.

> Grief since you saw me last
> And carefull hours with times deformed hand
> Hath written strange the feature o're my face.[84]

She wrote this same message to Thomas Jefferson and Francis Vanderkemp. Not given to self-indulgence, Abigail described her visage to
herself as well as to others. She presented physical evidence of her grief.
She saw herself as deformed by grief.

Historians tell us that death in that period was an event in cultural
transition, and that New England society with its Puritan heritage was
unique in its rites of passage. The mentality that comprehended death and
the protocols of death differed, but they were also in the process of changing from a traditional to a modern social world. The case of the Adamses
confirms this analysis. Some aspects of the older tradition, what Philippe
Ariès has called "tame death" and some of what everyone calls the nineteenth-century stance, "romantic" or "sentimental" death, describe Abigail
Smith's death.[85]

It hardly bears repeating, especially in light of the events described in
this episode, that death and dying were still ubiquitous in the early nineteenth century. Over a few short years, Abigail Adams experienced the
deaths of her niece Elizabeth Cranch Norton, her sister, and her brother-in-
law Cranch. A child of her son Thomas Boylston Adams died, as did the
infant daughter of John Quincy in St. Peterburg. She wrote a letter of
condolence to her widowed friend, Mrs. Black. Benjamin Rush died less
than six months before Abigail Smith. Sally Adams lay near death both in
the summer of 1811 and 1813 in the Adams home, but she recovered. Most
of those who died were either very young or very old; the death of a mature
but not aged person, while not untypical, was regarded as most unfortunate. "Bitter is the loss of a sweet Infant," wrote Abigail, "but how much
more increased are the pangs which rent the Heart of a Mother, when
called to part with the Head of a family, in the midst of her Days, and
usefulness? endeared by a thousand strong ties?"[86]

In fact, both of her sisters had lost adult daughters. Elizabeth Cranch
Norton had died, leaving eight small children, who were placed among
relatives.[87] Betsy Shaw had died of consumption in 1798. "Yes! my dear
sister, I fully know that a fond Parent suffers, at beholding a beloved Child
fatally arrested," Elizabeth wrote. "It makes Nature bleed at every pore and
can never be effaced from my memory."[88]

Abigail Smith took charge of her own death, mobilizing all her strength
to go to her mother, to die in her parents' home. Death was not yet
controlled by the medical or another social institution. Abigail died in the
place of her choice, among the people she cared for. Her death was not
considered private; she was surrounded by people. Children were not
shielded, could not be shielded from the obvious. "It is better to go to the
House of mourning than to the House of Feasting or Dancing. for the living
lay it to heart," Abigail Adams wrote to her grandsons. "You my dear
Children are now calld to the House of Mourning and sorrow, by the death

of your Dear Aunt Smith, and the only daughter of your grandparents, and the only sister of your Father."[89]

The "tame death," which was both familiar and near, characterized the early nineteenth century; simplicity of ritual and controlled emotions further distinguished traditional reactions to death. Whether the Adamses exhibited emotion or great self-control is unknown, for Abigail described only the funeral ritual: that Mrs. Smith's remains were deposited in the family vault after a service "attended by a numerous concourse of relative and Friends." Abigail approved of Mr. Whiting's eulogy, which did "ample Justice to her Life, Death and character."[90]

The intensity of grief that Abigail exhibited in letters, however, falls within the scope of modern sentimental responses to death. As the nineteenth century progressed, historians note, emotional expressiveness became appropriate. Abigail now idealized her daughter, partly because it reassured her of her daughter's redemption, but also because she had extolled Abigail Junior during her lifetime; in death her representations became more lofty. That idealization, historians suggest, represents one more modern trend, that of "separation," of individuating, of distinguishing between "my death" and "thy death," or myself from yourself, of giving worth to another by missing her.[91] Acceptance of her daughter's death did not come easily to Abigail, despite her religious convictions. She wrote of her ambivalence, wanting her daughter with her, but also knowing that she was freed from the pain of her illness in a better world. That juxtaposition of traditional and modern reactions, exhibited in her response to her daughter's death, was metaphoric of Abigail Adams's general approach to life. She contained within herself the strength of traditional New England Puritanism along with a forward-looking nineteenth-century vision, open to difference, to change, to opportunity.

Lights dimmed in Abigail's soul when her daughter died, but they did not go out. She began to emerge from her consuming grief, to focus on other people, to measure the tempo of the world again. "How great is the sum of the Blessings still left me," she wrote to Louisa Catherine. "She has left me a treasure." Abigail meant Caroline; and to Mercy Otis Warren, she described her granddaughter as "the dear representative of her mother: all that I can wish for. She is."[92] She described her "blessings" to John Quincy: "one of the first of these, is the Life, health, and cheerfullness of your Father. bowed down as he has been . . . he has not sunk under it."[93] She looked to her grandchildren—some of whom continued to live with her—for the future, and she hoped to see John Quincy again.

Her letters became an amalgam: doleful always about the death of Abigail Smith, a loss "which can never be effaced from my memory so long as breath remains"; hopeful when she wrote of the prospects of her children and grandchildren. Yet the old spark was ignited by politics: "We look

at the gigantic Armies of Russia and France [Napoleon had invaded]. . . .
Our own are in comparison as Lillyputians. Yet great deeds may be performed by small means." She described Perry's victory on Lake Erie,
thrilled with his words—"We have met them, and they are ours"—and she
compared him with Caesar.[94]

Yet Abigail felt old. She began to caution people who had not seen her
that her appearance had changed: "Years and affliction have made such
depredations upon your parents, more particularly upon your Mother, that
should she live to see you again, you would find her so changed in person,
that you would scarcly know her—." Her admonition continued, however,
to stress that surfaces were ephemeral. In the end, other attributes, "mental
graces," she called them, persisted, and she listed the qualities by which
she wished to be remembered:

> Yet at the darkened Eye, the witherd face
> or hoary hair, I never will repine:
> But Spair O time, what'er of mental grace
> of Candour, Love, or Sympathy divine
> What ever of fancys may or Friendship flame is mine.[95]

Epilogue

Reminiscing to her sister Elizabeth at the end of her life, Abigail observed: "You and I my dear Sister have gone through a long Life—with as few rubs of a rational nature as falls the Lot of Humanity." Abigail was recovering from a bad cold and suffering from rheumatism of the hip. Now that she was seventy years old, she confronted death with every illness, and her thoughts frequently turned to the past. Abigail peristed: "I have sometimes insisted upon my own way. and my opinion and sometimes yealded silently!" This account of life that she professed perhaps accurately reflected the past as she perceived it now that she was old and reflective. She had made peace with an imperfect world.

Abigail's uncanny optimism, which had sustained her since as a young girl she had written, "I am not made of a gloomy nature," survived into old age. Therefore, she painted her self-portrait, physical decay aside, in the same bright colors that limned the picture of her youthful character. She discounted the social and personal upheavals of fifty years as the understated "few rubs" that befall the lot of humanity.

She had made rational choices, she claimed, great choices such as the selection of her partner, that forecast her destiny. She considered her marriage: "After half a century, I can say. my choice would be the same if I again had youth. and opportunity to make it." She reflected also upon the somber irrevocability of that decision: "The die once cast, there is no retreat. untill death." In her youth she had described her marriage as formulated in love, the "tye more binding than humanity"; in old age she acknowledged the religious and contractual nature of the tie from which there was "no retreat."

History and biological nature had caused enormous upheavals in her life, to which she responded with the spiritual condition of acceptance—but she was not always so good as she professed at silence. It was only after she had emerged from her emotional battles, the price she paid for acceptance, that she retreated into silence. Her ability to confront and express grief, anger, fear, and loneliness led to the triumph of her reason and the spiritual condition of acceptance that she now claimed. It also accounts, in part, for the volumes of letters into which she poured her full character.

As she grew very old, she most feared that she would lose her reason. She did not. The letters continued, the hand more tremorous and weak, the writing more wispy, describing her daily activities and her infirmities. She died on October 28, 1818, just a few weeks short of her seventy-fourth birthday.

Notes

Introduction

1. Massachusetts Historical Society, Adams Papers, microfilm edition, 608 reels, Reel 122, June 26, 1818.
2. L. H. Butterfield et al., eds., *Adams Family Correspondence*, 4 volumes (Cambridge, Mass.: 1963, 1973), I, 154, Sept. 16, 1774.
3. Library of Congress, Shaw Papers, microfilm edition, 4 reels, Reel 1, Feb. 1814.
4. Stewart Mitchell, ed., *New Letters of Abigail Adams, 1788–1801* (Westport, Conn.: 1947), p. 182, May 26, 1798.

1. The Abigail Industry

1. Charles Francis Adams, "Memoir of Mrs. Adams," *Letters of Mrs. Adams, Wife of John Adams* (Boston: 1848), p. xxxi.
2. Charles Francis Adams edited liberally to present his family in the most favorable light. He suppressed passages, even destroyed whole letters that he considered unimportant or in poor taste, and changed spelling, grammar, and punctuation. The full corpus of family papers remained in the family library at Quincy until 1905, when the Adams Trust was created and the papers were moved for safekeeping to the Massachusetts Historical Society. In 1952 the trust transferred ownership from the Adams descendants to the society and appointed Lyman H. Butterfield editor. Under his stewardship, the full corpus of papers—which span three generations from the time of Abigail and John to the year 1890—became available for the first time on 608 reels of microfilm. More than one hundred reels cover Abigail-related correspondence. Since then, four volumes of Adams Family Correspondence, including Abigail's letters to the year 1782, have been made available in a letterpress edition, L. H. Butterfield et al., eds., *The Adams Family Correspondence*, 4 volumes (Cambridge, Mass.: 1963, 1973). Hereafter cited as AFC. For the full story of the Adams Papers, see L. H. Butterfield, "Introduction," *The Adams Papers: Diary and Autobiography of John Adams*, 4 volumes (Cambridge, Mass.: 1961), I, xiii–lxxiv, and "The Papers of the Adams Family: Some Account of Their History," Massachusetts Historical Society, *Proceedings* 71 (1959), pp. 328–56. For additional Abigail correspondence, see Charles Francis Adams, ed., *Correspondence between John Adams and Mercy Warren* (New York: 1972); L. H. Butterfield et al., eds., *The Book of Abigail and John: Selected Letters of the Adams Family 1762–1784* (Cambridge, Mass.: 1975); Lester Cappon, ed., *The Adams-Jefferson Letters: The Complete Correspondence between Thomas Jefferson and Abigail and John Adams* (Chapel Hill: 1959); Caroline Smith DeWindt, ed., *The Journal and Correspondence of Miss Adams, Daughter of John Adams*, 2 volumes (New York: 1841–42); and Stewart Mitchell, ed., *New Letters of Abigail Adams, 1788–1801* (Westport, Conn.: 1947).
3. The Abigail industry embraces much more than I show here, and includes children's books, graduate theses, patriotic memorabilia such as a recent collectors' coin, and a 1985 postage stamp.
4. In a typically newsy and chatty letter Abigail wrote to John in Philadelphia,

"I long to hear that you have declared an independancy—and by the way in the new Code of Laws which I suppose it will be necessary for you to make I desire you would Remember the Ladies, and be more generous and favorable to them than your ancestors. Do not put such unlimited power into the hands of the Husbands" (AFC, I, 370, Mar. 31, 1776).

5. L. H. Butterfield, "Abigail Adams," in Edward T. James et al., eds., *Notable American Women 1607–1950: A Biographical Dictionary* (Cambridge, Mass.: 1971), p. 6.

6. Little evidence survives about Abigail's youth. The earliest letter in her collected correspondence, written to her cousin Isaac Smith, Jr., is dated March 16, 1763, when she was eighteen years old (AFC, I, 3). References to her youth appear throughout the correspondence and are useful for reconstructing details of her early years. Her father's and her uncle's diaries provide insights into the environment in which Abigail grew up. See "Diaries of Rev. William Smith and Dr. Cotton Tufts, 1738–1784," Massachusetts Historical Society, *Proceedings*, 3d ser., 2 (1908–1909), pp. 444–70.

7. Laurel Thatcher Ulrich, writing of an earlier period, describes wives taking over absent men's duties as "deputy husbands," an accepted role: *Good Wives: Image and Reality in the Lives of Women in Northern New England, 1650–1750* (New York: 1980), pp. 35–50.

8. Elizabeth Ellet, *The Women of the American Revolution* (New York: 1848). For a similar interpretation, see Mary S. Logan, *The Part Taken by Women in American History* (New York: 1972).

9. Ellet, *Women of the Revolution*, p. 303.

10. Meade Minnigerode, *Some American Ladies: Seven Informal Biographies* (New York: 1926), p. 63.

11. Anne Husted Burleigh, *John Adams* (New Rochelle: 1969), p. 48.

12. Janet Whitney, *Abigail Adams* (Boston: 1947). Although this chapter does not review Irving Stone's fictionalized double biography of Abigail and John, *Those Who Love* (New York: 1965), it is one of the more accurate, detailed, and readable accounts of the Adamses' lives.

13. Whitney, *Abigail Adams*, p. 54. Catherine Drinker Bowen's fictionalized biography of John contains the same melodrama: "John left the chair, crossed the room to Abigail and inquired what she was reading. She held up the book: it was Locke on the 'Human Understanding.' John smiled looking down at the girl. . . . 'A big book for such a little head,' John said, taking the volume from her," *John Adams and the American Revolution* (Boston: 1950), p. 232.

14. Whitney, *Abigail Adams*, p. 123.

15. Ibid., p. 15.

16. Ibid., p. 270.

17. Phyllis Lee Levin, *Abigail Adams* (New York: 1987).

18. Ibid., p. xv.

19. Ibid., pp. 77–79, 121–23, 140–48, 286–93, 299–305.

20. Ibid., p. 97.

21. Ibid., p. 84.

22. Ibid., p. xv.

23. Ibid., pp. 526, n. 24; 536, n. 20.

24. Ibid., p. 20.

25. Ibid., p. 177.

26. Ibid., p. 431.

27. Page Smith, *John Adams*, 2 volumes (New York: 1962). Also see Smith, *Daughters of the Promised Land: Women in American History* (Boston: 1970).

28. Smith, *John Adams*, I, 71.

29. Ibid., 336.

30. Ibid., II, 608.

31. AA to Royall Tyler, Adams Papers, microfilm edition, Reel 364, Jan. 4, 1785. All references to the Adams Papers are to the microfilm edition published by the Massachusetts Historical Society, Boston. Hereafter cited as AP.

32. For her negative attitude toward France see AA to MOW, AP, Reel 363, Sept. 1784; AA to Cotton Tufts, ibid., Reel 363, Sept. 8, 1784; AA to Royall Tyler, ibid., Reel 364, Jan. 4, 1785; and AA to Charles Storer, ibid., Reel 364, Jan. 3, 1785.

33. Smith, *John Adams*, I, 431. Smith has not been alone in making the distinction between masculine and feminine qualities. Gamaliel Bradford described Abigail's "masculine" mind and nerves: "The wife of President John Adams and the mother of President John Quincy Adams is sometimes accused of being more man than woman in her temperament." See Bradford, *Portraits of American Women* (New York: 1919), p. 3.

34. Smith, *John Adams*, I, 336–37.

35. Elizabeth Evans, *Weathering the Storm: Women of the American Revolution* (New York: 1975).

36. Ibid., p. 5. The author identifies Abigail Adams by her husband and Mercy Otis Warren by her brother.

37. Richard B. Morris, *Seven Who Shaped Our Destiny: The Founding Fathers as Revolutionaries* (New York: 1973), p. 84. The term "feminism" was not used until the late nineteenth century. See Karen Offen, "Defining Feminism: A Comparative Historical Perspective," *Signs: Journal of Women in Culture and Society* 14 (1988), pp. 119–57.

38. "The Adams Chronicles," directed by Virginia Kassel (New York: WNET, 1975).

39. Joan Hoff-Wilson, "The Illusion of Change: Women and the American Revolution," in Alfred F. Young, ed., *The American Revolution: Explorations in the History of American Radicalism* (DeKalb, Ill.: 1976), p. 427.

40. Linda Grant DePauw, "The American Revolution and the Rights of Women: The Feminist Theory of Abigail Adams," in Larry R. Gerlach et al., eds., *The Legacy of the American Revolution* (Logan, Utah: 1978), p. 203.

41. Nancy F. Cott, "Passionlessness: An Interpretation of Victorian Sexual Ideology, 1790–1850," *Signs, Journal of Women in Culture and Society* 4 (1978), p. 229. Also see Cott, *The Bonds of Womanhood* (New Haven, Conn.: 1977), p. 162.

42. Mary Beth Norton, *Liberty's Daughters: The Revolutionary Experience of American Women, 1750–1800* (Boston: 1980), p. 50.

43. Carl N. Degler, *At Odds: Women and the Family in America from the Revolution to the Present* (New York: 1980), p. 190.

44. David F. Musto, "The Youth of John Quincy Adams," American Philosophical Society, *Proceedings* 113 (1969), pp. 269–82. Also see Musto, "The Adams Family," Massachusetts Historical Society, *Proceedings* 93 (1981), pp. 40–58; Joseph E. Illick, "John Quincy Adams: The Maternal Influence," *Journal of Psychohistory* 4 (1976), pp. 185–95. Illick addressed the absence of historical interest in Abigail's role as a parent: "Historians . . . have always recognized her presence though they have implicitly denied her importance" (p. 185).

45. Musto, "Youth," p. 269.

46. Ibid., p. 278.

47. Ibid., p. 280.

48. See Juliet Mitchell, *Psychoanalysis and Feminism* (New York: 1974), pp. 290–91. Also see David Spiegel, "Mothering, Fathering, and Mental Illness," in Barrie Thorne with Marilyn Yalom, eds., *Rethinking the Family* (New York: 1982), pp. 95–110. Spiegel wrote, "The relationship of families to mental illness is important from a feminist perspective because 'family' is a code word for 'mother.' . . . Most family

explanations for serious mental illness focus on problems in the mother-child, not the father-child interaction" (p. 95). Marilyn Yalom refers to the "blame-the-mother mode" in *Maternity, Mortality and the Literature of Madness* (University Park, Pa.: 1985), pp. 90, 109.

49. Musto, "Youth," p. 280.

50. For the most penetrating work on John's personality, see Peter Shaw, *The Character of John Adams* (Chapel Hill: 1976). Shaw probes for the private character behind the public figure, using literary technique and psychological theory to reveal the range of emotion and, often, the fragility of John's character.

51. AA to JQA, AP, Reel 359, Nov. 17, 1787.

52. Charles W. Akers, *Abigail Adams: An American Woman* (Boston: 1980); Lynne Withey, *Dearest Friend: A Life of Abigail Adams* (New York: 1981).

53. Withey, *Dearest Friend*, pp. ix–xiii.

54. Ibid., p. xii.

55. Ibid., p. 151.

56. AA to JA, AP, Reel 361, Dec. 17, 1783.

57. Withey, *Dearest Friend*, p. 70.

58. AA to JA, AP, Reel 361, Oct. 19, 1783.

59. AA to JA, ibid., Dec. 7, 1783.

60. For Mercy Otis Warren, see Lester H. Cohen, "Explaining the Revolution: Ideology and Ethics in Mercy Otis Warren's Historical Theory," *William and Mary Quarterly*, 3d series, 37 (1980), pp. 200–18. See also Lester H. Cohen, "Mercy Otis Warren: The Politics of Language and the Aesthetics of Self," *American Quarterly* 35 (1983), pp. 481–98.

61. AA to Isaac Smith Jr., AFC, I, 76, Apr. 20, 1771.

62. AA to Benjamin Waterhouse, AP, Reel 358, Oct. 6, 1782.

63. Edith B. Gelles, "Abigail Adams: Domesticity and the American Revolution," *New England Quarterly* 52 (1979), pp. 500–21.

64. Withey, *Dearest Friend*, p. ix. Wollstonecraft was not published until 1787.

65. Akers, *Abigail Adams*, p. 22.

66. Ibid., p. 3.

67. Ibid., p. 1.

68. Ibid., p. 114.

69. AA to JA, AP, Reel 361, July 21, 1783.

70. Linda K. Kerber, "The Republican Mother: Women and the Enlightenment—An American Perspective," *American Quarterly* 28 (1976), pp. 187–205. Linda K. Kerber, *Women of the Republic: Intellect and Ideology in Revolutionary America* (Chapel Hill: 1980). The stereotype of the republican woman, which originated in Kerber's analytic work, has now moved into the genre as a popular label, calling up imagery but covering up all the nuance, subtlety, and character of the women it labels. Its use as a vague descriptor both universalizes and diminishes individual women.

71. Akers, *Abigail Adams*, p. 146.

72. Ibid., pp. 156, 162.

73. Ibid., p. 178.

74. Paul C. Nagel, *Descent from Glory: Four Generations of the John Adams Family* (New York: 1983), p. 3.

75. Ibid., pp. 26, 77, 90, 110, 87, 118. John's situation was actually more acute, for "he frequently battled the melancholy . . . which occasionally incapacitated him," p. 15.

76. Ibid., pp. 60, 61.

77. Ibid., pp. 28, 52.

78. Ibid., p. 19.

79. Nagel, *Descent*, p. 19.
80. Gelles, "Abigail Adams," pp. 500–21.
81. Nagel, *Descent*, pp. 19, 50.
82. AA to John Thaxter, AP, Reel 361, July 1, 1783.
83. AA to Mary Cranch, Abigail Adams Papers, American Antiquarian Society, Jan. 20, 1787.
84. Nagel, *Descent*, p. 20. This comes from a letter Abigail wrote to John Quincy, when she thought he was overworking and neglecting exercise. AP, Reel 369, Nov. 28, 1786.
85. AA to Lucy Cranch, AP, Reel 369, Apr. 25, 1787.
86. Nagel, *Descent*, p. 20.
87. Ibid., p. 22.
88. Ibid., pp. 25–26.
89. Ibid., p. 20.
90. Ibid., pp. 20, 24.
91. Abigail criticized women for social ostentation and for frivolous display, but she generally cared for women. For Mme Lafayette, to whom she was immediately attracted, see AA to Mary Cranch, AP, Reel 363, Dec. 9–12, 1784. Abigail wrote of Martha Washington, "No Lady can be more deservedly beloved and esteemed than she is, and we have lived in habits of intimacy and Friendship." Mitchell, ed., *New Letters of Abigail Adams, 1788–1801* (Westport, Conn.: 1947), p. 57.
92. Nagel, *Descent*, p. 57. Carroll Smith-Rosenberg argues against the existence of mother-daughter tensions before the late nineteenth century because the continuity between the lives of women over generations encouraged close bonding. Daughters' lives repeated the patterns of mothers and grandmothers. Further, she points out that demographically, because of the number of offspring and the disparity in ages, there were many maternal figures within the extended family to diffuse the intensity of the mother-daughter relationship. *Disorderly Conduct: Visions of Gender in Victorian America* (New York: 1985), pp. 2–34.
93. AA to Mrs. Margaret Smith, AP, Reel 371, Apr. 22, 1788.
94. Nagel, *Descent*, p. 46.
95. Ibid., pp. 46–47.
96. Ibid., p. 80.
97. Ibid., p. 100.
98. Ibid., p. 109.
99. Ibid., p. 81.
100. Paul C. Nagel, *The Adams Women: Abigail and Louisa Adams, Their Sisters and Daughters* (New York: 1987).
101. Ibid., pp. 20, 32, 33, 35, 52, 53, 72, 76, 77, passim.
102. Ibid., p. 72.
103. Ibid., p. 99.
104. Ibid., p. 101.
105. Ibid., pp. 21–25, 60–62, 74.
106. Ibid., p. 103.
107. AA to JA, AP, Reel 361, Oct. 19, 1783. For the Nabby Adams-Royall Tyler romance, see chapter 5. Also see G. Thomas Tanselle, *Royall Tyler* (Cambridge, Mass.: 1967); Frederick Tupper and Helen Tyler Brown, eds., *Grandmother Tyler's Book: The Recollections of Mary Palmer Tyler, 1775–1866* (New York: 1925).
108. C. F. Adams, ed. *Correspondence between Adams and Warren*, pp. 493–94.
109. AA to JA, AFC, II, 133, Sept. 23, 1776; AFC, I, 310, Oct. 22, 1775.
110. For an analysis of gossip as a bonding agent within families, as well as distinctions between benign and malicious gossip, see chapter 5.
111. For women's life cycles, see Michael Kammen, "Changing Perceptions of the

Life Cycle in American Thought and Culture," Massachusetts Historical Society, *Proceedings* 91 (1979), pp. 35–66, especially pp. 48–52.

112. Shaw, *John Adams*, p. 94.

113. Smith-Rosenberg, *Disorderly Conduct*, p. 20.

114. By "domestic patriotism," I mean the work that women did at home to contribute to the war effort. AA to JA, AFC, IV, 328, June 17, 1782.

2. . . . a tye more binding . . .

1. Charles Francis Adams, ed., "Memoir of Mrs. Adams," in *Familiar Letters of John Adams and His Wife Abigail Adams, during the Revolution* (Boston: 1876), pp. xiv–xv.

2. Historians have variously calculated the average age at marriage for women in mid-eighteenth-century America as between 21 and 23; see Philip J. Greven, Jr., *Four Generations: Population, Land and Family in Colonial Andover, Massachusetts* (Ithaca, N.Y.: 1970), pp. 208–209; James A. Henretta, *The Evolution of American Society, 1700–1815* (Lexington, Mass.: 1973), p. 12; Daniel Scott Smith, "Parental Control and Marriage Patterns: An Analysis of Historical Trends in Hingham, Massachusetts," in Michael Gordon, ed., *The American Family in Social-Historical Perspective,* (New York: 1978), pp. 95–96.

3. For the emergence of the legal profession, see Richard D. Brown, *Knowledge Is Power: The Diffusion of Information in Early America, 1700–1865* (New York: 1989), pp. 82–84; Gerald W. Gawalt, *The Promise of Power: The Emergence of the Legal Profession in Massachusetts, 1760–1840* (Westport, Conn.: 1979); John M. Murrin, "The Legal Transformation: The Bench and Bar of Eighteenth-Century Massachusetts," in Stanley N. Katz and John M. Murrin, eds., *Colonial America: Essays in Politics and Social Development,* third edition (New York: 1983), pp. 540–72.

4. Charles Francis Adams, *Familiar Letters,* pp. xiv–vx.

5. Myths stabilize and integrate social organizations. They express or codify beliefs. They resolve contradictions, even prophesy. See Clifford Geertz, *Myth, Symbol, and Culture* (New York: 1971); Peter Novick, *That Noble Dream* (New York: 1988), pp. 4–5.

6. For changing marriage patterns, see Alan Macfarlane, *Marriage and Love in England, 1300–1840* (New York: 1986); Lawrence Stone, *The Family, Sex, and Marriage in England 1500–1800* (New York: 1977).

7. For cultural relativity, see Michel Foucault, *History of Sexuality,* 3 volumes (New York: 1978–1986); Clifford Geertz, *The Interpretation of Cultures* (New York: 1973); Richard Handler, "Boasian Anthropology and the Critique of American Culture," *American Quarterly,* 42 (1990), 252–73.

8. Macfarlane makes this point. *Marriage,* pp. 35–41.

9. For general remarks about sexuality in eighteenth-century New England, see John D'Emilio and Estelle B. Freedman, *Intimate Matters: A History of Sexuality in America* (New York: 1988), pp. 39–54.

10. Letter to Francis Vanderkemp, Feb. 3, 1814, cited in Charles Francis Adams, *Letters of Mrs. Adams, the Wife of John Adams* (Boston: 1848), p. 416.

11. See John Demos, *A Little Commonwealth: Family Life in Plymouth Colony* (New York: 1970); Philip Greven, *Four Generations;* Edmund S. Morgan, *The Puritan Family* (New York: 1944); Laurel Thatcher Ulrich, *Good Wives* (New York: 1980).

12. As an older woman, Abigail attributed her early education to her brother-in-law Richard Cranch, claiming that he first introduced the Smith sisters to literature. Library of Congress Shaw Papers, microfilm edition, 4 reels, AA to Elizabeth Shaw, Reel 1, Feb. 28, 1811. Hereafter cited as Shaw. It is clear, however, that after her marriage, Abigail began to read differently and broadly in history, religion, philoso-

phy, and more. She later read with her children.

13. The definition of the companionate marriage is, in fact, more complex. It may involve: choice of mate; the centrality of a couple in family life; the separation of household from either family of origin; the focus on children as economical drain on family resources rather than contributors; focus on family rather than lineage; equation of love, sex, and reproduction; monogamy, and until recently, durability. See Macfarlane, *Marriage*, pp. 154–58, 174–90 and Stone, *The Family, Sex, and Marriage*, pp. 378–90.

14. L. H. Butterfield et al., eds., *The Adams Family Correspondence*, 4 volumes (Cambridge, Mass.: 1963, 1973), I, 2, Oct. 4, 1762. Hereafter cited as AFC.

15. Ibid., 3, Feb. 14, 1763.

16. Ibid., 6, Aug. 11, 1763. Historians, philosophers, psychologists, theologians, and lovers attempt to define love; in this passage Abigail has done well. Following the convention for young women to use pen names in their correspondence, Abigail, until after her marriage, signed herself "Diana."

17. Ibid., 8, Aug. 1763.

18. For John Adams, see John Ferling, *John Adams: A Life* (Knoxville, Tenn.: 1992); Peter Shaw, *The Character of John Adams* (Chapel Hill: 1976).

19. AFC, I, 51, July 1765.

20. L. H. Butterfield et al., eds., *The Adams Papers: Diary and Autobiography of John Adams*, 4 volumes (Cambridge, Mass.: 1964–), I, 263, Dec. 18, 1765. Hereafter cited as DA.

21. Ibid., 312, May 26, 1766.

22. Ibid., III, 291–93. (References to the *Autobiography* are not dated as are *Diary* references.)

23. For John's "collapse," see John Ferling, *John Adams* (read in manuscript. No page citations) and Shaw, *John Adams*, pp. 64–65.

24. AFC, I, 76, Apr. 20, 1771. The source of the quote is not identified.

25. DA, III, 294. For events leading to the Revolution, see Edmund S. Morgan, *The Birth of the Republic, 1763–1789* (Chicago: 1956).

26. AFC, I, 88, Dec. 5, 1773.

27. DA, I, 338, n. 1.

28. AFC, I, 56, Oct. 6, 1766.

29. Ibid., 62, Sept. 13, 1767.

30. Ibid., 90, Dec. 30, 1773.

31. Ibid., 89, Dec. 5, 1773.

32. Ibid., 172–73, Oct. 16, 1774.

33. Ibid., 150, Sept. 8, 1774.

34. Ibid., 151–54, Sept. 14–16, 1774.

35. Ibid., 166, Oct. 9, 1774.

36. Ibid., 172, Oct. 16, 1774. The Battle of Lexington was the opening skirmish of the Revolutionary War. See Morgan, *Birth*, pp. 1–3.

37. AFC, I, 183, Feb. 3, 1775.

38. Ibid., 182, Jan. 28, 1775.

39. Ibid., 190, May 2, 1775; 193, May 4, 1775.

40. Macfarlane, *Marriage*, pp. 35–40.

41. AFC, II, 301, Aug. 5, 1777.

42. Ibid., I, 276, Sept. 8, 1775.

43. Ibid., 278–79, Sept. 17, 1775. She also noted that she had sent Charles and Nabby to stay with relatives.

44. Ibid., 284, Sept. 25, 1775.

45. Ibid., 288, Oct. 1, 1775.

46. Ibid., 296, Oct. 9, 1775.

47. Ibid., 310, Sept. 22, 1775.
48. Ibid., 296, Oct. 9, 1775.
49. Ibid., 303, Oct. 19, 1775.
50. Ibid., 312, Oct. 23, 1775.
51. Ibid., II, 159, Feb. 10, 1777.
52. Ibid., 150, Jan. 1777.
53. Ibid., 173, Mar. 9, 1777.
54. Macfarlane, *Marriage*, p. 148.
55. AFC, II, 212, May 17, 1777. On childbirth, see Catherine M. Scholten, *Childbearing in American Society: 1650–1850* (New York: 1985), chap. 1; Laurel Thatcher Ulrich, *A Midwife's Tale* (New York: 1990).
56. AFC, II, 232, May 6, 1777.
57. Ibid., 241, May 18, 1777. During the spring of 1777, there were rumors in New England of an invasion by Admiral Howe. See Don Higginbotham, *The War of American Independence* (New York: 1971), pp. 182–83.
58. AFC, II, 250, June 1, 1777.
59. Ibid., 277, July 9, 1777.
60. Ibid., 278–79, July 10, 1777.
61. Ibid., 282, July 16, 1777.

3. Domestic Patriotism

1. L. H. Butterfield et al., eds., *Adams Family Correspondence*, 4 volumes (Cambridge, Mass.: 1963), I, 117, June 30, 1774. Hereafter cited as AFC.
2. By the time of the Revolution, land in New England was scarce enough that a substantial tenant population existed. For a discussion of land distribution and the declining availability of land, see Philip J. Greven, Jr., *Four Generations: Population, Land and Family in Colonial Andover, Massachusetts* (Ithaca: 1970).
3. AFC, I, 119, July 1, 1774.
4. Ibid., 359, Mar. 16, 1776.
5. Ibid., 375, Apr. 11, 1776.
6. Ibid., Apr. 7, 1776.
7. Ibid.
8. Ibid., 377, Apr. 13, 1776.
9. Ibid., 407, May 14, 1776.
10. Ibid., 416, May 27, 1776.
11. Ibid., 244–45, July 12, 1775.
12. Ibid., 267, July 28, 1775.
13. Ibid., 305, Oct. 21, 1775.
14. Ibid., III, 6, Apr. 9, 1778.
15. Ibid., II, 324, Aug. 22, 1777.
16. Ibid., III, 61, July 15, 1778.
17. Ibid., II, 406, May 12, 1776.
18. Ibid., 419, May 17, 1777.
19. Ibid., 238, May 15, 1777.
20. Ibid., 408, Mar. 1778.
21. Ibid., III, 61, July 15, 1778.
22. Ibid., II, 175, Mar. 14, 1777.
23. Ibid., 232, May 8, 1777.
24. Ibid., 248, May 27, 1777.
25. Ibid., 251, June 1, 1777.
26. Ibid., IV, 250, Dec. 2, 1781.
27. Ibid., II, 251, June 1, 1777.

28. Ibid., 269, June 23, 1777.
29. Ibid., 340, Sept. 10, 1777.
30. Ibid.
31. Ibid., III, 135, Dec. 13, 1778.
32. Ibid., IV, 191, Aug. 1, 1781.
33. Ibid., III, 135, Dec. 13, 1778.
34. Ibid., 96–97, Sept. 29, 1778.
35. Ibid., 66, July 26, 1778.
36. Ibid., 96, Oct. 29, 1778.
37. Ibid., 125, Dec. 2, 1778.
38. Ibid., 81, Aug. 27, 1778.
39. Ibid., 136, Dec. 13, 1778.
40. Ibid., 145, Jan. 2, 1779.
41. Ibid., IV, 316, Apr. 25, 1782.
42. Ibid., 347, Aug. 18, 1782.
43. Ibid., III, 290, Feb. 28, 1780.
44. Ibid., 321, Apr. 15, 1780.
45. Ibid., 371, July 5, 1780.
46. Ibid., 275, Feb. 16, 1780.
47. Ibid., IV, 81–82, Feb. 27, 1781.
48. Ibid., 42, Dec. 21, 1780.
49. Ibid., 87, Mar. 5, 1781.
50. Ibid., III, 240, Nov. 29, 1779.
51. Marylynn Salmon, "Republican Sentiment, Economic Change, and the Property Rights of Women in American Law," in Ronald Hoffman and Peter J. Albert, eds., *Women in the Age of the American Revolution* (Charlottesville: 1989), pp. 447–78.
52. AFC, I, 415, May 27, 1776. It should be noted here, too, that both the seller and the purchaser were women. Mrs. Peter Adams, however, being a widow, did own her property. See Salmon, "Republican Sentiment." Also see Gloria L. Main, "Widows in Rural Massachusetts on the Eve of the Revolution," in Hoffman, *Women*, pp. 67–90.
53. AFC, II, 12, Jan. 16, 1776.
54. Ibid., III, 321, Apr. 15, 1780.
55. Ibid., 335, May 1, 1780.
56. Ibid., IV, 106, Apr. 23, 1781.
57. Ibid., 257, Dec. 9, 1781.
58. Charles Francis Adams, ed., *The Works of John Adams, Second President of the United States: With a Life of the Author, Notes and Illustrations, by His Grandson Charles Francis Adams*, 10 volumes (Boston: 1851–1856), IX, 513, June 17, 1782.
59. AFC, IV, 345, July 12, 1782.
60. Ibid.
61. Ibid., I, 359, Mar. 16, 1776.
62. Ibid., 376, Apr. 12, 1776.
63. Ibid., 389, Apr. 21, 1776.
64. Ibid., III, 289, Feb. 28, 1780. Lovelace is the seducer of Clarissa in Samuel Richardson's novel.
65. John's statement from a letter to William Cunningham, March 15, 1804, is often cited: "The people are Clarissa." See Jay Fliegelman, *Prodigals and Pilgrims: The American Revolution against Patriarchal Authority, 1750–1800* (New York: 1982), p. 237.
66. AFC, IV, 75, Feb. 3, 1781.
67. Ibid., II, 133, Sept. 23, 1776.
68. Ibid., III, 43, June 13, 1778.

69. Ibid., 48, June 24, 1778.
70. Ibid., II, 302, May 18, 1778.
71. Ibid., I, 370, Mar. 31, 1776.
72. Ibid., 329, Nov. 27, 1775.
73. See Gelles, " 'The Anchor of Our Hope': Abigail and Religion," *Religion and Public Education* 14 (1988), pp. 359–64.
74. AFC, I, 370, Mar. 31, 1776.
75. Ibid., II, 94, Aug. 14, 1776.
76. Ibid., 109, Aug. 25, 1776.
77. Ibid., 391, Jan. 15, 1778.
78. Ibid., 391, Jan. 15, 1778.
79. Ibid., IV, 306, Apr. 10, 1782.
80. Ibid., I, 97, Feb. 27, 1774.

4. A Virtuous Affair

1. On the politics of the American Revolution, see James H. Henderson, *Party Politics in the Continental Congress* (New York: 1974); Merrill D. Jensen, *The Founding of a Nation* (New York: 1968); Pauline Maier, *From Resistance to Revolution* (London: 1973); Jack N. Rakove, *The Beginnings of National Politics* (New York: 1979). For military history, see Don Higginbotham, *The War of American Independence* (New York: 1971); Howard Peckham, *The War for Independence* (Chicago: 1958); Willard M. Wallace, *Appeal to Arms* (New York: 1951); Christopher Ward, *The War of the Revolution*, 2 volumes (New York: 1952). For the diplomacy of the Revolution, see Samuel Flagg Bemis, *The Diplomacy of the American Revolution* (New York: 1935); Richard B. Morris, *The Peacemakers* (New York: 1965). For social change, see Robert Brown, *Middle Class Democracy and the Revolution in Massachusetts, 1691–1780* (New York: 1955); Robert Gross, *The Minutemen and Their World* (New York: 1976); Jackson T. Main, *The Social Structure of Revolutionary America* (Princeton: 1961); Christine Leigh Heyrman, *Commerce and Culture* (New York: 1984). For the history of thought, see Bernard Bailyn, *The Ideological Origins of the American Revolution* (Cambridge, Mass.: 1967); John P. Diggins, *The Lost Soul of American Politics* (New York: 1984); Gary Wills, *Inventing America* (New York: 1978); Gordon Wood, *The Creation of the American Republic, 1776–1787* (Chapel Hill: 1969).

2. For woman's different perspective, see Nancy Chodorow, *The Reproduction of Mothering* (Berkeley: 1978); Carol Gilligan, *In a Different Voice* (Cambridge, Mass.: 1982); Nel Noddings, *Caring* (Berkeley: 1984). See also Gerda Lerner, "New Approaches to the Study of Women in American History," *Journal of Social History* 3 (1969), pp. 53–63; Joan Kelly-Gadol, "The Social Relations of the Sexes: Methodological Implications of Women's History," in Elizabeth and Emily K. Abel, eds., *The Signs Reader* (Chicago: 1983).

3. The interesting debate in the growing literature focuses on the issue of how the Revolution changed the lives of women. For an overview of the literature, see Mary Beth Norton, "The Evolution of White Women's Experience in Early America," *American Historical Review* 89 (1984), especially pp. 614–19. For the lives of women, see Nancy Cott, *The Bonds of Womanhood* (New Haven: 1977); Linda Kerber, *Women of the Republic* (Chapel Hill: 1980); Suzanne Lebsock, *The Free Women of Petersburg* (New York: 1984); Mary Beth Norton, *Liberty's Daughters* (Boston: 1980); Mary P. Ryan, *Cradle of the Middle Class: The Family in Oneida County, New York, 1790–1865* (New York: 1981). See also Joan Hoff-Wilson's provocative essay, "The Illusion of Change: Women and the American Revolution," in Alfred F. Young, ed., *The American Revolution* (DeKalb, Ill.: 1976).

4. L. H. Butterfield et al., eds., Adams Papers, microfilm edition, 608 reels

(Boston: Massachusetts Historical Society, 1956). Hereafter cited as AP. The four-volume letterpress edition, which includes Abigail's letters to the year 1782, contains most of her correspondence with James Lovell. L. H. Butterfield et al., eds., *The Adams Family Correspondence*, 4 volumes (Cambridge, Mass.: 1963–). Cited hereafter as AFC.

5. See Charles W. Akers, *Abigail Adams: An American Woman* (Boston: 1980), pp. 64-65; AFC, III, xxxiv; Page Smith, *John Adams*, 2 volumes (New York: 1962), 236–37; Lynne Withey, *Dearest Friend: A Life of Abigail Adams* (New York: 1981), pp. 105–106. For a different assessment of Abigail, see Paul Nagel, *Descent from Glory: Four Generations of the John Adams Family* (New York: 1983), pp. 20, 56, 62. Nagel describes Abigail as "prudish" where sensuality is concerned.

6. Carroll Smith-Rosenberg observes the restraint in communications between women and men as part of her discussion of the intimacy among female correspondents. While her analysis focuses on the nineteenth century, her sample includes late eighteenth-century people. See, Smith-Rosenberg, "The Female World of Love and Ritual: Relations between Women in Nineteenth-Century America," *Signs: A Journal of Women in Culture and Society* 1 (1975), pp. 1–29. See especially p. 6.

7. *The Warren-Adams Letters*, volumes 72–73, Massachusetts Historical Society (1917, 1925), passim. When John became vice president, Mercy asked for political patronage for her husband and son; John refused. Later, and because he believed it not unrelated, John was piqued at Mercy's portrayal of him in her *History of the Rise, Progress and Termination of the American Revolution* (Boston: 1805). They tangled in a series of letters, and neither conceded. See Charles Francis Adams, ed., *Correspondence between John Adams and Mercy Warren* (New York: 1972). For a discussion of this correspondence, see Lester H. Cohen, "Mercy Otis Warren: The Politics of Language and the Aesthetics of Self," *American Quarterly* 35 (1983), pp. 481–98; Lester H. Cohen, "Explaining the Revolution: Ideology and Ethics in Mercy Otis Warren's Historical Theory," *William and Mary Quarterly* 37 (1980), pp. 200–18.

8. See AP and AFC, passim, for Abigail's correspondence with Samuel Adams, Elbridge Gerry, Thomas Jefferson, Cotton Tufts (her uncle), and John Thaxter (John Adams's law clerk and a family friend). See also Lester J. Cappon, ed., *The Adams-Jefferson Letters: The Complete Correspondence between Thomas Jefferson and Abigail and John Adams* (Chapel Hill: 1959), passim.

9 In contrast to non-intimate correspondents, Abigail and John Adams, like other married couples, did write to each other both loving and teasing messages. As husband and wife, they were free to address each other without social constraints. They used the conventional eighteenth-century "Dearest Friend" as salutation and concluded in various ways: "yours," "affectionately yours," or merely by a signature.

10. Robert Halsband, "Lady Mary Wortley Montagu as Letter-Writer," in Howard Anderson, Philip B. Daghlian, Irvin Ehrenpreis, eds., *The Familiar Letter in the Eighteenth Century* (Lawrence, Kans.: 1966), p. 70.

11. Robert Adams Day, *Told in Letters: Epistolary Fiction before Richardson* (Ann Arbor: 1966), pp. 1–8, 48–67; Margaret Drabble, "Introduction" in Jane Austen, *Lady Susan* (New York: 1974), pp. 9–11; Jay Fliegelman, *Prodigals and Pilgrims* (New York: 1982), p. 29.

I am grateful to Professor Fliegelman for interesting discussions about letter-writing conventions and for the loan of several volumes of teaching manuals from his personal collection. The partial title of the manual for women is *The New Pleasing Instructor, or Young Lady's Guide to Virtue and Happiness, Consisting of Essays, Relations, Descriptions, Epistles, Dialogues, and Poetry . . . Designed Principly for the Use of Female Schools: But Calculated for General Instruction and Amusement.* It was written "By a Lady" and published in Boston in 1799. The other volume, by George Fisher

"Accountant," is *The Instructor or Young Man's Best Companion*, the 25th edition published at Burlington in 1775; it contains a chapter on "How to Write Letters on Business or Friendship."

12. Howard Anderson and Irvin Ehrenpreis, "The Familiar Letter in the Eighteenth Century: Some Generalizations," in Anderson, *Familiar Letter*, pp. 269–75; Day, *Told in Letters*, pp. 48–67.

13. Anderson and Ehrenpreis, "Some Generalizations," p. 275.

14, Ibid., 274–75; Day, *Told in Letters*, p. 63; Herbert Davis, "The Correspondence of the Augustans," in Anderson, *Familiar Letter*, p. 13.

15. AFC, III, 150, Jan. 19, 1779.

16. Abigail recalled that as a young woman she had met Lovell, but she could hardly remember what he looked like. AFC, IV, 215, Sept. 20, 1781.

17. By "gender politics" I mean the dialogue, the struggle between women and men in which the issue is the social and political power of one sex over the other; more specifically, the issue is the use of power by men over women and the struggle by women to gain equitable status with men. For a discussion of gender politics, see Ethel Klein, *Gender Politics* (Cambridge, Mass.: 1984). The tension between dominance and subordination is the theme, as acknowledged by the title, of Lyle Koehler's *A Search for Power* (Urbana, Ill.: 1980).

18. In 1792 the town of Braintree was renamed Quincy to honor Abigail's grandfather, Col. John Quincy, a wealthy landowner and public figure. The house in which Abigail resided throughout the war has been restored and is maintained as a public monument by the Quincy Historical Society. See Wilhelmina S. Harris, *Adams National Historic Site* (Washington, D.C.: 1983); Waldo Chamberlain Sprague, *The President John Adams and President John Quincy Adams Birthplaces* (Quincy, Mass.: 1959).

19. After John Adams first left home to serve in the Continental Congress in 1774, he served in Philadelphia, Baltimore, and York, Pa., wherever the Congress met until 1778 when he left for his first trip to France. He returned home for a few months before he was reassigned to another ministerial post in Paris. He remained in Europe, either in The Hague or in Paris, where Abigail joined him in 1784.

20. John Thaxter was Abigail's nephew and a law student and clerk to John Adams. During the early war years he lived with Abigail and tutored her children. In 1779 he accompanied John to Paris as his private secretary. Louisa Smith was the daughter of Abigail's brother; she lived much of her lifetime in Abigail's household and served as amanuensis to John in his old age.

21. An anecdote illustrates Lovell's manner. Congress in the early years of the war was beleaguered by Frenchmen who came to volunteer their services to the colonial army. Lovell, as the only member of Congress who spoke fluent—and reputedly excellent—French, was assigned the task of meeting and, it was hoped, discouraging them. In late July 1777, a party of Frenchmen, including the Marquis de Lafayette, presented themselves in Philadelphia. The story was later recounted by a member of the Lafayette party. Lovell emerged from the Congress chamber, did not invite the waiting officers into his chambers, and said to them, not too politely, that "French officers seemed to have a great fancy for entering the American service without being invited, that Congress had already obtained all the French officers desired, and more. Whereupon he turned upon his heel and strode back to his seat." Edmund C. Burnett, *The Continental Congress* (New York: 1941), pp. 244–45.

Lovell was probably a part of the failed intrigue during the winter of 1777–78, the Conway Cabal, to replace George Washington as commander-in-chief with Gen. Horatio Gates. Burnett, *Continental Congress*, pp. 279–85.

22. For almost a year after Lexington, the British held Boston. In the summer of

1776, with a shift in military strategy, they abandoned Boston in favor of a plan to cut off all of New England, beginning with an invasion of New York City. Higginbotham, *War*, pp. 148–50.

23. In late 1776, fearing that the British would take Philadelphia, Congress adjourned briefly to Baltimore. Burnett, *Continental Congress*, p. 210. Lovell had been elected to the Continental Congress in November 1776, and in January 1777, he and John traveled on horseback to Baltimore, an arduous journey in the cold of midwinter, taking more than three weeks. AFC, II, 143–51.

24. By 1779 the Committee on Foreign Affairs had dwindled to one man—Lovell. Burnett, *Continental Congress*, p. 489.

25. There is no biography of James Lovell. The fullest sketch of his life that I have found is Clifford K. Shipton, *Sibley's Harvard Graduates* (Boston: 1968), XIV, 31–47. Other sources seem to draw on this for fact, character description, and anecdote. A sympathetic sketch based on contemporary correspondence appears in Rakove, *Beginnings*, pp. 226–28. Otherwise he is known through his letters which survive in the collections of his correspondents, such as the Adams Papers, and of course, in Edmund C. Burnett, *Letters of Members of the Continental Congress*, 8 volumes (Washington D.C.: 1921–36). See also Dumas Malone, ed., *Dictionary of American Biography* (New York: 1933), XI, 438–39; *Biographical Dictionary of American Congress, 1774–1971* (Washington, D.C.: 1971), p. 1310.

26. AFC, II, 333, Aug. 29, 1777.

27. AFC, II, 344, Sept. 17, 1777. This letter to Lovell was enclosed in a letter to John Adams.

28. The commission from the Committee on Foreign Affairs signed by Lovell, reads less like an appointment than as an order: "With great pleasure to ourselves we discharge our duty by inclosing to you your Commission for representing these United States at the Court of France. We are by no means willing to indulge a thought of your declining this important service, and therefore we send duplicates of the Commission and the late Resolves. . . ." Robert J. Taylor et al., eds., *Papers of John Adams*, 6 volumes (Cambridge: 1977–), V, 333, Nov. 27, 1777; also V, 342, Dec. 3, 1777. Hereafter cited as PJA.

29. PJA, V, 337, Nov. 28, 1777.

30. AFC, II, 370, Dec. 15, 1777.

31. Henry Adams, *The Education of Henry Adams: An Autobiography* (Boston: 1918), p. 17.

32. AFC, III, 41, June 12, 1778.

33. Ibid., 1, Apr. 1, 1778.

34. Ibid., 48, June 24, 1778.

35. Ibid., IV, 21, Nov. 27, 1780.

36. In early December 1776, after his release from prison, Lovell was elected to serve as a Massachusetts delegate to the Continental Congress along with John Hancock, Samuel Adams, John Adams, Robert Treat Paine, Elbridge Gerry, and Francis Dana. John Adams assessed Lovell to Gerry as ". . . a Man of Spirit Fortitude, and Patience, three Virtues the most Usefull of any in these Times. But besides these he has Taste Sense and Learning." PJA, V, 55, Dec. 10, 1776; also V, 56, Dec. 31, 1776. Lovell's admiration for John is apparent throughout their correspondence, although his subtle allusions sometimes require the interpretation by the editors of the AP; they explain that "I hope soon to have from you Sic Canibus Catulos similes. . . ." means that Lovell sees himself as the lesser of the two men. PJA, VI, 125–26, May 16, 1778. Prior to John's embarkation in January 1778, as an affirmation of his friendship, Lovell offered his assistance in family affairs. He wrote, "I expect you will tell me in the most free confidential manner how I may do my duty to you or to your family. . . ." PJA, V, 391, Jan. 20, 1778.

37. AFC, III, 370, Dec. 15, 1777.
38. Ibid., 210, July 15, 1779.
39. Ibid., 214, July 28, 1779.
40. Ibid., II, 396, Mar. 1, 1778.
41. Ibid., III, 1, Apr. 1, 1778.
42. Ibid., 147, Jan. 4, 1779. Lovell edited the Journals of Congress.
43. Ibid., 248, Dec. 13, 1779.
44. Ibid., 256, Jan. 6, 1780.
45. Ibid., 257, Jan. 13, 1780.
46. Ibid., 248, Dec. 13, 1779. In a later age, this might be considered "insider trading."
47. Ibid., 314, Mar. 21, 1780. As an interesting aside, John too saw opportunities to profit in Europe, though true to his character, he resisted the temptation. He wrote to Lovell, "If I were capable of Speculating in English Funds, or of conducting private Trade, I might find opportunities here to make a private Profit, and might have Inducements from private considerations to continue here: But this will never be my Case." PJA, VI, 319, July 26, 1778.
48. AFC, III, 121, Nov. 14, 1778.
49. Ibid., IV, 81, Feb. 27, 1781.
50. Ibid., 196, Aug. 23, 1781.
51. Ibid., III, 83, Sept. 1, 1778. This is a quote from the Scottish poet Allan Ramsay. See AFC, III, 84, n. 2.
52. Ibid., 257, Jan. 13, 1780.
53. Ibid., IV, 208, Sept. 4, 1781.
54. Ibid., III, 43, June 13, 1778.
55. Ibid., 236, Nov. 18, 1779.
56. Ibid., 362, June 11, 1780. Lovell was intrigued with the use of codes. For the cipher invented by Lovell, see AFC, IV, Appendix, pp. 393–99.
57. AFC, III, 31, Feb. 13, 1780.
58. Ibid., IV, 91, Mar. 17, 1781.
59. Abigail did not write explicitly—if she were even consciously aware—of such suspicion. At moments of great loneliness, however, she wrote oblique comments which might be so construed. "It is painfull to me to tell you that I have never received a line from you since . . . April," she wrote in late September 1778. "I will not suggest an idea that you have not wrote, or entertain a suspicion that distance, length of time, change of climate or any other cause could render you less mindfull of your country, less thoughtfull of your Friends or less solicitious [sic] for the welfare of your family, since so many hazardous circumstances may have arisen and deprived me of the repeated testimonies of your affection." AFC, III, 94, Sept. 29, 1778.
60. For example, "Let me entreat you to consider," John wrote, "if some of your Letters had by any Accident been taken, what a figure they would have made in a Newspaper to be read by the whole world." AFC, III, 177, Feb. 21, 1779. For a situation in which diplomatic dispatches between John Adams and Congress were intercepted, see PJA, VI, 71–75.
61. AFC, IV, 111, May 10, 1781.
62. A letter from Lovell to Elbridge Gerry, dated Nov. 20, 1780, was intercepted and published by the British in Rivington's New York Royal Gazette. The scandalous paragraph read: "Is it not Time to pay a Visit to Mass.? Does my Wife look as if she wanted a toothless grey headed sciatic Husband near her? I am more Benefit to her at a Distance than in   as the Almanac has it." AFC, IV, 151–52.
63. Ibid., 111, May 10, 1781.
64. Ibid., 112, May 13, 1781.

65. Ibid., 114, May 14, 1781.
66. Ibid.
67. Ibid., 111, May 10, 1781.
68. Ibid., 148, June 16, 1781.
69. Ibid., 151, June 16, 1781.
70. Ibid., 160, June 23, 1781.
71. Ibid., 61, Jan. 8, 1781.
72. Ibid., 193–94, Aug. 10, 1781.
73. Ibid., 208–209, Sept. 12, 1781.
74. Ibid., 215, Sept. 20, 1781.
75. Ibid., 225, Oct. 9, 1781.
76. Ibid., 254, Dec. 4, 1781.
77. Ibid., 284, note 2. I have not seen evidence of the resumption of either the correspondence or the friendship. Lovell did seek John's patronage in later years, and the Adamses continued to be sympathetic, though somewhat incredulous at his plight. See AP, passim.
78. For Tyler, see chapter 5.
79. In contrast, Linda Kerber identifies a real flirtation between two late eighteenth-century people, the poet Joel Barlow and Elizabeth Whitman, in which the correspondents, although unmarried, referred to each other as husband and wife. ". . . these endearments," writes Kerber, "may signify a physical relationship between the two." Kerber, *Women*, p. 249, note 32.
80. Lester H. Cohen notes, but does not develop at length, an interesting exchange between Mercy Warren and John Adams. Cohen writes that Mercy "jousted amiably with her friend John Adams, at once calling attention to the impropriety (and therefore the hint of wickedness) in women discussing politics, and engaging in the most insightful political analysis." The author asks, "Was Warren, then, posturing . . . ?" And he concludes, ". . . that she paid them [her words] more than lip service." Cohen takes Mercy at her word. Cohen, "Mercy Otis Warren," p. 489. Lyle Koehler describes the use of deferential language as a form of manipulation for power. Koehler, *Search*, pp. 182–83. My own reading is that this was Mercy's way of acknowledging the convention which she had every intention of violating.
81. Cappon, *The Adams-Jefferson Letters*, p. 33. A friendship had developed between Abigail Adams and Thomas Jefferson during the ten months she had lived in Paris.
82. Ibid., pp. 268, 270.
83. AFC, IV, 111, May 10, 1781.
84. Ibid., I, 370, May 21, 1776.
85. For woman's dependent and submissive role as a reflection of a hierarchical scheme, see Edmund S. Morgan, *The Puritan Family* (New York: 1944), pp. 44–45. Also see Koehler, *Search*, p. 31; Ulrich, *Good Wives*, p. 8.

5. Gossip

1. L. H. Butterfield *et al.*, eds., *Diary and Autobiography of John Adams*, 4 volumes (Cambridge, Mass.: 1961), II, 61.
2. I have chosen to define gossip simply and broadly, as do most students of the subject. A more complex definition would incorporate the moral or ethical issues (telling secrets or lies), instrumental issues (who, how many, and when), or the distinctions between gossip, scandal (usually malicious gossip), and rumor (does not have to be about people). The OED notes the first use of the word as early as the eleventh century and certainly by the thirteenth century. The word is both a

noun and a verb, refers to the person who talks, the person who listens, the content of the message, and the process. See *Compact Edition of the Oxford English Dictionary*, 2 volumes (New York: 1971), I, 1179.

3. Leviticus 19:16, *The Oxford Annotated Bible*, edited by Herbert G. May and Bruce M. Metzger (New York: 1965), p. 146. Maimonides, *Code*, "Laws Concerning Moral Despositions and Ethical Conduct," chapter 7, sections 1–4. Aristotle, *Nichomachean Ethics*, book 4, chapter 3., p. 31. Thomas Aquinas, *Summa Theologica* (New York: 1918), II, 290–303. For literary references since Shakespeare, see Patricia Meyer Spacks, *Gossip* (New York: 1985).

4. The debate about gossip as a social phenomenon as opposed to behavior serving the individual ego developed in the mid-1960s, beginning with an article by Max Gluckman and a response by Robert Paine. See Gluckman, "Gossip and Scandal," *Current Anthropology* 4 (1963), pp. 307–16; Paine, "What Is Gossip About? An Alternative Hypothesis," *Man*, n.s., 2 (1967), pp. 278–85. For a psychoanalytic approach, see Jean B. Rosenbaum and Mayer Subrin, "The Psychology of Gossip," *Journal of the American Psychoanalytic Association* 2 (1963), pp. 817–31. Freud alluded to gossip in "Group Psychology and the Analysis of the Ego," in *The Standard Edition of the Complete Psychological Works of Sigmund Freud*, volume 18, translated and edited by James Strachey (London: 1955), pp. 67–134. See also C. G. Jung, "A Contribution to the Psychology of Rumor (1910–11)," *The Collected Works of C. G. Jung*, volume 4 (London: 1961), pp. 35–48. For the moral aspects of gossip, see Sissela Bok, *Secrets: On the Ethics of Concealment and Revelation* (New York: 1982), chapter 7, pp. 89–102. For history, see John Demos, *Entertaining Satan: Witchcraft and the Culture of Early New England* (New York: 1982), especially pp. 246–51. Lyle Koehler discusses gossip as a weapon attributed to the "weaker sex," in *A Search for Power: The "Weaker Sex" in Seventeenth-Century New England* (Urbana, Ill.: 1980), pp. 197–98. Mary Beth Norton cleverly matches gossip and slander to the reputations of women in "Gender and Defamation in Seventeenth-Century Maryland," *William and Mary Quarterly* 44 (1987), pp. 3–39.

5. Peter Wilson, "Filcher of Good Names: An Enquiry into Anthropology and Gossip," *Man* 9 (1974), p. 99; Gluckman, "Gossip and Scandal," p. 312.

6. For the most imaginative and exhaustive discussion of gossip in the contemporary literature, see Spacks, *Gossip*. In this analysis of literary texts from early medieval to the present time, Spacks examines the pervasiveness of gossip as a technique, as a medium, and as a device in literature, and she draws inference to real life. See also Roger Abrahams, "A Performance-Centered Approach to Gossip," *Man* 5 (1970), pp. 291–303; Don Handelman, "Gossip in Encounters: The Transmission of Information in a Bounded Social Setting," *Man* 8 (1973), pp. 210–27; Peter Wilson, "Filcher of Good Names," pp. 93–103.

7. For instance, Michel Foucault writes about the influence of "talk" in the formulation of sexual mores in fourth-century Athens. See *The Use of Pleasure*, volume 2 of *The History of Sexuality*, translated by Robert Hurley, 3 volumes (New York: 1985), p. 194.

8. No consensus emerges from the literature about how marriage partners were chosen in the eighteenth century. Edmund S. Morgan and John Demos suggest strong parental influence during the seventeenth century, and this argument has persisted in studies of the entire colonial period. See Morgan, *The Puritan Family: Religion and Domestic Relations in Seventeenth-Century New England* (New York: 1944), pp. 55–57; Demos, *A Little Commonwealth: Family Life in Plymouth Colony* (New York: 1970), pp. 154–56. Philip Greven argues that in the eighteenth century, in the fourth generation, parental control over marriages was declining: *Four Generations: Population, Land, and Family in Colonial Andover, Massachusetts* (Ithaca: 1970), pp. 208–10, 230. Page Smith claims, on the other hand, that by the late eighteenth century,

"For perhaps the first time in history, young men chose their brides and brides their husbands." *Daughters of the Promised Land: Women in American History* (Boston: 1970), p. 41. Claims for affective relationships and the companionate marriage in Lawrence Stone's *The Family, Sex, and Marriage in England, 1500–1800* (New York: 1977), pp. 282–90, have influenced subsequent interpretations in America, as has Alan Macfarlane's *Marriage and Love in England, 1300–1840* (New York: 1986). Carl N. Deger in *At Odds: Women and the Family in America from the Revolution to the Present* (New York: 1980), pp. 19–25, cites Greven (see above) and Daniel Scott Smith ("Parental Control and Marriage Patterns: An Analysis of Historical Trends in Hingham, Massachusetts," *Journal of Marriage and the Family* 35 [Aug. 1973], pp. 423–24) and notes the decline in parental influence by the late eighteenth century. In *Liberty's Daughters: The Revolutionary Experience of American Women, 1750–1800* (Boston: 1980), pp. 57–58, Mary Beth Norton claims that daughters sought parental approval. Suzanne Lebsock, describing the southern experience and stressing the "companionate marriage," states that with love at the center of marriage, choice of partners "could be decided only by the young people themselves." *The Free Women of Petersburg: Status and Culture in a Southern Town, 1784–1860* (New York: 1984), p. 17. Laurel Thatcher Ulrich, on the other hand, notes the irony that for "the very classes that had first begun to romanticize marriage," the economic alliances of families was the primary consideration of choice of mates (*Good Wives: Images and Reality in the Lives of Women in Northern New England, 1650–1750* [New York: 1980], p. 119). Nancy Woloch suggests that although a woman welcomed parental approval, she alone chose her marriage partner, the only independent decision she made in her lifetime (*Women and the American Experience* [New York: 1984], p. 67). In her expansive study of courtship in America, Ellen K. Rothman states that most couples, although they preferred to have parental approval, were prepared to marry without it (*Hands and Hearts: A History of Courtship in America* [New York: 1984], p. 29).

9. Abigail Adams to John Adams, Dec. 23, 1782, Adams Papers, microfilm edition, Reel 359. All references to the Adams Papers are to the microfilm edition published by the Massachusetts Historical Society. Hereafter cited as AP. For stages of gossip see Spacks, *Gossip,* p. 48.

10. JA to AA, AP, Reel 360, Jan. 22, 1783.

11. AA to JA, Reel 359, Dec. 23, 1782.

12. At sixteen years old, Nabby's age is below the presumed average for late eighteenth-century marriage, which demographers set at about twenty-three. It should be noted, however, that her mother had met John Adams when she was sixteen and had married at nineteen. See Daniel Smith, "Parental Control and Marriage Patterns," pp. 423–24.

13. For Tyler, especially for rumors about his Harvard life, see Clifford K. Shipton, *Sibley's Harvard Graduates* (Boston: 1960), XI, 313–18. See also G. Thomas Tanselle's sensitive literary biography, *Royall Tyler* (Cambridge, Mass.: 1967) and the uncritical memorial to Tyler in his wife's autobiography, Frederick Tupper and Helen Tyler Brown, eds., *Grandmother Tyler's Book: The Recollections of Mary Palmer Tyler, 1775–1866* (New York: 1925).

14. AA to JA, AP, Reel 360, Apr. 28, 1783; AP, Reel 360, May 7, 1783; Reel 361, June 20, 1783; ibid., Oct. 19, 1783; ibid., Dec. 27, 1783.

15. JA to AA, AP, Reel 360, Feb. 4, 1783; AP, Reel 361, Oct. 14, 1783.

16. Elizabeth Shaw to Mary Cranch, Library of Congress, Shaw Papers, microfilm edition, 4 reels, Reel 1, Feb. 1, 1783. Hereafter cited as Shaw.

17. The letters exchanged within the family are not always as explicit as the latter-day gossip would wish. Elizabeth Shaw frequently wrote provocative phrases, followed by two sentence lengths of dashes. "I saw all the furious Passions rioting in my Nabbys Face—I saw ___ ___ ___ ___ etc." ES to MC, Shaw, Reel 1,

June 1784.

18. AA to JA, AP, Reel 361, Oct. 19, 1783.

19. See John Adams's assent to Tyler in a letter to AA, ibid., Reel 362, Jan. 25, 1784; Tyler's suit to John Adams, ibid., Jan. 13, 1784; and John Adams to Tyler, Apr. 3, 1784: "Sir, you and the young Lady have my Consent to arrange your Plans according to your own Judjments, and I pray God to bless and prosper you both together or assunder," ibid. For Tyler's grief after the departure, see ES to MC, Shaw, Reel 1, Aug. 24, 1784; and Tupper and Brown, *Grandmother Tyler's Book*, p. 80.

20. MC to AA, AP, Reel 365, Aug. 14, 1785.

21. AA to JQA, AP, Reel 365, Aug. 23, 1785.

22. ES to MC, Shaw, Reel 1, Nov. 6, 1785. See also June 6, 1785.

23. For Abigail Adams to Tyler, see, AP, Reel 364, Jan. 4, 1785. Most of young Abigail's papers that were in the possession of her daughter's family were destroyed when the family home burned. See Caroline deWindt, ed., *Journal and Correspondence of Miss Adams, Daughter of John Adams*, 2 volumes (New York: 1841), Introduction.

24. MC to AA, AP, Reel 365, Aug. 14, 1785.

25. Tupper and Brown, *Grandmother Tyler's Book*, pp. 73, 75, 95.

26. Abigail assured John Quincy, "We are all rejoiced because it came of her own accord free and unsolicited from her and was the result of many months anxiety as you were witness" (AP, Reel 365, Aug. 11, 1785). AA to C. Tufts, Reel 367, Jan. 10, 1786; C. Tufts to AA, Reel 368, July 6, 1786; AA to JQA, AP, Reel 367, Feb. 16, 1786.

27. MC to AA, AP, Reel 366, Oct. 1785.

28. ES to AA, AP, Reel 366, Nov. 6, 1785.

29. JQA to AA, AP, Reel 366, Dec. 28, 1785.

30. C. Tufts to AA, AP, Reel 366, Oct. 12, 1785.

31. MC to AA, AP, Reel 366, Nov. 8, 1785; ibid., JQA to AA, Dec. 28, 1785.

32. JQA to AA, ibid.; Tupper and Brown, *Grandmother Tyler's Book*, pp. 95–96; ES to MC, Shaw, Reel 1, Aug. 24, 1784; ibid., Jan. 9, 1785; ibid., Jan. 30, 1785.

33. Royall Tyler to AA, AP, Reel 366, Oct. 13, 1785; Royall Tyler to JA, ibid., Oct. 15, 1785.

34. In forming their interpretations of this story, historians have relied on two versions recorded in *Grandmother Tyler's Book:* one in a letter of Mary Tyler's mother, Elizabeth Hunt Palmer, and a second that is probably based on Tyler's explanation to his wife of Mary Cranch's role (see Tupper and Brown, pp. 76–80). I think that the Palmer-Tyler version of Cranch's jealousy and interference, the retelling of a family myth in the oral tradition, has to be discounted as less reliable than the recorded Adams version.

35. ES to AA2, Shaw, Reel 1, Nov. 19, 1785; ibid., Feb. 14, 1786.

36. Gluckman, "Gossip and Scandal," p. 312.

37. The most remarkable letter of the series on Tyler, remarkable for its irony, is one written by young Abigail before she had met Tyler. Nabby visited Boston where she first heard rumors about Tyler and repeated that gossip to her cousin Betsy Cranch, in whose house Tyler was now living, as a warning not to be attracted by this man who was "practicing upon Chesterfeilds [sic] plan" and not to be trusted. See L. H. Butterfield et al., eds., *The Adams Family Correspondence*, 4 volumes (Cambridge, Mass.: 1963–73), IV, 335.

38. Gluckman emphasizes that gossip enforces conformity of values and objectives within a community ("Gossip and Scandal," p. 312).

39. AA to JA, AP, Reel 359, Dec. 23, 1782; JA to AA, Reel 360, Jan. 22, 1783.

40. Gluckman, "Gossip and Scandal," p. 314.

41. JA to AA, AP, Reel 360, Feb. 4, 1783.

42. See Spacks, *Gossip,* pp. 229–33.

43. For the Adams "myth," see David F. Musto, "The Youth of John Quincy Adams," American Philosophical Society, *Proceedings* 113 (1969), pp. 269–82.

44. AA to JA, AP, Reel 359, Dec. 23, 1782.

45. JA to AA, AP, Reel 360, Jan. 29, 1783.

46. JA to AA, Apr. 8, 1783. A copy of this letter in Elizabeth's hand is in the Shaw Papers, suggesting that Elizabeth had read it and was impressed, specifically that it expressed family values (Shaw, Reel 1).

47. AA to C. Tufts, AP, Reel 367, Jan. 10, 1786.

48. Rosenbaum and Subrin, "Psychology of Gossip," p. 819; Spacks *Gossip,* pp. 27–34.

49. Nor are stories about group members interesting to outsiders. Gluckman, "Gossip and Scandal," pp. 309, 313, 314. Gluckman points out, in fact, that gossip is a "duty" of the group (p. 313).

50. ES to MC, Shaw, Reel 1, Aug. 15, 1785; MC to AA, AP, Reel 366, Nov. 8, 1785.

51. Abrahams, "A Performance-Centered Approach," p. 291; Handelman, "Gossip in Encounters"; Paine, "What Is Gossip About?" p. 281; Rosenbaum and Subrin, "Psychology of Gossip," pp. 822–23, 830.

52. Mary Cranch told Abigail that she had not informed on Tyler for two reasons: she did not wish to cause trouble, and she "plainly perceived that he would do his own business for himself without the assistance of any body else" (AP, Reel 366, Nov. 8, 1785).

53. Within this perspective, gossip is especially associated with women. See Demos, *Entertaining Satan,* pp. 246–51; Koehler, *Search,* pp. 197–98; Norton, "Gender and Defamation," pp. 3–39; Spacks, *Gossip,* pp. 38–42, 150–53.

54. Spacks, *Gossip,* p. 38.

55. "Gossip" probably derives from "God" and "sib" meaning kin or relation, in other words, "god-related." It was first used in the thirteenth century to describe a spiritual friend, especially one who was present at a baptism, probably then, a godmother. Later it came to mean women friends who were present at childbirth. It was associated with women and by the sixteenth century was used to mean "a woman of light and trifling character who engages in idle talk." That definition has persisted to the present time, emphasizing the triviality (dictionaries variously refer to "small talk," "idle talk," "tattle," and "private affairs") of the content of gossip. See *Compact Edition of Oxford English Dictionary,* II, 1179.

56. In truth, the power of gossip is underestimated. In our own time, we note the controversial legal issue of private men's clubs; their claim to be purely social may be accurate, a fact that works to the greater disadvantage of professional women who wish access to the clubs. Talk does not have to be directly related to business to accomplish business; the "ins" and the "outs" of the group are defined by "who talks."

57. AA to MC, AP, Reel 368, June 13, 1786; AA to JQA, ibid.

58. See Tanselle, *Royall Tyler,* and Tupper and Brown, *Grandmother Tyler's Book.* It falls beyond the scope of this chapter to analyze *The Contrast* for autobiographical content about his romance with Nabby Adams. The subject is touched upon in Tanselle and in Richard S. Pressman, "Class Positioning and Shays' Rebellion: Resolving the Contradictions of *The Contrast," Early American Literature* 29 (1986), pp. 87–102.

59. AA to MC, AP, Reel 368, June 13, 1786.

60. AA to Charles Storer, AP, Reel 368, May 22, 1786.

6. Faithful Are the Wounds of a Friend

1. Lester J. Cappon, ed., *The Adams-Jefferson Letters: The Complete Correspondence between Thomas Jefferson and Abigail and John Adams* (Chapel Hill: 1959), pp. 268–69, May 20, 1804. Hereafter cited as Cappon.

2. Abigail Adams to Mary Cranch, Massachusetts Historical Society, Adams Papers, microfilm edition, Reel 364, May 8, 1785. Hereafter cited as AP. A few letters concerning the business of transferring the office did take place. For the Adams-Jefferson friendship, its stresses and breakdown, see Cappon, passim; Dumas Malone, *Jefferson and the Ordeal of Liberty* (Boston: 1962); Malone, *Jefferson the President, First Term 1801–1805* (Boston: 1970); Adrienne Koch, ed., *Adams and Jefferson: "Posterity Must Judge"* (Chicago: 1963); Merrill D. Peterson, *Thomas Jefferson and the New Nation* (New York: 1970), pp. 438–43, 568–69; Peter Shaw, *The Character of John Adams* (Chapel Hill: 1976), passim; Page Smith, *John Adams*, 2 volumes (New York: 1962), passim.

3. For Paris, see Howard C. Rice, Jr., *The Adams Family in Auteuil 1784–1785* (Boston: 1956); Howard C. Rice, Jr., *Thomas Jefferson's Paris* (Princeton: 1976).

4. See TJ to JA, AP, Reel 364, May 25, 1785; AA to TJ, ibid., June 1785; AA to TJ, AP, Reel 370, July 6, 1787.

5. Cappon, p. 269, May 20, 1804.

6. For eighteenth-century letter-writing conventions, see Howard Anderson, Philip B. Daghlian, and Irvin Ehrenpreis, eds., *The Familiar Letter in the Eighteenth Century* (Lawrence, Kans.: 1966); Robert Adams Day, *Told in Letters* (Ann Arbor: 1966); Jay Fliegelman, *Prodigals and Pilgrims* (New York: 1982), p. 29.

7. Cappon, p. 273, July 1, 1804.

8. Ibid., p. 274.

9. TJ to AA, Cappon, p. 270, June 13, 1804. For the Judiciary Act of 1801, see Max Farrand, "The Judiciary Act of 1801," *American Historical Review* 5 (1899–1900), pp. 681–86. Also see note 2 above.

10. Cappon, p. 277, Aug. 18, 1804. See also Samuel Flagg Bemis, *John Quincy Adams and the Foundations of American Foreign Policy* (New York: 1949), p. 112.

11. Cappon, pp. 272–74, July 1, 1804.

12. For the Sedition Act, see Bernard Bailyn and John B. Hench, eds., *The Press and the American Revolution* (Worcester, Mass.: 1980); Leonard W. Levy, *Emergence of a Free Press* (New York: 1985); Levy, *Jefferson and Civil Liberties: The Darker Side* (Cambridge, Mass.: 1963); John C. Miller, *Crisis in Freedom: The Alien and Sedition Acts* (Boston: 1951); James Morton Smith, *Freedom's Fetters: The Alien and Sedition Laws and American Civil Liberties* (Ithaca: 1956). Also see note 2 above.

13. Nancy Chodorow, *The Reproduction of Mothering: Psychoanalysis and the Sociology of Gender* (Berkeley: 1978); Carol Gilligan, *In a Different Voice: Psychological Theory and Women's Development* (Cambridge: 1982); Jean Baker Miller, *Toward a New Psychology of Women* (Boston: 1976). Also see Mary Field Belenky et al., *Women's Ways of Knowing: The Development of Self, Voice, and Mind* (New York: 1986); Jean Strouse, ed., *Women and Analysis: Dialogues on Psychoanalytic Views of Femininity* (Boston: 1974). For the debate on "difference," see Diana Baumrind, "Sex Differences in Moral Reasoning: Response to Walker's (1984) Conclusion That There Are None," *Child Development* 57 (1986), pp. 511–21; Linda Kerber et al., "On 'In a Different Voice': An Interdisciplinary Forum," *Signs: Journal of Women in Culture and Society* 11 (1987), pp. 304–33; L. J. Walker, "Sex Differences in the Development of Moral Reasoning: A Critical Review," *Child Development* 55 (1984), pp. 677–91.

14. For language as representative of culture, see Fliegelman, *Prodigals*; Cathy N. Davidson, *Revolution and the Word: The Rise of the Novel in America* (New York: 1986); Margaret Homans, *Bearing the Word: Language and Female Experience in Nine-*

teenth-Century Women's Writings (Chicago: 1986); Joan Lidoff, *Fluid Boundaries: The Origins of a Distinctive Women's Voice in Literature* (Chicago: forthcoming). For a useful dialogue about the compatibility of deconstruction and feminist theory, see *Feminist Studies* 14 (1988), especially Leslie Wahl Rabine, "A Feminist Politics of Non-Identity," pp. 11–32, and Joan W. Scott, "Deconstructing Equality-Versus-Difference: On the Uses of Post-Structuralist Theory for Feminism," pp. 33–50.

15. Nancy F. Cott, *The Bonds of Womanhood: "Woman's Sphere" in New England, 1780–1835* (New Haven: 1977); Carl N. Degler, *At Odds: Women and the Family in America from the Revolution to the Present* (New York: 1980); Linda K. Kerber, *Women of the Republic: Intellect and Ideology in Revolutionary America* (Chapel Hill: 1980); Suzanne Lebsock, *The Free Women of Petersburg: Status and Culture in a Southern Town, 1784–1860* (New York: 1984); Linda J. Nicholson, *Gender and History: The Limits of Social Theory in the Age of the Family* (New York: 1986); Mary Beth Norton, *Liberty's Daughters: The Revolutionary Experience of American Women, 1750–1800* (Boston: 1980); Marylynn Salmon, *Women and the Law of Property in Early America* (Chapel Hill: 1986); Laurel Thatcher Ulrich, *Good Wives: Images and Reality in the Lives of Women in Northern New England, 1650–1750* (New York: 1982).

16. There are several problems with using the term "republican" to represent women's lives in the post-revolutionary era. First, most of the sources used by historians for evidence of republicanism turn out to be prescriptive; often written by men, either politicians or clergymen, they define roles that are idealized to enforce a certain kind of behavior. Otherwise, literary sources, such as novels, of which very few were indigenous until the mid-nineteenth century, also idealized and romanticized women's lives. They were prescriptive, not descriptive; they told women how to live rather than explaining existing conditions of life for most women. The Republican Woman, wife or mother, was a prescription for women, not an analysis of lives. The whole consideration of Republican Mother is troublesome, furthermore, because what it suggests is that women could act as citizens by raising their sons to be good citizens, in other words, raising their sons for the state. Finally, the use of the rubric "republican" so generalizes women as to lose sight of any active impulses that women might possess. Women become passive and plastic images in an historical framework that immobilizes individual character. See chapter 8, "Mother and Citizen."

17. By "vantage" and "emphasis," I mean the perspective that women brought to thinking about politics—more specifically to notions of power and authority—and the value that political considerations had to their lives. The women of Abigail's milieu talked (or wrote) about politics. But they also wrote about domestic matters. Latter-days historians tend to look for the political statements and overlook the domestic commentary. They look for evidence of women's political involvement, and they find it, but by their selective use of sources, they skew the record so that it may appear that politics occupied too great a dimension in women's lives.

18. See Natalie Zemon Davis, "On the Lame," a response to Robert Finlay, "The Refashioning of Martin Guerre," both in *American Historical Review* 93 (1988), pp. 572–603, 553–71, for use of historical sources and methods for probing *mentalité*.

19. The antagonism generated over the case of the EEOC v. Sears, Roebuck, and Company was a high point of this debate among feminists. For an overview, see "Women's History Goes to Trial," *Signs: Journal of Women in Culture and Society* 2 (1986), pp. 751–79. See also essays by Linda Kerber, Catherine G. Greeno, and Eleanor E. Maccoby, Zella Luria, Carol B. Stack and Carol Gilligan in the *Signs* "Forum," ibid.

20. On the "corruption" of female imagery by language, see Jean Bethke Elshtain, "Feminist Discourse and Its Discontents: Language, Power, and Meaning,"

Feminist Studies 7 (1982), pp. 603–21; Sara Ruddick, "Maternal Thinking," in Barrie Thorne with Marilyn Yalom, eds., *Rethinking the Family: Some Feminist Questions* (New York: 1982), pp. 76–94.

21. Jean Baker Miller suggests the creation of a separate female language to express female *mentalité* that the conventional "masculine" language cannot capture. See Miller, *New Psychology*, pp. 83–86. For other advocates of a separate female language, see Hélène Cixous, "The Laugh of the Medusa," translated by Keith Cohen and Paula Cohen, *Signs: Journal of Culture and Society* 1 (1976), pp. 875–93; Mary Daly, *Gyn/Ecology: The Metaethics of Radical Feminism* (Boston: 1978).

22. When Abigail reminded John to "Remember the Ladies" in the new "Code of Laws," her appeal concluded: "Regard us then as Beings placed by providence under your protection and in immitation of the Supreem Being make use of that power only for our happiness." She did not demand equality or even political rights; she asked for just treatment of women by men. Similarly, Mercy Otis Warren, commenting to Abigail about the imminence of war in January 1774, wrote, "But as our weak and timid sex is only the Echo of the other, and like some pliant peace of Clock Work the springs of our souls move slow or more Rapidly . . . so I build much on the high key that at present seems to Animate the American patriots." Both of these bright and articulate women who wrote volumes on politics—as well as about child rearing, crops, household affairs, and gossip—accepted the subordinate role of women in a patriarchal political world. And the patriarchy extended into the family. For quotations, see L. H. Butterfield et al., eds., *The Adams Family Correspondence*, 4 volumes (Cambridge, Mass.: 1963), I, 92, 370.

23. For anthropological corroboration, see Michelle Zimbalist Rosaldo, "Women, Culture, and Society: A Theoretical Overview," in Rosaldo and Louise Lamphere, eds., *Woman, Culture, and Society* (Stanford: 1974), pp. 17–42. At the same time, anthropologists debate the issue of difference. See ibid., passim.; also see Jane Fishburne Collier and Sylvia Junko Yanagisako, eds., *Gender and Kinship: Essays toward a United Analysis* (Stanford: 1987).

24. Freud admits that "our insight into . . . developmental processes in girls is unsatisfactory, incomplete, and vague." He nevertheless claims that "women have less sense of justice than men, are overwhelmed by jealousy and shame, are vain, are unable to submit to life's requirements, and have made no contribution to civilization." Sigmund Freud, *The Dissolution of the Oedipus Complex* (1924), p. 179; and *New Introductory Lectures* (New York: 1933), p. 132. Cited in Chodorow, *Reproduction*, pp. 142–43.

25. Chodorow, *Reproduction*, p. 110.

26. Ibid., p. 109.

27. Ibid., p. 169.

28. Ibid., p. 167. See also Miller, *New Psychology*, pp. 70–71, 87–88, for her formulation of the connectedness/autonomy distinction. Miller considers that the social imagery of the autonomous male is imposed from youth and that to violate this model is threatening for men, although they long for relationships. "It is not that men are not concerned about relationships. . . . I do think men are yearning for an affiliated mode of living. . . . Men have deprived themselves of this mode, left it with women," pp. 87–88.

29. Sigmund Freud, "Some Psychical Consequences of the Anatomical Distinction between the Sexes," (1925) in *The Standard Edition of the Complete Psychological Works of Sigmund Freud*, translated by James Strachey (London: 1961), cited in Gilligan, *Different Voice*, p. 7.

30. Gilligan, *Different Voice*, p. 19. See chapters 1–3 for the development of her theory.

31. Ibid., p. 18. Elshtain refers to the "double standard" in language. "Feminist

Discourse," p. 608.

32. Cappon, p. 268, May 20, 1804.

33. TJ to AA, Cappon, pp. 269–71, June 13, 1804.

34. AA to TJ, ibid., pp. 271–73, July 1, 1804.

35. The tie in the electoral vote was broken after six days of voting in the House of Representatives, on February 17, 1801, several weeks before the inauguration on March 4. See Malone, *Ordeal*, pp. 499–506.

36. On the issue of "denial," I am not arguing that Jefferson deliberately distorted the past, but rather that he considered and wrote in good faith, perhaps unconsciously, or politely, or tactfully changing facts in order to facilitate a reconciliation by not rehearsing a decade of grievances.

37. AA to TJ, Cappon, p. 273, July 1, 1804.

38. Abigail was a religious woman who believed in earthly providence as well as rewards in the hereafter. See Edith B. Gelles, " 'The Anchor of Our Hope': Abigail Adams and Religion," *Religion and Public Education* 14 (1988), pp. 359–64.

39. She refers to Callender's accusations that earlier Jefferson had an affair with a married woman, and that later Sally Hemings, the slave-girl who had accompanied Polly to Europe, became his mistress. These stories were printed during Jefferson's presidency and were largely ignored for over a century until Fawn Brodie developed the Sally Hemings story in *Thomas Jefferson: An Intimate History* (New York: 1974), pp. 29–32. Dumas Malone repudiates the accusation in *Jefferson the President*, Appendix, pp. 494–98. Most recently, the story was refuted by Sidney P. Moss and Carolyn Moss in "The Thomas Jefferson Miscegenation Legend in British Travel Books," *Journal of the Early American Republic* 7 (1987), pp. 253–74.

40. On virtue, see Ruth H. Bloch, "The Gendered Meanings of Virtue in Revolutionary America," *Signs: Journal of Women in Culture and Society* 13 (1987), pp. 37–58.

41. Edmund G. Burrows and Michael Wallace, "The American Revolution: The Ideology and Psychology of National Liberation," *Perspectives in American History* 6 (1972), pp. 167–306; also Fliegelman, *Prodigals*; Winthrop D. Jordan, "Familial Politics: Thomas Paine and the Killing of the King," *Journal of American History* 60 (1973), pp. 294–308; Karen Greenberg, "American Androgyny: Gender Distinctions and the Rhetoric of the Revolutionary Era" (paper presented at the 1988 annual meeting of the Society for Historians of the Early American Republic. Cited by permission of the author).

42. AA to TJ, Cappon, p. 274, July 1, 1804.

43. TJ to AA, ibid., pp. 274–76, July 22, 1804.

44. Dueling was widespread into the nineteenth century, although there was considerable opinion against it. Burr had previously stood in a duel and Hamilton had lost a son as well as stood as a second to what Jefferson had called "the most barbarous of appeals." For an account of the Burr-Hamilton duel of July 11, 1804, see Milton Lomask, *Aaron Burr: The Conspiracy and Years of Exile 1805–1836* (New York: 1982), pp. 344–58.

45. AA to TJ, Cappon, pp. 276–78, Aug. 18, 1804.

46. Ibid., pp. 278–80, Sept. 11, 1804. This reflected the Anti-Federalist position on the Sedition Act. See James Morton Smith, *Freedom's Fetters*, passim.

47. Cappon, pp. 279–80, Sept. 11, 1804.

48. AA to TJ, ibid., pp. 280–82, Oct. 25, 1804.

49. TJ to AA, ibid., p. 280, Sept. 11, 1804.

50. AA to TJ, ibid., p. 272, July 1, 1804.

51. See note 2 above.

52. The idea for this section came to me after reading Mitchell Robert Breitweiser, *Cotton Mather and Benjamin Franklin: The Price of Representative Personality* (Cambridge: 1987). The concept of one man representing or imaging an age sug-

gests the significance of probing beyond the surface for explanations.

53. JA to TJ, Cappon, p. 264, March 24, 1801.

54. Benjamin Rush, friend to both men, had attempted to negotiate a truce between them on several occasions. It was Rush who ultimately brought about the reconciliation in 1812—when Adams was ready.

55. Another example of Abigail's loyalty to John in his feuds was her breaking with her former close friend Mercy Otis Warren after John became irritated with her presentation of him in her *History of the Rise, Progress and Termination of the American Revolution* (1805). See "Correspondence between John Adams and Mercy Otis Warren, July–August 1807," Massachusetts Historical Society *Proceedings*, 5th ser., 4 (Boston: 1878).

56. For a caring Jefferson, see Helen Duprey Bullock, *My Head and My Heart: A Little History of Thomas Jefferson and Maria Cosway* (New York: 1945).

57. TJ to AA, Cappon, p. 278, Sept. 11, 1804.

58. AA to TJ, ibid., p. 281, Oct. 25, 1804.

59. Ibid.

60. John Locke, *Two Treatises of Government*, edited by Peter Laslett (Cambridge, Eng.: 1960), p. 339. Quoted in Mary Beth Norton, "The Constitutional Status of Women in 1787," *Law and Inequality: A Journal of Theory and Practice* 6 (1988), pp. 7–15, which also asserts that, in the era of the Constitution, "women had no status," p. 7.

61. An appropriate addendum is fixed to the end of the last letter in John's hand: "Quincy Nov. 19, 1804. The whole of this Correspondence was begun and conducted without my Knowledge or Suspicion. Last Evening and this Morning at the desire of Mrs. Adams I read the whole. I have no remarks to make upon it at this time and in this place. J. Adams." Cappon, p. 282.

7. The Threefold Cord

1 L. H. Butterfield et al., eds., *Adams Family Correspondence*, 4 volumes (Cambridge, Mass., 1963–1973), I, 135, July 9, 1774. Hereafter cited as AFC.

2. For the Adams family myth, see David F. Musto, "The Youth of John Quincy Adams," American Philosophical Society, *Proceedings* 113 (1969), pp. 269–82; Musto, "The Adams Family," Massachusetts Historical Society, *Proceedings* 93 (1981), pp. 40–58.

3. John P. Diggins, *The Lost Soul of American Politics: Virtue, Self-Interest, and the Foundations of Liberalism* (New York: 1984); Ann Douglas, *The Feminization of American Culture* (New York: 1977); Philip J. Greven, Jr., *Four Generations: Population, Land, and Family in Colonial Andover, Massachusetts* (Ithaca: 1970); Peter Laslett, *The World We Have Lost: England Before the Industrial Age* (New York: 1965); Edmund S. Morgan, *The Puritan Family: Religion and Domestic Relations in Seventeenth-Century New England* (New York: 1966); Lawrence Stone, *The Family, Sex, and Marriage in England 1500–1800* (New York: 1977).

4. In the early nineteenth century, Tocqueville observed that American men were inspired by "enlightened self-interest," while women were the guardians of morality. "America is still the place where the Christian religion has kept the greatest real power over men's souls; . . . [Religion] reigns supreme in the souls of women, and it is women who shape mores." Alexis de Tocqueville, *Democracy in America* (Garden City, N.Y.: 1969), p. 291. For virtue in revolutionary and republican America, see Ruth H. Bloch, "The Gendered Meaning of Virtue in Revolutionary America," *Signs: Journal of Women and Culture in Society* 13 (1987), pp. 37–58; Diggins, *Lost Soul*, especially chapter 8, "Society, Religion, and the Feminization of Virtue"; Gordon Wood, *The Creation of the American Republic, 1776–1787* (Chapel Hill: 1969), pp. 65–70, 606–15; J. G. A. Pocock, *The Machiavellian Moment: Florentine Political*

Thought and the Atlantic Republican Tradition (Princeton: 1975), pp. 506–52.

5. AFC, I, 242, July 7, 1775.

6. In order to distinguish between kin sisters and sisters as friends, the latter will appear in quotes—"sisters." *Socrates*, the Stanford library's computerized card catalogue of books published since 1962, carries 255 entries under the subject of "sisters." They include references to: all women; Black women; Catholic, sorority, Victorian, reformer, suffragist, Quaker, Mormon, labor union, and club women; and seven colleges.

7. Mary Cranch to her husband's uncle, John Cranch of Westminster, England. Boston Public Library, MS ENG 483 (397), Oct. 11, 1784.

8. Library of Congress, Shaw Papers, microfilm edition, 4 reels, Reel 1, Feb. 28, 1811. Hereafter cited as Shaw.

9. For Mary's letters, see Massachusetts Historical Society, Adams Papers, microfilm edition, 608 reels, especially reels 343–445, which include the family Papers. Hereafter cited respectively as MHS and AP. Also see the Cranch Papers, Library of Congress. Cited hereafter as Cranch Papers.

10. For Cranch, see Clifford K. Shipton, *Sibley's Harvard Graduates* (Boston: 1873–), XI, 1741–45, 370–76.

11. For Mary's letters to her son, William, see LC, Cranch papers, passim.

12. For the death of Mary and Richard Cranch, see AP, Reel 398. For affectionate letters from Richard to Mary, see MHS, Cranch Family Papers, AC62-M54, passim.

13. For family portraits, see Andrew Oliver, *Portraits of John and Abigail Adams* (Cambridge, Mass.: 1967).

14. The average age at marriage in late eighteenth-century America was about twenty-three. See James A. Henretta, *The Evolution of American Society, 1700–1815* (Lexington, Mass.: 1973), p. 12; Daniel Scott Smith, "Parental Control and Marriage Patterns: An Analysis of Historical Trends in Hingham, Massachusetts," *Journal of Marriage and the Family* 35 (1973), pp. 423–24; Smith and Michael Hindus, "Premarital Pregnancy in America, 1640–1971: An Overview and Interpretation," *Journal of Interdisciplinary History* 5 (1975), pp. 537–70.

15. For health in the eighteenth century, see Richard H. Shyrock, *Medicine and Society in America, 1660–1860* (Ithaca: 1960).

16. Shaw, Dec. 14, 1784.

17. Shaw, Feb. 8, 1771.

18. Shaw, Mar. 1788.

19. Shaw, Aug. ?? [*sic*].

20. AFC, II, 381, Jan. 10, 1778. Emphasis mine.

21. For Elizabeth's letters to students and their parents, see Shaw.

22. Michael Kammen, "Changing Perceptions of the Life Cycle in American Thought and Culture," MHS, *Proceedings* 91 (1979), pp. 35–66, 35.

23. Ibid. See also, Tamara Hareven, "Family Time and Historical Time," in Hareven, ed., *Family and Kin in Urban Communities, 1700–1930* (New York: 1977), pp. 187–207.

24. AFC, I, 92, Jan. 19, 1774.

25. Primarily women were acknowledged in laws of inheritance. See Richard B. Morris, "Women's Rights in Early American Law," in *Studies in the History of American Law* (New York: 1964); Carole Shammas, Marylynn Salmon, and Michael Dahlin, *Inheritance in America: From Colonial Times to the Present* (New Brunswick, N.J.: 1987).

26. Elizabeth Fishel, *Sisters: Love and Rivalry Inside the Family and Beyond* (New York: 1979); Esther N. Goody, *Contexts of Kinship* (Cambridge, Eng.: 1973), p. 221.

27. AFC, I, 1–2, Dec. 30, 1761.

28. It is estimated that 95 percent of women were married in late eighteenth-

century America. See Henretta, *Evolution*, pp. 171–72; Mary Beth Norton, *Liberty's Daughters: The Revolutionary Experience of American Women* (Boston: 1980), pp. 41–42; Lee Chambers-Schiller, *Liberty: A Better Husband* (New Haven: 1984).

29. AFC, I, 169, Oct. 14, 1774.
30. AFC, 104, Mar. 7, 1774.
31. Shaw [1768–78] Aug. ?? [*sic*].
32. AFC, I, 65, Apr. 18, 1768.
33. Shaw, Aug. ?? [*sic*].
34. AFC, I, 168, Oct. 14, 1774.
35. AFC, I, 94–96, Feb. 8, 1774.
36. AFC, I, 103–106, Mar. 7, 1774.
37. AFC, II, 159, Feb. 20, 1777. For Abigail's consistent opinion on Calvinism, see Stewart Mitchell, ed., *New Letters of Abigail Adams, 1788–1801* (Westport, Conn.: 1947), p. 117, Dec. 12, 1797. Hereafter cited as NL.
38. AFC, II, 173, Mar. 8, 1777.
39. AFC, II, 356, Oct. 22, 1777.
40. AFC, II, 403, 7, 78. Nevertheless some negative feelings persisted. After the birth of Elizabeth's first child, Abigail wrote, "I have a new Nephew at Haverhill (betterd I hope by the mother's side)" AFC, III, 78, Aug. 19, 1778.
41. See Charles Francis Adams, ed., *Letters of Mrs. Adams, the Wife of John Adams* (New York: 1848), p. 226, Jan. 18, 1785. Hereafter cited as CFA.
42. AFC, I, 55, Oct. 6, 1766.
43. AFC, I, 53–54, July 15, 1766.
44. AFC, I, 59, Jan. 15, 1767; AFC, I, 53–54, July 15, 1766.
45. AP, Reel 364, Apr. 25, 1785.
46. AFC, I, 59, Jan. 15, 1767.
47. Shaw, Feb. 28, 1811.
48. L. H. Butterfield et al., eds., *Diary and Autobiography of John Adams*, 4 volumes (Cambridge, Mass.: 1961), I, 108, Summer 1759.
49. AFC, I, 61, Jan. 31, 1767.
50. AFC, I, 55, Oct. 6, 1766.
51. AFC, I, 59, Jan. 15, 1767.
52. AFC, I, 57–58, Jan. 12, 1767.
53. AFC, I, 54, Jan. 15, 1766.
54. AFC, I, 57, Oct. 13, 1766.
55. AP, Reel 358, Oct. 8, 1782.
56. AP, Reel 359, Nov. 8, 1782.
57. AP, Reel 360, Feb. 18, 1783.
58. AP, Reel 361, Oct. 19, 1783.
59. AP, Reel 361, Nov. 8, 1783.
60. AP, Reel 362, Dec. 15, 1783.
61. Shaw, Apr. 6, 1781.
62. Shaw, Mar. 15, 1782. Letter may be misdated by one year.
63. Ibid.
64. AP, Reel 360, Apr. 7, 1783.
65. Shaw, June 1784.
66. See below, chapter 8.
67. Tamara Hareven, *Family Time and Industrial Time* (Cambridge: 1982).
68. AP, Reel 363, Dec. 5, 1784.
69. AP, Reel 364, Apr. 25, 1785.
70. Shaw, Mar. 18, 1786.
71. AP, Reel 365, Sept. 7, 1785.
72. Shaw, Mar. 18, 1786.

73. Shaw, Nov. 8, 1811.
74. Ibid.
75. AP, Reel 369, Feb. 9, 1787.
76. Ibid., Oct. 22, 1786.
77. Shaw, June 1784.
78. Shaw, Aug. 24, 1784.
79. AP, Reel 362, Apr. 12, 1784.
80. Shaw, Nov. 19, 1785.
81. AP, Reel 368, May 21, 1786.
82. AP, Reel 363, Nov. 6, 1784.
83. MC to AA, AP, Reel 369, Apr. 22, 1787.
84. NL, p. 92, May 24, 1797.
85. NL, pp. 111–12, Nov. 15, 1797.
86. NL, pp. 92–93, May 24, 1797.
87. AP, Reel 369, Apr. 22, 1787; MC to AA, Reel 370, June 13, 1787.
88. Shaw, Mar. 1784.
89. Shaw, Nov. 26, 1788.
90. NL, pp. 14–15, July 12, 1789.
91. NL, pp. 15–16, July 12, 1789.
92. NL, p. 139, Mar. 5, 1798.
93. For Abigail's care of William Cranch, see NL, 232–33; LC, Cranch Papers. For his judicial appointment, see Page Smith, *John Adams*, 2 volumes (Garden City, N.J.: 1962), II, 1065.
94. Abigail's niece, Louisa Smith, the daughter of her derelict brother William Smith, remained a spinster and lived in the Adams household until after John's death.
95. Micaela di Leonardo, "The Female World of Cards and Holidays: Women, Families, and the Work of Kinship," *Signs: Journal of Women in Culture and Society* 12 (1987), pp. 440–53. Di Leonardo distinguishes kin work as maintenance of "cross-household kin ties, including visits, letters, telephone calls, presents," and the like, i.e., those rituals that are nonessential to economic survival and that depend upon adult women, (pp. 442–43).
96. NL, p. 174, May 18, 1798.
97. NL, p. 178, May 21, 1798.
98. Shaw, May 1788.
99. Shaw, Mar. 20, 1785.
100. For the role of gossip in family life, see chapter 5.
101. AP, Reel 365, July 19, 1785.
102. AP, Reel 368, Sept. 24, 1786.
103. AP, Reel 369, Feb. 9, 1787.
104. Shaw, Jan. 20, 1783.
105. CFA, p. 256, June 24, 1785.
106. NL, p. 13, June 28, 1789.
107. NL, pp. 15–16, July 12, 1789.
108. The Adamses' first son was named for Abigail's maternal grandfather. For Col. John Quincy, see Charles Francis Adams, Jr., *Three Episodes of Massachusetts History*, 2 volumes (Boston: 1892); Daniel M. Wilson, *Colonel John Quincy of Mt. Wollaston, 1689–1767, a Public Character of New England's Provincial Period* (Boston: 1909); Also see Shipton, *Sibley's*, V, 445.
109. AP to C. Tufts, Reel 365, Aug. 18, 1785.
110. CFA, p. 288, May 21, 1786.
111. AP, Reel 368, Sept. 24, 1786.
112. For Shays' Rebellion, see Jack N. Rakove, *The Beginnings of National Politics*

(New York: 1979), pp. 391–92; Wood, *American Republic*, pp. 412–13.
113. AP, Reel 368, July 10–11, 1786.
114. AP, Reel 369, Feb. 9, 1787.
115. ES to AA, ibid., Feb. 8, 1787.
116. AP, Reel 369, Apr. 29, 1787.
117. AP, Abigail Adams Papers, American Antiquarian Society, Mar. 8–10, 1787.
118. For more evidence of women's political reticence, see Richard D. Brown, *Knowledge Is Power: The Diffusion of Information in Early America, 1700–1865* (New York: 1989), chapter 7.
119. Abigail did write to many men about politics: to John certainly, but also notably to James Lovell, Thomas Jefferson, Benjamin Rush (but not to Mrs. Rush), and others. She wrote voluminously on political topics to John Quincy. See above chapters 4 and 6. Charles Francis Adams, who inherited the responsibility of sorting family letters in the nineteenth century, discarded many of Abigail's letters to her women friends because he considered them trivial, i.e., they dealt with domestic matters and gossip.
120. NL, p. 143, Mar. 13, 1798. The XYZ Affair refers to a diplomatic episode in which President John Adams had sent envoys to negotiate with the French Directory. They were approached with bribes by French agents, dubbed "X," "Y," and "Z." Considered an insult to the American government, the incident developed into a diplomatic crisis. See Page Smith, *John Adams*, II, 952–65.
121. Shaw, June 26, 1813.
122. Several times Abigail did complain about the subordination of women, but she would immediately recover and express acceptance. See chapter 1.
123. AP, Reel 405, Dec. 28, 1807.
124. AP, Reel 412, Oct. 21, 1811. "A threefold cord is not quickly broken." Ecclesiastes 4:12. For this cite I am grateful to Ruth Stimpson, who called it to my attention.
125. Shaw, Apr. 11, 1815.
126. Shaw, I, Mar. 20, 1785.
127. Carroll Smith-Rosenberg wrote the first significant article describing female friendships in the late eighteenth and nineteenth centuries. Nancy Cott agreed on the timing, claiming that "sisterhood," which emerged in the late eighteenth through the mid-nineteenth centuries, was "characterized by a newly self-conscious and idealized concept of female friendship." Carroll Smith-Rosenberg, "The Female World of Love and Ritual: Relations between Women in Nineteenth-Century America," *Signs: Journal of Women in Culture and Society* 1 (1975), pp. 1–29; Nancy F. Cott, *The Bonds of Womanhood: Woman's Sphere in New England, 1780–1835* (New Haven: 1977), p. 160.
128. Smith-Rosenberg charts a continuum of female connections, which had as its heart the "mother-daughter relationship" with its "closeness and mutual emotional dependency," after which "sisters, aunts, first cousins and nieces" provide the central core of an expanding realm of female relations (pp. 62, 64). Cott sees women's friendships growing out of prescriptions that "identified women with qualities of heart. . . . The identification of woman with the heart meant that she was defined in relation to other persons" (pp. 164–65). While Smith-Rosenberg and Cott have researched broadly in the diaries and letters of many eighteenth- and nineteenth-century women, other historians have focused attention on specific friendships, sometimes exploring the dimensions of the sisterhood, sometimes probing for its significance, sometimes for its nature. For literature on "sisters" and sisters, see Elizabeth Fishel, *Sisters;* Estelle B. Freedman, *Their Sisters' Keepers: Women's Prison Reform, 1830–1930* (Ann Arbor: 1981); Margo Horn, " 'Sisters Worthy of Respect': Family Dynamics and the Women's Roles in the Blackwell Family,"

Journal of Family History (Winter 1983), pp. 367–82; Carol Lasser, " 'Let Us Be Sisters Forever': The Sororal Model of Nineteenth-Century Female Friendship," *Signs* 14 (1988), pp. 158–81; Gerda Lerner, *The Grimke Sisters from South Carolina* (New York: 1971); Robin Morgan, *Sisterhood Is Powerful* (New York: 1970); Marilyn Ferris Motz, *True Sisterhood: Michigan Women and Their Kin, 1820–1920* (Albany: 1983); Dorothy Sterling, ed., *We Are Your Sisters: Black Women in the Nineteenth Century* (New York: 1984).

129. Nel Noddings describes the role of memory in caring-i.e., we care because we remember being cared for. Noddings, *Caring: A Feminine Approach to Ethics and Moral Education* (Berkeley: 1984). See also Jan Lewis and Kenneth A. Lockridge, " 'Sally Has Been Sick': Pregnancy and Family Limitation among Virginia Gentry Women, 1780–1830," *Journal of Social History* 22 (1988), pp. 5–20, especially p. 6.

130. Sara Ruddick describes exercising authority as one function of maternal work. Ruddick, *Maternal Thinking: Toward a Politics of Peace* (Boston: 1989), pp. 37–38, 44.

131. Perhaps the contemporary concept bears closer resemblance to the eighteenth-century prototype of sisterhood than its twentieth-century model. That is, the ideal of "sisterhood" is less identified with twentieth-century family relationships, which seem to be more contentious, than with a myth of what family relationships were in an earlier period when family ties were stronger.

132. Here I am drawing primarily on the work of Meyer Fortes and other British anthropologists. Fortes, *Kinship and the Social Order* (Chicago: 1969); Goody, *Contexts of Kinship*; Maurice Block, "The Long Term and the Short Term," in Jack Goody, ed., *The Character of Kinship* (New York: 1973), pp. 75–88; Derek Freeman, "Kinship, Attachment Behavior and the Primary Bond," in Jack Goody, ed., *Character*, pp. 109–20; Julian Pitt-Rivers, "The Kith and the Kin," in Jack Goody, ed., *Character*, pp. 89–106.

133. Fortes, *Kinship*, p. 247.

134. Pitt-Rivers, "Kith and Kin," p. 96.

135. The term is used by Noddings to distinguish the "cared-for" from the "one-caring." *Caring*, p. 4.

136. Fortes, *Kinship*, p. 249.

8. Mother and Citizen

1. Adrienne Rich, *Of Woman Born: Motherhood as Experience and Institution* (New York: 1986), p. 13.

2. Ibid., xxiii–xxiv. For patriarchy, see also Michelle Zimbalist Rosaldo and Louise Lamphere, eds., *Woman, Culture, and Society* (Stanford, Cal.: 1974) and Gerda Lerner, *The Creation of the Patriarchy* (New York: 1986).

3. Rich, *Woman*, p. 57.

4. Ibid., p. 61. It is interesting to observe the shift in meaning attributed to the word "patriarchy" over the past twenty years. Not long ago, historians of the Revolution used "patriarchy" to refer to an authoritarian British empire. See Edmund G. Burrows and Michael Wallace, "The American Revolution: The Ideology and Psychology of National Liberation," in *Perspectives in American History* 6 (1972), pp. 167–306. Jay Fliegelman, *Prodigals and Pilgrims: The American Revolution against Patriarchal Authority, 1750–1800* (New York: 1982). For the theory of patriarchy, see Johann P. Sommerville, ed., *Filmer: Patriarchs and Other Writings* (Cambridge, Eng.: 1991); Gordon Schochet, *Patriarchalism in Political Thought* (Oxford: 1975). See also Carole Pateman, *The Sexual Contract* (Stanford, Cal.: 1988), pp. 19–38.

5. For a different view of the effects of the Revolution, see Joan Hoff-Wilson, "The Illusion of Change: Women and the American Revolution," in Alfred F. Young,

ed., *The American Revolution: Explorations in the History of American Radicalism* (De-Kalb, Ill.: 1976). Also see Ruth H. Bloch, "The Gendered Meanings of Virtue in Revolutionary America," *Signs: Journal of Women in Culture and Society* 13 (1987), pp. 37–58; Bloch, "American Feminine Ideals in Transition: The Rise of the Moral Mother, 1785–1815," *Feminist Studies* 4 (1978), pp. 101–26. Also see Joan R. Gunderson, "Independence, Citizenship, and the American Revolution," *Signs* 13 (1987), pp. 59–77; Ronald Hoffman and Peter J. Albert, eds., *Women in the Age of the American Revolution* (Charlottesville: 1989); Mary Beth Norton, *Liberty's Daughters: The Revolutionary Experience of American Women, 1750–1800* (Boston: 1980); Norton, "The Evolution of White Women's Experience in Early America," *American Historical Review* 89 (1984), pp. 593–619.

6. Linda K. Kerber, "The Republican Mother: Women and the Enlightenment—An American Perspective," *American Quarterly* 28 (1976), p. 188. See also Kerber, *Women of the Republic: Intellect and Ideology in Revolutionary America* (Chapel Hill: 1980).

7. Kerber, "Republican Mother," p. 202.

8. See Nina Baym, "Women and the Republic: Emma Willard's Rhetoric of History," *American Quarterly* 43 (1991), pp. 1–23; Jan Lewis, "The Republican Wife: Virtue and Seduction in the Early Republic," *William and Mary Quarterly*, 3rd ser., 44 (1987), pp. 689–721; Rosemarie Zagarri, "Morals, Manners, and the Republican Mother" (paper read at the 1990 annual meeting of the American Historical Association); Charles W. Akers, *Abigail Adams: An American Woman* (Boston: 1980); Sara M. Evans, *Born for Liberty: A History of Women in America* (New York: 1989).

9. L. H. Butterfield et al., eds., *The Adams Family Correspondence*, 4 volumes (Cambridge, Mass.: 1963–73), I, 142–43, Aug. 19, 1774. Hereafter cited as AFC. Charles Rollin's histories were popular among revolutionary Americans "because they were a principal medium through which they learned about classical heroes." AFC, I, 143, n. 2. For Rollin, see Henry F. May, *The Enlightenment in America* (New York: 1976), p. 39.

10. Abigail was operating fully within the Lockean tradition, attempting to inspire interest rather than invoking her authority as teacher. See, James L. Axtell, *The Educational Writings of John Locke* (Cambridge, Eng.: 1968), especially pp. 145–77. Furthermore, concerned that he would learn rough manners from other children, Abigail had John Quincy tutored at home rather than sending him to public school. Benjamin Rush agreed, noting that "the vices of young people are generally learned from each other." Rush, "Of the Mode of Education Proper in the Republic," in *Essays, Literary, Moral, and Philosophical* (Philadelphia: 1798), p. 14.

11. Edmund S. Morgan, *The Puritan Family: Religion and Domestic Relations in Seventeenth-Century New England* (New York: 1944). See also Carol F. Karlsen, *The Devil in the Shape of a Woman: Witchcraft in Colonial New England* (New York: 1987); Lyle Koehler, *A Search for Power: The "Weaker Sex" in Seventeenth-Century New England* (Urbana, Ill.: 1980); Mary P. Ryan, *Cradle of the Middle Class: The Family in Oneida County, New York, 1790–1865* (New York: 1981); Laurel Thatcher Ulrich, *Good Wives: Images and Reality in the Lives of Women in Northern New England, 1650–1750* (New York: 1980); Ulrich, *A Midwife's Tale: The Life of Martha Ballard, Based on Her Diary, 1785–1812* (New York: 1990).

12. Philip J. Greven, Jr., *The Protestant Temperament: Patterns of Child Rearing, Religious Experience, and the Self in Early America* (New York: 1977), pp. 178–79. For a contemporary family to the Adamses in which duty was central, see Joy Day Buel and Richard Buel, Jr., *The Way of Duty: A Woman and Her Family in Revolutionary America* (New York: 1984).

13. John Adams's first mission to France in 1778 ended within a year, as Benjamin Franklin was appointed sole minister plenipotentiary. Adams returned

home, only to sail again in June 1779 to participate in the negotiations of a French alliance. On the first trip he took John Quincy. Charles accompanied his father and brother on the second trip. See Page Smith, *John Adams*, 2 volumes (New York: 1962), I, 349–435.

14. AFC, III, 37, June [10?] 1778.

15. AFC, II, 390, Feb. 15, 1778, to John Thaxter.

16. AFC, III, 268, Jan. 19, 1780.

17. Benjamin Rush wrote in strikingly similar language to Abigail, invoking religion as the basis of republicanism and civic virtue. He wrote: "I beg leave to remark, that the only foundation for a useful education in a republic is to be laid in Religion. Without this there can be no virtue, and without virtue there can be no liberty, and liberty is the object and life of all republican governments" (*Essays*, p. 8). Also: "A Christian cannot fail of being useful to the republic, for his religion teaches him, that no man 'liveth to himself.' And lastly, a Christian cannot fail of being wholly inoffensive, for his religion teaches him, in all things to do to others what he would wish, in like circumstances, they should do to him" (ibid., p. 9).

18. AFC, III, 310–13, Mar. 20, 1780.

19. Ibid., pp. 97–98, Sept. 29, 1778.

20. For continuity of religious themes in late eighteenth-century America, see Ruth H. Bloch, "Religion and Ideological Change in the American Revolution," in Mark A. Noll, ed., *Religion and American Politics* (New York: 1990), pp. 44–61; also see John P. Diggins, *The Lost Soul of American Politics: Virtue, Self-Interest, and the Foundations of Liberalism* (New York: 1984); Greven, *Protestant Temperament*: John M. Murrin, "Religion and Politics in America from the First Settlements to the Civil War," in Noll, *Religion*, pp. 19–43; Edmund S. Morgan, "The Puritan Ethic and the American Revolution," *William and Mary Quarterly*, 3d ser., 24 (1967), pp. 3–43. Morgan refers to a "set of values (and ideas) inherited from the age of Puritanism," p. 3; Ulrich, *Good Wives*.

21. Adams Papers, microfilm edition, Reel 411, June 30, 1811. Hereafter cited as AP.

22. James Madison to AA, AP, Reel 410, Aug. 15, 1810; Madison to JQA, ibid., Oct. 16, 1810.

23. AP, Reel 411, June 30, 1811.

24. In each of their letters, at least one paragraph at the beginning described letters received and sent with dates and ships where possible. Thus the Adamses kept a kind of running index or catalogue of their correspondence.

25. AP, Reel 411, June 21, 1811.

26. Ibid., Mar. 4, 1811.

27. Ibid.

28. AP, Reel 398, Sept. 1, 1800.

29. For AA2 in upstate New York, see chapter 9.

30. AP, Reel 411, June 21, 1811.

31. Ibid., Feb. 22, 1811.

32. AA to Louisa Catherine, ibid., Apr. 28, 1811.

33. For a similar interpretation of republicanism as a "rationale," or as "vocabulary for explaining" political participation, see Daniel Walker Howe, "The Evangelical Movement and Political Culture in the North during the Second Party System," *Journal of American History* 77 (1991), pp. 1216–39, especially p. 1234.

34. AFC, III, 37, June 10, 1778.

35. AP, Reel 361, Nov. 20, 1783.

36. AFC, I, 377, Apr. 13, 1777.

37. AP, Reel 361, Nov. 11, 1783.

38. AFC, I, 118, July 1, 1774.

39. Ibid., 148, Aug. 28, 1774. See also AFC, I, 113–14, June 29, 1774; ibid., 384, Apr. 14, 1776.

40. Ibid., I, 308, Mar. 17, 1780. For JQA's success, see ibid., IV, 113, May 13, 1781. Benjamin Rush advocated a similar formula for a proper education, including the admonition to write well: "Too much pains cannot be taken to teach our youth to read and write our American language with propriety and elegance" (*Essays*, p. 15). Also, "I shall only remark, that there is one thing in which all mankind agree upon this subject, and that is, in considering writing that is blotted, crooked, or illegible, as a mark of vulgar education." See p. 78.

41. Ibid., IV, 113, May 13, 1781. The rote learning of Greek especially contrasts with the Lockean approach noted earlier. See note 10 above.

42. Ibid., pp. 55–56, Dec. 28, 1780. Again, Rush concurred: A student "must be indulged occasionally in amusements, but he must be taught that study and business should be his principle pursuits in life" (*Essays*, p. 12). Also an advocate of physical fitness, Rush recommended exercise as well as diet. "The black broth of Sparta, and the barley broth of Scotland, have been alike celebrated for their beneficial effects upon the minds of young people" (*Essays*, p. 13).

43. AP, Reel 412, Sept. 1–8, 1811.

44. Ibid., Sept. 10, 1811.

45. Ibid., Sept. 1–8, 1811.

46. Ibid., Nov. 30, 1811.

47. For a similar conclusion, see Leonard L. Richards, *The Life and Times of Congressman John Quincy Adams* (New York: 1986), p. 17. For other works on JQA, see Samuel Flagg Bemis, *John Quincy Adams and the Foundations of American Foreign Policy* (New York: 1949); Robert A. East, *John Quincy Adams: The Critical Years, 1785–1794* (New York: 1962); and especially George A. Lipsky, *John Quincy Adams: His Theory and Ideas* (New York: 1950).

48. AP, Reel 415, Jan. 9, 1813; Reel 411, Mar. 4, 1811.

49. For family continuity over generations, see Philip J. Greven, Jr., *Four Generations: Population, Land, and Family in Colonial Andover, Massachusetts* (Ithaca, N.Y.: 1970); Carroll Smith-Rosenberg, *Disorderly Conduct: Visions of Gender in Victorian America* (New York: 1985), pp. 32–34.

50. See Cathy N. Davidson, *Revolution and the Word: The Rise of the Novel in America* (New York: 1986), p. 39. Also see Anthony Giddens, *Central Problems in Social Theory: Action, Structure and Contradiction in Social Analysis* (Berkeley: 1979), p. 6. Giddens, as noted in Davidson, reformulates Marx's aphorism that "the ideas of the ruling class are in every epoch the ruling ideas." Davidson, p. 40.

51. Rich, *Woman*, p. 275.

52. See Edith B. Gelles, " 'The Anchor of Our Hope': Abigail Adams and Religion," *Religion and Public Education* 14 (1988), pp. 359–64.

53. John Adams also advised his son to return—in more forceful language: "One thing is clear in my mind, and that is that you ought to be at home; if there you should be obliged to live on Turnips, Potatoes and Cabbage, as I am. My Sphere is reduced to my Garden; and So must yours be. The wandering Life that you have lived, as I have done before you, is not compatible with human nature. It was not made for it. We must move in narrower Circles. Chicanery I expect will keep you in Europe another Winter, and more Winters." Then this remarkable statement: "And what is this World, and this Life to me? You were the greatest Comfort of my life, and of that I have been and am deprived." AP, Reel 416, Nov. 28, 1813.

54. AFC, I, 139, Aug. 9, 1774. John believed that Mercy retaliated for his failure to appoint her family members by representing him unfavorably in her *History of the American Revolution*. Lester Cohen refers to Warren as a "neo-Puritan republican lady," in "Mercy Otis Warren: The Politics of Language and the Aesthetics of Self,"

American Quarterly 35 (1983), pp. 481–98, especially p. 487. See also John Ferling, *John Adams: A Life* (Knoxville, Tenn.: 1992); Page Smith, *John Adams*, II, 1087–88; Peter Shaw, *The Character of John Adams* (Chapel Hill: 1976), pp. 287–95.

55. Anthropologist Mary Catherine Bateson comments that contemporary American men are encouraged to separate from their mothers, as strong ties are considered "pathological, not quite manly." *Composing a Life* (New York: 1989), p. 104. See also Alan Riding, *Distant Neighbors: A Portrait of the Mexicans* (New York: 1984), chapter 1, in which he points out that Latino men remain closely bonded with their mothers. For the impact of cultural relativism on history, see Richard Handler, "Boasian Anthropology and the Critique of American Culture," *American Quarterly* 42 (1990), pp. 252–73.

56. AP, Reel 418, June 30, 1814.

57. AP, Reel 411, Jan. 12, 1811.

58. AP, Reel 416, Sept. 13, 1813.

59. Jürgen Habermas has argued that an ideology is always a response to a counter-force in the culture and is therefore reactionary. Habermas, *Towards a Rational Society*, translated by Jeremy J. Shapiro (Boston: 1968), p. 99.

9. My Closest Companion

1. WSS to AA, Adams Papers, microfilm edition, Reel 416, July 20, 1813. Hereafter cited as AP.

2. AA to Lucy Cranch Greenleaf, Abigail Adams Papers, American Antiquarian Society, July 1813; AA to JQA, AP, Reel 416, Aug. 30, 1813; AA to Julia Rush, ibid., Sept. 24, 1813; AA to MOW, ibid., July 1813.

3. AA to Mrs. Black, AP, Reel 415, Jan. 24, 1813. Almost universally, Abigail Adams Smith is referred to as Nabby in the secondary literature. I have chosen not to use the diminutive but rather to refer to her as Mrs. Smith or Abigail Junior. The reason is that nowhere in the letters have I seen Mrs. Smith, as an adult, called Nabby. The diminutive, I believe, is reserved for children.

4. AA to JQA, AP, Reel 416, July 1, 1813.

5. She suffered chronic rheumatism, colds, fevers, and inflammations in various parts of her body which remain undiagnosed.

6. Stewart Mitchell, ed., *New Letters of Abigail Adams, 1788–1801* (Westport, Conn.: 1947), p. xxxiv. Hereafter cited as NL.

7. Caroline deWindt, ed., *Journal and Correspondence of Miss Adams, Daughter of John Adams* (New York: 1841–42), Dec. 9, 1809, p. 219.

8. AA to JQA, AP, Reel 415, June 14, 1813.

9. AA to JQA, AP, Reel 411, Jan. 20, 1811; AA to JQA, Reel 411, Mar. 4, 1811.

10. AA to Mrs. Margaret Smith, AP, Reel 371, Apr. 22, 1788.

11. AA to MC, AP, Reel 368, June 13, 1786.

12. AA to MC, NL, p. 3, Nov. 24, 1788.

13. AA to MC, NL, p. 20, Aug. 9, 1789.

14. AA to MC, NL, p. 60, Oct. 10, 1790.

15. AA to MC, NL, p. 65, Dec. 12, 1790.

16. TJ to AA, AP, Reel 366, Nov. 20, 1785.

17. AA to MC, NL, p. 66, Dec. 12, 1790.

18. AA to MC, NL, p. 77, Feb. 5, 1792. If Abigail Smith was pregnant, no child was born that year, nor is there another mention of her "circumstances." Abigail regretted, if not disapproved of, her daughter's repeated pregnancies.

19. Katharine Metcalf Roof, *Colonel William Smith and Lady* (Boston: 1929), p. 219.

20. AA to MC, NL, p. 89, May 16, 1797.

21. AA to MC, NL, p. 90, May 16, 1797.

22. Ibid., p. 119, Dec. 16, 1797.
23. Ibid., pp. 130–31, Feb. 6, 1798.
24. Ibid., p. 8, May 16, 1789.
25. Another sad development within the family, Charles's alcoholism, had progressed to the point where hope for his survival had vanished. Abigail had visited with Sally Adams and learned the worst information. Charles would die in 1800. Abigail grieved for her son; John grieved but was angry. See NL, pp. 89, 254.
26. AA to MC, NL, Sept. 31, 1779; ibid., p. 262, Dec. 8, 1800; AA to JQA, July 1, 1813, AP, Reel 416.
27. AA to MC, NL, p. 211, Dec. 8, 1800, p. 262.
28. AA to JQA, Dec. 8, 1811, AP, Reel 412; AA to JQA, AP, Reel 416, Aug. 30, 1813.
29. Charles Francis Adams, ed., *The Works of John Adams*, 10 volumes (Boston: 1851–1856), VIII, 617–18. John wrote to Smith: "Upon this occasion I must be plain with you. Your pride and ostentation which I myself have seen with inexpressible grief for many years, have excited among your neighbors so much envy and resentment . . . it will never be forgiven or forgotten. He whose vanity has been indulged and displayed to the humiliation and mortification of others, may depend on meeting their revenge whenever they shall find an opportunity," p. 618. Hereafter cited as *Works*.
30. When friends in Washington offered to intercede on behalf of young William Steuben Smith, John Adams refused, insisting that he wanted no special privileges for his grandson. Young Smith was eventually released along with other prisoners. He returned home, completed his studies at Columbia, and then traveled to St. Petersburg as secretary to John Quincy Adams. For the Miranda Affair, see Claude G. Bowers, *Jefferson in Power* (Boston: 1967), pp. 320–23; Roof, *Colonel Smith*, 265–72; Page Smith, *John Adams*, 2 volumes (New York: 1962), pp. 1090–91.
31. AA to MC, NL, p. 67, Dec. 12, 1790.
32. Ibid., p. 88, May 5, 1797.
33. AA to JQA, AP, Reel 412, Sept. 24, 1811.
34. In 1791, Abigail wrote to Mary about her poor health, adding: "A critical period of life augments my complaints." NL, p. 81, Apr. 20, 1792. Referring to a miscarriage of her niece, she wrote: "She poor thing has had a mishap." NL, p. 244, Apr. 7, 1800. Some letters have been lost or edited, which may also account for the silence. For attitudes about sexuality, see John D'Emilio and Estelle B. Freedman, *Intimate Matters: A History of Sexuality in America* (New York: 1988).
35. Describing a "stile of dress" that she considered an outrage, Abigail wrote to Mary, "The arm naked almost to the shoulder and without stays or Bodice. A tight girdle round the waist, and the 'rich Luxurience of naturs Charms' without a hankerchief fully displayd." NL, p. 241, Mar. 18, 1800.
36. Audre Lorde, *The Cancer Journals* (San Francisco: 1980), p. 49.
37. Susan Sontag, *Illness as Metaphor* (New York: 1977), p. 9.
38. AA to JQA, AP, Reel 412, Sept. 24, 1811.
39. For the history of breast cancer, see William A. Cooper, "The History of the Radical Mastectomy," *Annals of Medical History* 3 (1941), pp. 36–54. Daniel DeMoulin, *A Short History of Breast Cancer* (Boston/The Hague: 1983); L. J. Rather, *The Genesis of Cancer: A Study in the History of Ideas* (Baltimore: 1978).
40. Ibid.
41. Philip Cash, Eric H. Christianson, J. Worth Estes, eds., *Medicine in Colonial Massachusetts, 1620–1820* (Boston: 1980), especially Part II, "The Practitioners."
42. WSS to AA, AP, Reel 412, Aug. 12, 1811.
43. AA to WSS, Massachusetts Historical Society, DeWindt Collection, Aug. 29, 1811.

44. Although John Adams's attitude toward Smith mellowed with age (and distance), he was at times barely able to suppress his contempt. Following one of Smith's indiscretions, he wrote: "I have received your letter . . . with a great deal of pain. . . . I will not interfere with the discipline and order of the army, because you are my son-in-law." *Works*, May 22, 1799, p. 652.

45. WSS to AA, AP, Reel 412, Sept. 15, 1811.

46. The physician mentioned most often in the family correspondence is Dr. John Warren (1753–1815), brother of Dr. Joseph Warren, a good friend of the Adamses who died at Bunker Hill. After graduating from Harvard in 1771, John Warren apprenticed with his brother, who in turn had apprenticed under Dr. James Lloyd, who had received his medical training in England. During the Revolution, John Warren served valiantly under fire and presumably learned surgery, for after passing an examination before a medical board, he was appointed senior surgeon. The common term of medical apprenticeship was two years, there being no medical school in Boston until after 1781, when the first courses were introduced at Harvard. Nor did apprenticeship confer the title of M.D. Warren was awarded an honorary M.D. by Harvard in 1786. He was Boston's leading surgeon. He seems to have adopted a conservative course with Abigail Smith's breast tumor, waiting to see if it would become worse before recommending surgery. Dr. Cotton Tufts, Abigail's ancient uncle, was not convinced that the tumor was cancerous. The other physicians who participated in the surgical arena (Warren was probably chief surgeon) for her operation were Dr. Amos Holbrook (1754–1842), who trained by apprenticeship, but who in 1780 "walked London and Paris hospitals" and later practiced in Quincy; Dr. Thomas Welsh (1751–1831); and John Warren's son, Dr. John Collins Warren (1778–1856), who trained in London at Guys Hospital. See Philip Cash, "The Professionalization of Boston Medicine, 1760–1803," in Cash, *Medicine in Colonial Massachusetts*, pp. 69–95, 117 and Howard A. Kelly and Walter L. Burrage, *Dictionary of American Medical Biography* (Boston: 1928).

47. For the Adams-Rush correspondence, see John A. Schutz and Douglass Adair, eds., *The Spur of Fame: Dialogues of John Adams and Benjamin Rush, 1805–1813* (San Marino: 1966). This edition omits all references to Abigail Smith's operation, although Rush's letter is found in the Adams Papers. BR to JA, AP, Reel 412, Sept. 20, 1811.

48. I wish to thank the archivists at the Historical Society of Pennsylvania who tracked this letter for me, especially Ellen Slack, who transcribed it. I suspected that if it survived, the letter was among the Rush Papers, some of which are housed at the Library Company of Philadelphia. The letter was not immediately apparent because it was cataloged under the prosaic name of A. Smith, not Abigail Adams Smith. AAS to Rush, Benjamin Rush Papers, vol. 15, p. 111.

49. See Julia Epstein's fascinating article "Writing the Unspeakable: Fanny Burney's Mastectomy and the Fictive Body," *Representations* 16 (Fall 1986), pp. 131–66. Also see Epstein, *The Iron Pen: Frances Burney and the Politics of Women's Writing* (Madison: 1989), chapter 2. Epstein cites Michel Foucault, *The Birth of the Clinic: An Archaeology of Medical Perception*, translated by A. M. Sheridan Smith (New York: 1975), for the idea that "the turn of the nineteenth century was the time when clinical experience becomes a form of knowledge." Foucault attributed the change to the invention of the stethoscope. Epstein futher posits that change was influenced by the development of autopsy as common procedure in the eighteenth century: "it inaugurated this shift from theory and word to observation and touch," p. 161.

50. BR to JA, AP, Reel 412, Sept. 20, 1811.

51. Rush (1745–1813) trained at Edinburgh and later studied in London and Paris. In 1789 he became professor of theory and practice of medicine at the College of Philadelphia, where he soon established himself as a critic of prevailing medical

theories; this earned him many detractors. His dedication to patients during the yellow fever epidemic of 1797 is renowned. His favorite remedies were bleeding and purgation. See David Hawke, *Benjamin Rush* (New York: 1971); Kelly, *Dictionary,* pp. 1066–68; Schutz, *Spur,* chapter 1.

52. Some patients who lived long lives after breast surgery may not have had malignant tumors, but rather fibrosis. I have seen it argued both ways for patients who did survive, such as Sarah Winslow, who lived thirty-nine years to the age of eighty-five. Her surgeon, interestingly enough, was John Adams's ancestor Zabdiel Boylston, best known for introducing the smallpox inoculation to the Colonies. Winslow's mastectomy in 1718 is the earliest known in America. See Alan D. Steinfeld, "A Historical Report of Mastectomy for Carcinoma of the Breast," *Surgery, Gynecology & Obstetrics* 141 (1975), pp. 616–17. An example of a woman who delayed surgery too long was the famous English philosopher Mary Astell, who died after her 1731 mastectomy. See Ruth Perry, *The Celebrated Mary Astell* (Chicago: 1986), pp. 318–22.

53. AA to JQA, AP, Reel 412, Nov. 17, 1811.

54. Ibid.

55. Ibid., Sept. 24, 1811.

56. Joyce Hemlow et al., eds., *The Journals and Letters of Fanny Burney (Madam d'Arblay),* 12 volumes (Oxford: 1972–84), VI, 596–616. In her biography of Burney, Hemlow suggests that if readers are too sensitive "to enter the gruesome operating-theater, feel the cutting and hear the screams," they may prefer to "turn over the leaf and choose another tale." Hemlow, *The History of Fanny Burney* (Oxford: 1958), p. 322.

57. Using the term "sisters," Burney was referring to her friends. (See above, chapter 7.) She had, in fact, rejected the offer of several friends to remain with her during the operation.

58. Julia Epstein translated this letter. "Writing the Unspeakable," p. 151.

59. AA to LCA, AP, Reel 412, Nov. 26, 1811.

60. AA to JQA, AP, Reel 412, Dec. 8, 1911.

61. ESP to AA, AP, Reel 412, Dec. 18, 1811.

62. BR to JA, Reel 413, Jan. 15, 1812.

63. AA to JQA, Reel 413, Feb. 17, 1812.

64. AA to LCA, AP, Reel 412, Nov. 26, 1811.

65. AA to JQA, AP, Reel 412, Dec. 8, 1811.

66. ESP to JQA, AP, Reel 413, Feb. 26, 1812.

67. AA to Caroline, de Windt, *Journal,* p. 231, Aug. 6, 1812.

68. AA to Mrs. Black, AP, Reel 415, Jan. 24, 1813. Mrs. Black was a Boston friend of Abigail Adams.

69. AA to JQA, AP, Reel 415, Apr. 5, 1813.

70. ESP to AA, AP, Reel 415, June 22, 1813.

71. MOW to AA, AP, Reel 415, June 15, 1813.

72. AA to JQA, Reel 416, July 1, 1813.

73. AA to Lucy Cranch Greenleaf, Abigail Adams Papers, American Anti-quarian Society, Jan. 1813.

74. ESP to AA, AP, Reel 416, July 12, 1813.

75. AA to JQA, AP, Reel 416, July 14, 1813.

76. AA to Lucy Cranch Greenleaf, Abigail Adams Papers, Aug. 17, 1813.

77. AA to JQA, AP, Reel 416, Sept. 24, 1813.

78. AA to JQA, AP, Reel 416, Sept. 13, 1813.

79. AA to JQA, AP, Reel 416, Oct. 22, 1813.

80. AA to MOW, AP, Reel 416, July 1813.

81. See, for instance, Nancy Chodorow, *The Reproduction of Mothering: Psycho-*

analysis and the Sociology of Gender (Berkeley: 1978); Jean Baker Miller, *Toward a New Psychology of Women* (Boston: 1976); Jean Strouse, ed., *Women and Analysis: Dialogues on Psychoanalytic Views of Femininity* (Boston: 1974).

82. AA to AA2, deWindt, *Journal*, Apr. 10, 1810, p. 211. For Puritan attitudes about parents limiting worldly affection for children, see Edmund S. Morgan, *The Puritan Family* (New York: 1944), pp. 75–78.

83. AA to JQA, AP, Reel 416, Aug. 30, 1813.

84. AA to JQA, AP, Reel 416, Sept. 24, 1813; AA to Vanderkemp, ibid., Oct. 15, 1813; AA to TJ, MHS, Cranch Family Papers, AC 62-M54, 9/20/13. She quotes Shakespeare, *The Comedy of Errors*, act V, scene 1, lines 396–99. I am grateful to Woof Kurtzman of *TheatreWorks* in Palo Alto for tracking this quote for me.

85. For literature about death in history, see Philippe Ariès, *The Hour of Our Death* (New York: 1981); Ariès, *Western Attitudes toward Death* (Baltimore: 1974); David E. Stannard, *The Puritan Way of Death* (New York: 1977); also see the special issue, "Death in America," *American Quarterly* 26 (Dec. 1974).

86. AA to LCA, AP, Reel 416, Dec. 6, 1813.

87. The Reverend Norton eventually remarried, but until he did, his wife's relatives searched widely for a woman who would be willing to undertake the management of his household. See Library of Congress, Shaw Papers, microfilm edition.

88. ESP to AA, AP, Reel 416, Aug. 19, 1813.

89. AA to George Washington Adams and John Adams, AP, Reel 416, Aug. 15, 1813. Quote is Ecclesiastes 7:2.

90. AA to JQA, Reel 416, Aug. 30, 1813.

91. Philippe Ariès describes part of the transformation from medieval to modern attitudes to death as concern for self, the hereafter, immersion in a community, all seen as part of "My Death." Sentimental or Romantic attitudes emphasize "Thy Death," separation, the sense of bereavement of the living for the dead. See Ariès, *Western Attitudes*, pp. 27–82; Stannard, *Puritan Way*, pp. 135–63.

92. AA to MOW, AP, Reel 416, Sept. 13, 1813.

93. AA to JQA, ibid., Oct. 22, 1813.

94. Ibid.

95. AA to JQA, ibid., Nov. 8, 1813.

Bibliography

Manuscript Sources

American Antiquarian Society. Worcester, Mass.
    Abigail Adams Papers.
Boston Public Library. Boston.
    MS ENG 483 (397).
Historical Society of Pennsylvania. Collections of the Library Company of Philadelphia. Philadelphia.
    Benjamin Rush Papers.
Library of Congress. Manuscript Division. Washington, D.C.
    Cranch Papers. Microfilm edition.
    Shaw Papers. Microfilm edition.
Massachusetts Historical Society. Boston.
    Adams Papers. Microfilm edition.
    Cranch Family Papers.
    DeWindt Collection.

Printed Sources

Adams, Charles Francis, ed. *Correspondence between John Adams and Mercy Warren.* New York: Arno Press, 1972.
————. *The Familiar Letters of John Adams and His Wife Abigail Adams during the Revolution.* Boston: Hurd & Houghton, 1876.
————. *Letters of Mrs. Adams, the Wife of John Adams.* Boston: Hurd & Houghton, 1848.
————. "Memoir of Mrs. Adams," *Letters of Mrs. Adams, Wife of John Adams.* 4th ed. Boston: Charles C. Little & James Brown, 1848.
————. *The Works of John Adams, Second President of the United States: With a Life of the Author, Notes and Illustrations, by His Grandson Charles Francis Adams.* 10 volumes. Boston: Books for Libraries Press, 1851–1856.
Bell, Susan Groag, and Karen Offen. *Women, the Family, and Freedom: The Debate in Documents.* 2 volumes. Stanford, Cal.: Stanford University Press, 1983.
Burnett, Edmund C. *Letters of Members of the Continental Congress.* 8 volumes. Washington, D.C.: Carnegie Institute of Washington, 1921–1936.
Butterfield, L. H., et al., eds. *The Adams Papers: Adams Family Correspondence.* 4 volumes. Cambridge, Mass.: Harvard University Press, Belknap Press, 1963, 1973.
————. *The Adams Papers: Diary and Autobiography of John Adams.* 4 volumes. Cambridge, Mass.: Harvard University Press, Atheneum, 1961.
————. *The Book of Abigail and John: Selected Letters of the Adams Family 1762–1784.* Cambridge, Mass.: Harvard University Press, 1975.
Cappon, Lester, ed. *The Adams-Jefferson Letters: The Complete Correspondence between Thomas Jefferson and Abigail and John Adams.* 2 volumes. Chapel Hill: University of North Carolina Press, 1959.

"Correspondence between John Adams and Mercy Otis Warren, July–August 1807." Massachusetts Historical Society, *Proceedings*, 5th ser., 4 (1878).

DeWindt, Caroline Smith, ed. *The Journal and Correspondence of Miss Adams, Daughter of John Adams*. 2 volumes. New York: Wiley & Putnam, 1841–1842.

"Diaries of Rev. William Smith and Dr. Cotton Tufts, 1738–1784." Massachusetts Historical Society, *Proceedings*, 3rd ser., 2 (1908–1909): 444–70.

Hemlow, Joyce, et al., eds. *The Journals and Letters of Fanny Burney (Madam d'Arblay)*. 12 volumes. Oxford: Oxford University Press, 1972–1984.

Mitchell, Stewart, ed. *New Letters of Abigail Adams, 1788–1801*. Westport, Conn.: Greenwood Press, 1947.

Oliver, Andrew. *Portraits of John and Abigail Adams*. Cambridge, Mass.: Harvard University Press, Belknap Press, 1967.

Schutz, John A., and Douglass Adair, eds. *The Spur of Fame: Dialogues of John Adams and Benjamin Rush, 1805–1813*. San Marino, Cal.: Huntington Library, 1966.

Taylor, Robert J., et al., eds. *The Adams Papers: Papers of John Adams*. 6 volumes. Cambridge, Mass.: Harvard University Press, Belknap Press, 1977–.

Tupper, Frederick, and Helen Tyler Brown, eds. *Grandmother Tyler's Book: The Recollections of Mary Palmer Tyler, 1775–1866*. New York: G. P. Putnam's, 1925.

Tyler, Royall. *The Contrast, a Comedy in Five Acts*. 1790. Reprinted in *Representative Plays by American Dramatists, 1765–1819*. Edited by Montrose J. Moses. New York: E. P. Dutton, 1918.

Warren, Mercy Otis. *History of the Rise, Progress and Termination of the American Revolution*. 3 volumes. 1805. Reprint. New York: AMS Press, 1970.

The Warren-Adams Letters. Volumes 72–73. Boston: Massachusetts Historical Society, 1917, 1925.

Secondary Sources

Abrahams, Roger. "A Performance-Centered Approach to Gossip." *Man* 5 (1970): 291–303.

Adams, Charles Francis, Jr. *Three Episodes of Massachusetts History: The Settlement of Boston Bay; the Antinomian Controversy; A Study of Church and Town Government*. 2 volumes. Boston: Houghton Mifflin, 1892.

Adams, Henry. *The Education of Henry Adams: An Autobiography*. Boston: Houghton Mifflin, 1918.

"The Adams Chronicles," directed by Virginia Kassel. New York: WNET, 1975.

Ahlstrom, Sidney E. *A Religious History of the American People*. New Haven: Yale University Press, 1972.

Akers, Charles W. *Abigail Adams: An American Woman*. Boston: Little, Brown, 1980.

Anderson, Howard, Philip B. Daghlian, and Irvin Ehrenpreis, eds. *The Familiar Letter in the Eighteenth Century*. Lawrence, Kans.: University of Kansas Press, 1966.

Anderson, Howard, and Irvin Ehrenpreis. "The Familiar Letter in the Eighteenth Century: Some Generalizations." In *The Familiar Letter in the Eighteenth Century*, edited by Anderson et al. Lawrence, Kans.: University of Kansas Press, 1966.

Appleby, Joyce. *Capitalism and a New Social Order: The Republican Vision of the 1790's*. New York: New York University Press, 1984.

Ariès, Philippe. *The Hour of Our Death*. New York: Alfred A. Knopf, 1981.

———. *Western Attitudes toward Death*. Baltimore: Johns Hopkins University Press, 1974.

Axtell, James L. *The Educational Writings of John Locke*. Cambridge, Eng.: Cambridge University Press, 1968.

Bailyn, Bernard. *The Ideological Origins of the American Revolution.* Cambridge, Mass.: Harvard University Press, 1967.

Bailyn, Bernard, and John B. Hench, eds. *The Press and the American Revolution.* Worcester, Mass.: American Antiquarian Society, 1980.

Baker, Paula. "The Domestication of Politics: Women and American Political Society 1780–1920." *American Historical Review* 89 (1984): 620–47.

Baumrind, Diana. "Sex Differences in Moral Reasoning: Response to Walker's (1984) Conclusion That There Are None." *Child Development* 57 (1986): 511–21.

Baym, Nina. "Women and the Republic: Emma Willard's Rhetoric of History." *American Quarterly* 43 (1991): 1–23.

Belenky, Mary Field, Blythe McVicker Clinchy, Nancy Rule Goldberger, and Jill Mattuck Tarule. *Women's Ways of Knowing: The Development of Self, Voice, and Mind.* New York: Basic Books, 1986.

Bemis, Samuel Flagg. *The Diplomacy of the American Revolution.* New York: A. Appleton-Century, 1935.

————. *John Quincy Adams and the Foundations of American Foreign Policy.* New York: W. W. Norton, 1949.

Biographical Directory of American Congress, 1774–1989. Washington, D.C.: U.S. Government Printing Office, 1989.

Bloch, Ruth H. "American Feminine Ideals in Transition: The Rise of the Moral Mother, 1785–1815." *Feminist Studies* 4 (1978): 101–26.

————. "The Gendered Meanings of Virtue in Revolutionary America." *Signs: Journal of Women in Culture and Society* 13 (1987): 37–58.

————. "Religion and Ideological Change in the American Revolution." In *Religion and American Politics from the Colonial Period to the 1980's*, edited by Mark A. Noll. New York: Oxford University Press, 1990.

————. *Visionary Republic: Millennial Themes in American Thought, 1750–1800.* New York: Cambridge University Press, 1985.

Block, Maurice. "The Long Term and the Short Term." In *The Character of Kinship*, edited by Jack Goody. New York: Cambridge University Press, 1973.

Bok, Sissela. *Secrets: On the Ethics of Concealment and Revelation.* New York: Pantheon, 1982.

Bonomi, Patricia U. *Under the Cope of Heaven: Religion, Society and Politics in Colonial America.* New York: Oxford University Press, 1987.

Bowen, Catherine Drinker. *John Adams and the American Revolution.* Boston: Little, Brown, 1950.

Bowers, Claude G. *Jefferson in Power.* Boston: Houghton Mifflin, 1967.

Bradford, Gamaliel. *Portraits of American Women.* Boston: Houghton Mifflin, 1919.

Breitweiser, Mitchell Robert. *Cotton Mather and Benjamin Franklin: The Price of Representative Personality.* New York: Cambridge University Press, 1987.

Brodie, Fawn. *Thomas Jefferson: An Intimate History.* New York: W. W. Norton, 1974.

Brown, Richard D. *Knowledge Is Power: The Diffusion of Information in Early America, 1700–1865.* New York: Oxford University Press, 1989.

Brown, Robert. *Middle Class Democracy and the Revolution in Massachusetts, 1691–1780.* New York: Harper & Row, 1955.

Buel, Joy Day, and Richard Buel, Jr. *The Way of Duty: A Woman and Her Family in Revolutionary America.* New York: W. W. Norton, 1984.

Bullock, Helen Duprey. *My Head and My Heart: A Little History of Thomas Jefferson and Maria Cosway.* New York: G. P. Putnam's, 1945.

Burleigh, Anne Husted. *John Adams.* New Rochelle, N.Y.: Arlington House, 1969.

Burnett, Edmund C. *The Continental Congress: A Definitive History of the Continental Congress from Its Inception in 1774 to March 1789.* New York: W. W. Norton, 1941.

Burrows, Edmund G., and Michael Wallace. "The American Revolution: The Ide-
    ology and Psychology of National Liberation." *Perspectives in American History*
    6 (1972): 167–306.
Butterfield, L. H. "Abigail Adams." In *Notable American Women 1607–1950: A Bio-
    graphical Dictionary*, edited by Edward T. James et al. Cambridge, Mass.:
    Harvard University Press, 1971.
———. Introduction to *The Adams Papers: Diary and Autobiography of John Adams*. 4
    volumes. Cambridge, Mass.: Harvard University Press, 1961.
———. "The Papers of the Adams Family: Some Account of Their History." Massa-
    chusetts Historical Society, *Proceedings* 71 (1959): 328–56.
Cash, Philip. "The Professionalization of Boston Medicine, 1760–1803." In *Medicine
    in Colonial Massachusetts* edited by Philip Cash et al. Boston: The Society,
    1980.
Cash, Philip, Eric H. Christianson, and J. Worth Estes, eds. *Medicine in Colonial
    Massachusetts, 1620–1820*. Boston: The Society, 1980.
Chambers-Schiller, Lee. *Liberty: A Better Husband*. New Haven: Yale University
    Press, 1984.
Chodorow, Nancy. *The Reproduction of Mothering: Psychoanalysis and the Sociology of
    Gender*. Berkeley and Los Angeles: University of California Press, 1978.
Cixous, Hélène. "The Laugh of the Medusa." Translated by Keith Cohen and Paula
    Cohen. *Signs: Journal of Women in Culture and Society* 1 (1976): 875–93.
Clinton, Catherine. *The Plantation Mistress*. New York: Pantheon, 1983.
Cohen, Charles Lloyd. *God's Caress: The Psychology of Puritan Religious Experience*.
    New York: Oxford University Press, 1986.
Cohen, Lester H. "Explaining the Revolution: Ideology and Ethics in Mercy Otis
    Warren's Historical Theory." *William and Mary Quarterly* 37 (1980): 200–18.
———. "Mercy Otis Warren: The Politics of Language and the Aesthetics of Self."
    American Quarterly 35 (1983): 481–98.
Collier, Jane Fishburne, and Sylvia Junko Yanagisako, eds. *Gender and Kinship:
    Essays toward a United Analysis*. Stanford, Cal.: Stanford University Press,
    1987.
Cooper, William A. "The History of the Radical Mastectomy." *Annals of Medical
    History* 3 (1941): 36–54.
Cott, Nancy F. *The Bonds of Womanhood: "Woman's Sphere" in New England, 1780–1835*.
    New Haven: Yale University Press, 1977.
———. "Passionlessness: An Interpretation of Victorian Sexual Ideology, 1790–
    1850." *Signs: Journal of Women in Culture and Society* 4 (1978): 219–36.
Daly, Mary. *Gyn/Ecology: The Metaethics of Radical Feminism*. Boston: Beacon Press,
    1978.
Davidson, Cathy N. *Revolution and the Word: The Rise of the Novel in America*. New
    York: Oxford University Press, 1986.
Davis, Herbert. "The Correspondence of the Augustans." In *The Familiar Letter in the
    Eighteenth Century*, edited by Howard Anderson et al. Lawrence, Kans.:
    University of Kansas Press, 1966.
Davis, Natalie Zemon. "On the Lame." *American Historical Review* 93 (1988): 572–
    603.
Day, Robert Adams. *Told in Letters: Epistolary Fiction before Richardson*. Ann Arbor:
    University of Michigan Press, 1966.
"Death in America." Special issue, edited by David E. Stannard. *American Quarterly*
    26 (December 1974).
Degler, Carl N. *At Odds: Women and the Family in America from the Revolution to the
    Present*. New York: Oxford University Press, 1980.

D'Emilio, John, and Estelle B. Freedman. *Intimate Matters: A History of Sexuality in America.* New York: Harper & Row, 1988.

Demos, John. *Entertaining Satan: Witchcraft and the Culture of Early New England.* New York: Oxford University Press, 1982.

———. *A Little Commonwealth: Family Life in Plymouth Colony.* New York: Oxford University Press, 1970.

———. *Past, Present and Personal: The Family and the Life Course in American History.* New York: Oxford University Press, 1986.

Demoulin, Daniel. *A Short History of Breast Cancer.* Boston and The Hague: Martinus Nijhoff, 1983.

DePauw, Linda Grant. "The American Revolution and the Rights of Women: The Feminist Theory of Abigail Adams." In *The Legacy of the American Revolution,* edited by Larry R. Gerlach et al. Logan, Utah: Utah State University Press, 1978.

Diggins, John P. *The Lost Soul of American Politics: Virtue, Self-Interest, and the Foundations of Liberalism.* New York: Basic Books, 1984.

di Leonardo, Micaela. "The Female World of Cards and Holidays: Women, Families, and the Work of Kinship." *Signs: Journal of Women in Culture and Society* 21 (1987): 440–53.

Douglas, Ann. *The Feminization of American Culture.* New York: Alfred A. Knopf, 1977.

Drabble, Margaret. "Introduction" in Jane Austen, *Lady Susan.* New York: Viking Penguin, 1974.

East, Robert A. *John Quincy Adams: The Critical Years, 1785–1794.* New York: Bookman, 1962.

Ellet, Elizabeth. *The Women of the American Revolution.* New York: McMenanery & Hess, 1848.

Elshtain, Jean Bethke. "Feminist Discourse and Its Discontents: Language, Power, and Meaning." *Feminist Studies* 7 (1982): 603–21.

———. *Public Man, Private Woman: Women in Social and Political Thought.* Princeton: Princeton University Press, 1981.

Epstein, Julia. *The Iron Pen: Frances Burney and the Politics of Women's Writing.* Madison: University of Wisconsin Press, 1989.

———. "Writing the Unspeakable: Fanny Burney's Mastectomy and the Fictive Body." *Representations* 16 (1986): 131–66.

Erikson, Erik H. *Childhood and Society.* New York: W. W. Norton, 1950.

Evans, Elizabeth. *Weathering the Storm: Women of the American Revolution.* New York: Charles Scribner's, 1975.

Evans, Sara M. *Born for Liberty: A History of Women in America.* New York: Free Press, 1989.

Farrand, Max. "The Judiciary Act of 1801." *American Historican Review* 5 (1899–1900): 681–86.

Ferling, John. *John Adams: A Life.* Knoxville, Tenn.: University of Tennessee Press, 1992.

Fishel, Elizabeth. *Sisters: Love and Rivalry inside the Family and Beyond.* New York: William Morrow, 1979.

Fisher, George. *The Instructor or Young Man's Best Companion.* 25th ed. Burlington: 1775.

Fliegelman, Jay. *Prodigals and Pilgrims: The American Revolution against Patriarchal Authority, 1750–1800.* New York: Cambridge University Press, 1982.

Fortes, Meyer. *Kinship and the Social Order.* Chicago: University of Chicago Press, 1969.

Foucault, Michel. *The Birth of the Clinic: An Archaeology of Medical Perception.* Translated by A. M. Sheridan Smith. New York: Pantheon, 1975.
——. *History of Sexuality.* 3 volumes. New York: Pantheon, 1978–1986.
Freedman, Estelle B. *Their Sisters' Keepers: Women's Prison Reform, 1830–1930.* Ann Arbor: University of Michigan Press, 1981.
Freeman, Derek. "Kinship, Attachment Behavior and the Primary Bond." In *The Character of Kinship,* edited by Jack Goody. Cambridge, Eng.: Cambridge University Press, 1973.
Freud, Sigmund. "The Dissolution of the Oedipus Complex." (1924). In *The Standard Edition of the Complete Psychological Works of Sigmund Freud.* Translated and edited by James Strachey. Vol. 19. London: Hogarth Press, 1961.
——. "Group Psychology and the Analysis of the Ego." (1921) In *The Standard Edition of the Complete Psychological Works of Sigmund Freud.* Translated and edited by James Strachey. Vol. 18. London: Hogarth Press, 1955.
——. *New Introductory Lectures.* New York: W. W. Norton, 1933.
——. "Some Psychical Consequences of the Anatomical Distinction between the Sexes." In *The Standard Edition of the Complete Psychological Works of Sigmund Freud.* Translated and edited by James Strachey. Vol. 19. London: Hogarth Press, 1961.
Gaustad, Edwin S. *Dissent in American Religion.* Chicago: University of Chicago Press, 1973.
Gawalt, Gerald W. *The Promise of Power: The Emergence of the Legal Profession in Massachusetts, 1760–1840.* Westport, Conn.: Greenwood Press, 1979.
Geertz, Clifford. *The Interpretation of Cultures.* New York: Basic, 1973.
——. *Myth, Symbol, and Culture.* New York: W. W. Norton, 1971.
Gelles, Edith B. "Abigail Adams: Domesticity and the American Revolution." *New England Quarterly* 52 (1979): 500–21.
——. "The Abigail Industry." *William and Mary Quarterly* 45 (1988): 656–83.
——. " 'The Anchor of Our Hope': Abigail Adams and Religion." *Religion and Public Education* 14 (1988): 359–64.
——. "Gossip: An Eighteenth-Century Case." *Journal of Social History* 22 (1989): 667–83.
——. "A Virtuous Affair: The Correspondence between Abigail Adams and James Lovell." *American Quarterly* 39 (1987): 252–69.
Gilligan, Carol. *In a Different Voice: Psychological Theory and Women's Development.* Cambridge, Mass.: Harvard University Press, 1982.
Gluckman, Max. "Gossip and Scandal." *Current Anthropology* 4 (1963): 307–16.
Goody, Esther N. *Context of Kinship.* Cambridge, Eng.: Cambridge University Press, 1973.
Greenberg, Karen. "American Androgyny: Gender Distinctions and the Rhetoric of the Revolutionary Era." Paper read at the annual meeting of the Society for Historians of the Early American Republic, 1988, at Sturbridge Village, Mass.
Greven, Philip J., Jr. *Four Generations: Population, Land and Family in Colonial Andover, Massachusetts.* Ithaca, N.Y.: Cornell University Press, 1970.
——. *The Protestant Temperament: Patterns in Child Rearing, Religious Experience, and the Self in Early America.* New York: Alfred A. Knopf, 1977.
Gross, Robert. *The Minutemen and Their World.* New York: Hill & Wang, 1976.
Halsband, Robert. "Lady Mary Wortley Montagu as Letter-Writer." In *The Familiar Letter in the Eighteenth Century,* edited by Howard Anderson, Philip B. Daghlian, and Irvin Ehrenpreis. Lawrence, Kans.: University of Kansas Press, 1966.
Handelman, Don. "Gossip in Encounters: The Transmission of Information in a Bounded Social Setting." *Man* 8 (1973): 210–27.

Hareven, Tamara. "Family Time and Historical Time." In *Family and Kin in Urban Communities, 1700–1930*. New York: Franklin Watts, 1977.
————. *Family Time and Industrial Time*. New York: Cambridge University Press, 1982.
Harris, Wilhelmina S. *Adams National Historic Site*. Washington, D.C.: U.S. Government Printing Office, 1983.
Hawke, David. *Benjamin Rush*. New York: Bobbs-Merrill, 1971.
Hemlow, Joyce. *The History of Fanny Burney*. Oxford: Clarendon Press, 1958.
Henderson, James H. *Party Politics in the Continental Congress*. New York: McGraw-Hill, 1974.
Henretta, James A. *The Evolution of American Society, 1700–1815*. Lexington, Mass.: D. C. Heath, 1973.
Heyrman, Christine Leigh. *Commerce and Culture*. New York: W. W. Norton, 1984.
Higginbotham, Don. *The War of American Independence*. New York: Macmillan, 1971.
Hindus, Michael S., and Daniel Scott Smith. "Premarital Pregnancy in America, 1640–1971: An Overview and Interpretation." *Journal of Interdisciplinary History* 5 (1975): 537–70.
Hoffman, Ronald, and Peter J. Albert, eds. *Women in the Age of the American Revolution*. Charlottesville: University Press of Virginia, 1989.
Hoff-Wilson, Joan. "The Illusion of Change: Women and the American Revolution." In *The American Revolution: Explorations in the History of American Radicalism*, edited by Alfred F. Young. DeKalb, Ill.: Northern Illinois University Press, 1976.
Homans, Margaret. *Bearing the Word: Language and Female Experience in Nineteenth-Century Women's Writings*. Chicago: University of Chicago Press, 1986.
Horn, Margo. " 'Sisters Worthy of Respect': Family Dynamics and the Women's Roles in the Blackwell Family." *Journal of Family History* 8 (1983): 367–82.
Howe, Daniel Walker. "The Evangelical Movement and Political Culture in the North during the Second Party System." *Journal of American History* 77 (1991): 1216–39.
Illick, Joseph E. "John Quincy Adams: The Maternal Influence." *Journal of Psychohistory* 4 (1976): 185–95.
Jensen, Merrill D. *The Founding of a Nation*. New York: Oxford University Press, 1968.
Johnson, Michael P. "Planters and Patriarchy: Charleston, 1800–1860." *Journal of Southern History* 46 (1980): 45–72.
Jordan, Winthrop D. "Familial Politics: Thomas Paine and the Killing of the King." *Journal of American History* 60 (1973): 294–308.
Jung, C. G. "A Contribution to the Psychology of Rumor (1910–11)." In *The Collected Works of C. G. Jung*. Vol. 4. London: Routledge & Kegan Paul, 1961.
Kammen, Michael. "Changing Perceptions of the Life Cycle in American Thought and Culture." Massachusetts Historical Society, *Proceedings* 91 (1979): 5–66.
Karlsen, Carol F. *The Devil in the Shape of a Woman: Witchcraft in Colonial New England*. New York: W. W. Norton, 1987.
Kelly, Howard A., and Walter L. Burrage. *Dictionary of American Medical Biography*. Boston: D. Appleton, 1928.
Kelly-Gadol, Joan. "The Social Relations of the Sexes: Methodological Implications of Women's History." In *The Signs Reader: Women, Gender and Scholarship*, edited by Elizabeth Abel and Emily K. Abel. Chicago: University of Chicago Press, 1983.
Kerber, Linda K. "The Republican Mother: Women and the Enlightenment—An American Perspective." *American Quarterly* 28 (1976): 187–205.

———. "Separate Spheres, Female Worlds, Women's Place: The Rhetoric of Women's History." *Journal of American History* 75 (1988): 9–39.

———. *Women of the Republic: Intellect and Ideology in Revolutionary America.* Chapel Hill: University of North Carolina Press, 1980.

Klein, Ethel. *Gender Politics.* Cambridge, Mass.: Harvard University Press, 1984.

Koch, Adrienne, ed. *Adams and Jefferson: "Posterity Must Judge."* Chicago: University of Chicago Press, 1963.

Koehler, Lyle. *A Search for Power: The "Weaker Sex" in Seventeenth-Century New England.* Urbana, Ill.: University of Illinois Press, 1980.

Koonz, Claudia. *Mothers in the Fatherland: Women, the Family, and Nazi Politics.* New York: St. Martin's Press, 1987.

Laslett, Peter. *The World We Have Lost: England Before the Industrial Age.* New York: Charles Scribner's, 1965.

Lasser, Carol. "'Let Us Be Sisters Forever': The Sororal Model of Nineteenth-Century Female Friendship." *Signs: Journal of Women in Culture and Society* 14 (1988): 158–81.

Lebsock, Suzanne. *The Free Women of Petersburg: Status and Culture in a Southern Town, 1784–1860.* New York: W. W. Norton, 1984.

Lerner, Gerda. *The Creation of the Patriarchy.* New York: Oxford University Press, 1986.

———. *The Grimke Sisters from South Carolina.* New York: Schocken, 1971.

———. "New Approaches to the Study of Women in American History." *Journal of Social History* 3 (1969): 53–63.

Levin, Phyllis Lee. *Abigail Adams.* New York: St. Martin's Press, 1987.

Levy, Leonard W. *Emergence of a Free Press.* New York: Oxford University Press, 1985.

———. *Jefferson and Civil Liberties: The Darker Side.* Cambridge, Mass.: Harvard University Press, 1963.

Lewis, Jan. "The Republican Wife: Virtue and Seduction in the Early Republic." *William and Mary Quarterly,* 3rd ser., 44 (1987): 689–721.

Lewis, Jan, and Kenneth A. Lockridge. "'Sally Has Been Sick': Pregnancy and Family Limitation among Virginia Gentry Women, 1780–1830." *Journal of Social History* 22 (1988): 5–20.

Lidoff, Joan. *Fluid Boundaries: The Origins of a Distinctive Women's Voice in Literature.* Chicago: University of Chicago Press, forthcoming.

Lipsky, George A. *John Quincy Adams: His Theory and Ideas.* New York: Thomas Y. Crowell, 1950.

Locke, John. *Two Treatises of Government.* Edited by Peter Laslett. Cambridge, Eng.: Cambridge University Press, 1960.

Logan, Mary S. *The Part Taken by Women in American History.* New York: Arno Press, 1972.

Lomask, Milton. *Aaron Burr: The Conspiracy and Years of Exile 1805–1836.* New York: Farrar, Straus & Giroux, 1982.

Lorde, Audre. *The Cancer Journals.* San Francisco: spinsters/aunt lute, 1980.

Macfarlane, Alan. *Marriage and Love in England, 1300–1840.* New York: Basil Blackwell, 1986.

Maier, Pauline. *From Resistance to Revolution: Colonial Radicals and the Development of American Opposition to Britain, 1765–1776.* London: Routledge & Kegan Paul, 1973.

Main, Jackson T. *The Social Structure of Revolutionary America.* Princeton: Princeton University Press, 1961.

Malone, Dumas. *Jefferson and the Ordeal of Liberty.* Boston: Little, Brown, 1962.

————. *Jefferson the President, First Term 1801–1805*. Boston: Little, Brown, 1970.

May, Henry F. *The Enlightenment in America*. New York: Oxford University Press, 1976.

Middlekauff, Robert. *Ancients and Axioms: Secondary Education in Eighteenth-Century New England*. New Haven: Yale University Press, 1963.

————. *The Glorious Cause*. New York: Oxford University Press, 1982.

Miller, Jean Baker. *Toward a New Psychology of Women*. Boston: Beacon Press, 1976.

Miller, John C. *Crisis in Freedom: The Alien and Sedition Acts*. Boston: Little, Brown, 1951.

Minnigerode, Meade. *Some American Ladies: Seven Informal Biographies*. New York: G. P. Putnam's, 1926.

Mitchell, Juliet. *Psychoanalysis and Feminism*. New York: Vintage, 1974.

Morgan, Edmund S. *American Slavery: American Freedom*. New York: W. W. Norton, 1975.

————. *The Birth of the Republic, 1763–1789*. Chicago: University of Chicago Press, 1956.

————. *The Puritan Family: Religion and Domestic Relations in Seventeenth-Century New England*. New York: Harper & Row, 1944.

————. *Virginians at Home: Family Life in the Eighteenth Century*. Charlottesville, Va.: University of Virginia Press, 1952.

Morris, Richard B. *The Peacemakers*. New York: Harper & Row, 1965.

————. *Seven Who Shaped Our Destiny: The Founding Fathers as Revolutionaries*. New York: Harper & Row, 1973.

————. "Women's Rights in Early American Law." In *Studies in the History of American Law*. New York: Columbia University Press, 1964.

Moss, Sidney P., and Carolyn Moss. "The Thomas Jefferson Miscegenation Legend in British Travel Books." *Journal of the Early American Republic* 7 (1987): 253–74.

Motz, Marilyn Ferris. *True Sisterhood: Michigan Women and Their Kin, 1820–1920*. Albany: State University of New York Press, 1983.

Murrin, John M. "The Legal Transformation: The Bench and Bar of Eighteenth-Century Massachusetts." In *Colonial America: Essays in Politics and Social Development*, edited by Stanley N. Katz and John M. Murrin. 3rd ed. New York: Alfred A. Knopf, 1983.

Musto, David F. "The Adams Family." Massachusetts Historical Society, *Proceedings* 93 (1981): 40–58.

————. "The Youth of John Quincy Adams." American Philosophical Society, *Proceedings* 113 (1969): 269–82.

Nagel, Paul C. *The Adams Women: Abigail and Louisa Adams, Their Sisters and Daughters*. New York: Oxford University Press, 1987.

————. *Descent from Glory: Four Generations of the John Adams Family*. New York: Oxford Universty Press, 1983.

The New Pleasing Instructor, or Young Lady's Guide to Virtue and Happiness, Consisting of Essays, Relations, Descriptions, Epistles, Dialogues, and Poetry . . . Designed Principly for the Use of Female Schools: But Calculated for General Instruction and Amusement. Boston: 1799.

Nicholson, Linda J. *Gender and History: The Limits of Social Theory in the Age of the Family*. New York: Columbia University Press, 1986.

Noddings, Nel. *Caring: A Feminine Approach to Ethics and Moral Education*. Berkeley and Los Angeles: University of California Press, 1984.

Noll, Mark A., ed., *Religion and American Politics from the Colonial Period to the 1980's*. New York: Oxford University Press, 1990.

Norton, Mary Beth. "The Constitutional Status of Women in 1787." *Law and Inequality: A Journal of Theory and Practice* 6 (1988): 7–15.

———. "The Evolution of White Women's Experience in Early America." *American Historical Review* 89 (1984): 593–619.

———. "Gender and Defamation in Seventeenth-Century Maryland." *William and Mary Quarterly* 44 (1987): 3–39.

———. *Liberty's Daughters: The Revolutionary Experience of American Women, 1750–1800.* Boston: Little, Brown, 1980.

Novick, Peter. *That Noble Dream.* New York: Cambridge University Press, 1988.

Offen, Karen. "Defining Feminism: A Comparative Historical Perspective." *Signs: Journal of Women in Culture and Society,* 14 (1988): 119–57.

Okin, Susan Moller. *Women in Western Political Thought.* Princeton: Princeton University Press, 1979.

"On 'In a Different Voice': An Interdisciplinary Forum." By Linda K. Kerber, Catherine G. Greeno, Eleanor E. Maccoby, Zella Luria, Carol B. Stack, and Carol Gilligan. *Signs: Journal of Women in Culture and Society* 11 (1987): 304–33.

Paine, Robert. "What Is Gossip About? An Alternative Hypothesis." *Man,* n.s. 2 (1967): 278–85.

Pateman, Carole. *The Sexual Contract.* Stanford, Cal.: Stanford University Press, 1988.

Perry, Ruth. *The Celebrated Mary Astell.* Chicago: University of Chicago Press, 1986.

Peterson, Merrill D. *Thomas Jefferson and the New Nation.* New York: Oxford University Press, 1970.

Pitt-Rivers, Julian. "The Kith and the Kin." In *The Character of Kinship,* edited by Jack Goody. Cambridge, Eng.: Cambridge University Press, 1973.

Pocock, J. G. A. *The Machiavellian Moment: Florentine Political Thought and the Atlantic Republic Tradition.* Princeton: Princeton University Press, 1975.

———. *Virtue, Commerce and History: Essays on Political Thought and History, Chiefly in the Eighteenth Century.* New York: Cambridge University Press, 1985.

Pressman, Richard S. "Class Positioning and Shays' Rebellion: Resolving the Contradictions of *The Contrast.*" *Early American Literature* 29 (1986): 87–102.

Rabine, Leslie Wahl. "A Feminist Politics of Non-Identity." *Feminist Studies* 14 (1988): 11–32.

Rakove, Jack N. *The Beginnings of National Politics: An Interpretive History of the Continental Congress.* New York: Alfred A. Knopf, 1979.

Rather, L. J. *The Genesis of Cancer: A Study in the History of Ideas.* Baltimore: Johns Hopkins University Press, 1978.

Rice, Howard, C., Jr. *The Adams Family in Auteuil 1784–1785.* Boston: Massachusetts Historical Society, 1956.

———. *Thomas Jefferson's Paris.* Princeton: Princeton University Press, 1976.

Rich, Adrienne. *Of Woman Born: Motherhood as Experience and Institution.* New York: W. W. Norton, 1986.

Richards, Leonard L. *The Life and Times of Congressman John Quincy Adams.* New York: Oxford University Press, 1986.

Roof, Katharine Metcalf. *Colonel William Smith and Lady.* Boston: Houghton Mifflin, 1929.

Rosaldo, Michelle Zimbalist. "Woman, Culture, and Society: A Theoretical Overview." In *Woman, Culture, and Society,* edited by Michelle Zimbalist Rosaldo and Louise Lamphere. Stanford, Cal.: Stanford University Press, 1974.

Rosaldo, Michelle Zimbalist, and Louise Lamphere, eds. *Woman, Culture, and Society.* Stanford, Cal.: Stanford University Press, 1974.

Rosenbaum, Jean B., and Mayer Subrin. "The Psychology of Gossip." *Journal of the American Psychoanalytic Association,* 2 (1963): 817–31.

Rothman, Ellen K. *Hands and Hearts: A History of Courtship in America.* New York: Basic, 1984.

Ruddick, Sara. "Maternal Thinking." In *Rethinking the Family: Some Feminist Questions*, edited by Barrie Thorne with Marilyn Yalom. New York: Longman, 1982.
―――. *Maternal Thinking: Toward a Politics of Peace*. Boston: Beacon Press, 1989.
Rush, Benjamin. *Essays, Literary, Moral, and Philosophical*. Philadelphia: Thomas and William Bradford, 1798.
Ryan, Mary P. *Cradle of the Middle Class: The Family in Oneida County, New York, 1790–1865*. New York: Cambridge University Press, 1981.
―――. *Womanhood in America from Colonial Times to the Present*. New York: New Viewpoints, 1975.
Salmon, Marylynn. *Women and the Law of Property in Early America*. Chapel Hill: University of North Carolina Press, 1986.
Schochet, Gordon. *Patriarchalism in Political Thought*. Oxford: Basil Blackwell, 1975.
Scholten, Catherine M. *Childbearing in American Society: 1650–1850*. New York: New York University Press, 1985.
Scott, Joan W. "Deconstructing Equality-Versus-Difference: On the Uses of Post-Structuralist Theory for Feminism." *Feminist Studies* 14 (1988): 33–50.
Shammas, Carole, Marylynn Salmon, and Michael Dahlin. *Inheritance in America: From Colonial Times to the Present*. New Brunswick, N.J.: Rutgers University Press, 1987.
Shaw, Peter. *The Character of John Adams*. Chapel Hill: University of North Carolina Press, 1976.
Shipton, Clifford K. *Sibley's Harvard Graduates*. Boston: Massachusetts Historical Society, 1873–.
Shryock, Richard H. *Medicine and Society in America, 1660–1860*. Ithaca, N.Y.: Cornell University Press, 1960.
Smith, Daniel Scott. "Parental Control and Marriage Patterns: An Analysis of Historical Trends in Hingham, Massachusetts." In *The American Family in Social-Historical Perspective*, edited by Michael Gordon. 2nd ed. New York: St. Martin's Press, 1978.
―――. "Parental Control and Marriage Patterns: An Analysis of Historical Trends in Hingham, Massachusetts." *Journal of Marriage and the Family* 35 (1973): 423–24.
Smith, James Morton. *Freedom's Fetters: The Alien and Sedition Laws and American Civil Liberties*. Ithaca, N.Y.: Cornell University Press, 1956.
Smith, Page. *Daughters of the Promised Land: Women in American History*. Boston: Little, Brown, 1970.
―――. *John Adams*. 2 volumes. New York: Doubleday, 1962.
Smith-Rosenberg, Carroll. *Disorderly Conduct: Visions of Gender in Victorian America*. New York: Oxford University Press, 1985.
―――. "The Female World of Love and Ritual: Relations between Women in Nineteenth-Century America." *Signs: Journal of Women in Culture and Society* 1 (1975): 1–29.
Soderlund, Jean. "Women in Eighteenth-Century Pennsylvania: Toward a Model of Diversity." *The Pennsylvania Magazine of History and Biography* 115 (1991): 163–183.
Sontag, Susan. *Illness as Metaphor*. New York: Farrar, Straus & Giroux, 1977.
Spacks, Patricia Meyer. *Gossip*. New York: Alfred A. Knopf, 1985.
Spiegel, David. "Mothering, Fathering, and Mental Illness." In *Rethinking the Family*, edited by Barrie Thorne with Marilyn Yalom. New York: Longman, 1982.
Sprague, Waldo Chamberlain. *The President John Adams and President John Quincy Adams Birthplaces*. Quincy, Mass.: Quincy Historical Society, 1959.

Spruill, Julia Cherry. *Women's Life and Work in the Southern Colonies*. New York: W. W. Norton, 1938.

Stannard, David E. *The Puritan Way of Death*. New York: Oxford University Press, 1977.

Stansell, Christine. *City of Women: Sex and Class in New York 1789–1860*. New York: Alfred A. Knopf, 1986.

Steinfeld, Alan D. "A Historical Report of Mastectomy for Carcinoma of the Breast." *Surgery, Gynecology & Obstetrics* 141 (1975): 616–17.

Sterling, Dorothy, ed. *We Are Your Sisters: Black Women in the Nineteenth Century*. New York: W. W. Norton, 1984.

Stone, Irving. *Those Who Love*. New York: Doubleday, 1965.

Stone, Lawrence. *The Family, Sex, and Marriage in England 1500–1800*. New York: Harper & Row, 1977.

Strouse, Jean, ed. *Women and Analysis: Dialogues on Psychoanalytic Views of Femininity*. Boston: G. K. Hall, 1974.

Tanselle, G. Thomas. *Royall Tyler*. Cambridge, Mass.: Harvard University Press, 1967.

Thorne, Barrie, ed., with Marilyn Yalom. *Rethinking the Family*. New York: Longman, 1982.

de Tocqueville, Alexis. *Democracy in America*. Garden City, N.Y.: Doubleday, 1969.

Ulrich, Laurel Thatcher. *Good Wives: Images and Reality in the Lives of Women in Northern New England, 1650–1750*. New York: Oxford University Press, 1980.

————. *A Midwife's Tale: The Life of Martha Ballard, Based on Her Diary, 1785–1812*. New York: Alfred A. Knopf, 1990.

Walker, L. J. "Sex Differences in the Development of Moral Reasoning: A Critical Review." *Child Development* 55 (1984): 677–91.

Welter, Barbara. "The Cult of True Womanhood: 1820–1860." *American Quarterly* 18 (1966): 258–70.

Whitney, Janet. *Abigail Adams*. Boston: Little, Brown, 1947.

Wills, Gary. *Inventing America: Jefferson's Declaration of Independence*. New York: Doubleday, 1978.

Wilson, Daniel M. *Colonel John Quincy of Mt. Wollaston, 1689–1767, a Public Character of New England's Provincial Period*. Boston: George Ellis, 1909.

Wilson, Peter. "Filcher of Good Names: An Enquiry into Anthropology and Gossip." *Man* 9 (1974): 93–103.

Withey, Lynne. *Dearest Friend: A Life of Abigail Adams*. New York: Free Press, 1981.

Woloch, Nancy. *Women and the American Experience*. New York: Alfred A. Knopf, 1984.

Wood, Gordon. *The Creation of the American Republic, 1776–1787*. Chapel Hill: University of North Carolina Press, 1969.

Yalom, Marilyn. *Maternity, Mortality and the Literature of Madness*. University Park, Pa.: Pennsylvania State University Press, 1985.

Index

EDITH GELLES is an historian and affiliated scholar at the Institute for Research on Women and Gender at Stanford. She has taught in the Humanities Program at the University of California, Irvine, and at Stanford.